Ohio Real Estate

APPRAISAL

8th Edition

HONDROS LEARNING™

4140 Executive Parkway

Westerville, Ohio 43081

www.hondroslearning.com

© 2020 by Hondros Learning™. All rights reserved

Published 2020. Printed in the United States of America

22 21 20   1 2 3

ISBN: 978-1-59844-403-2

Part of Hondros Education Group

For more information on or to purchase our products, please visit www.hondroslearning.com.

Suggested Syllabus

OHIO REAL ESTATE APPRAISAL—DAY CLASSES

COURSE DESCRIPTION: The course is designed to provide the student with a basic understanding of the theory, procedures, and methods of real estate appraising and the three approaches to appraisal.

COURSE OBJECTIVES: Upon completion of this course, students will be able to:

1. Demonstrate a basic knowledge of Ohio real estate appraisal and its methodology.
2. Demonstrate a basic knowledge of real estate appraisal terminology and principles.
3. Gain a general understanding of appraisal data sources.

COURSE TEXTBOOK: *Ohio Real Estate Appraisal*, 8ᵗʰ edition,, ©2020 Hondros Learning™

COURSE NUMBER: RE140

COURSE CREDIT HOURS: 20 clock hours or 2 credit hours awarded upon successful course completion.

INSTRUCTION METHOD: Lecture

MODULE 1 (a.m.)	Introduction and Overview
	Chapter 1 - Introduction to Appraisal
	Chapter 2 - Real Estate and Appraisal
	Chapter 3 - Value and the Real Estate Market
	Chapter 4 - The Appraisal Process
MODULE 2 (p.m.)	Chapter 4 - The Appraisal Process (continued)
	Chapter 5 - Appraisal Data
	Chapter 6 - External and Environmental Influences
	Chapter 7 - Residential Construction and Home Inspection
MODULE 3 (a.m.)	Chapter 8 - Site Valuation
	Chapter 9 - Sales Comparison Approach
	Chapter 10 - Cost Approach
	Chapter 11 - Income Approach
MODULE 4 (p.m.)	Chapter 11 - Income Approach (continued)
	Chapter 12 - Reconciling Estimates of Value and Reporting Conclusions
	Review
	Final Examination
	Review of Final Examination

CLASSROOM HOURS ALL CAMPUSES: 8:00 a.m. - 5:35 p.m.
    Module (a.m.): 8:00 a.m. - 12:35 p.m.
    Lunch Break: 12:35 p.m. - 1:05 p.m.
    Module (p.m.): 1:05 p.m. - 5:35 p.m.

ATTENDANCE: Attendance is mandatory to receive course credit.

GRADING: Final grade is based 25% on classroom participation and attendance, and 75% on Final Exam and Quiz grades.

NOTES: Recording devices are not permitted during class lecture sessions.

Rev. 07.01.20

OHIO REAL ESTATE APPRAISAL—NIGHT CLASSES

COURSE DESCRIPTION: The course is designed to provide the student with a basic understanding of the theory, procedures, and methods of real estate appraising and the three approaches to appraisal.

COURSE OBJECTIVES: Upon completion of this course, students will be able to:
1. Demonstrate a basic knowledge of Ohio real estate appraisal and its methodology.
2. Demonstrate a basic knowledge of real estate appraisal terminology and principles.
3. Gain a general understanding of appraisal data sources.

COURSE TEXTBOOK: *Ohio Real Estate Appraisal*, 8th edition, ©2020 Hondros Learning™

COURSE NUMBER: RE140

COURSE CREDIT HOURS: 20 clock hours or 2 credit hours awarded upon successful course completion.

INSTRUCTION METHOD: Lecture

MODULE 1	Introduction and Overview
	Chapter 1 - Introduction to Appraisal
	Chapter 2 - Real Estate and Appraisal
	Chapter 3 - Value and the Real Estate Market
	Chapter 4 - The Appraisal Process
MODULE 2	Chapter 4 - The Appraisal Process (continued)
	Chapter 5 - Appraisal Data
	Chapter 6 - External and Environmental Influences
	Chapter 7 - Residential Construction and Home Inspection
MODULE 3	Chapter 8 - Site Valuation
	Chapter 9 - Sales Comparison Approach
	Chapter 10 - Cost Approach
	Chapter 11 - Income Approach
MODULE 4	Chapter 11 - Income Approach (continued)
	Chapter 12 - Reconciling Estimates of Value and Reporting Conclusions
	Review
	Final Examination
	Review of Final Examination

CLASSROOM HOURS: 6:00 p.m. - 10:30 p.m.

ATTENDANCE: Attendance is mandatory to receive course credit.

GRADING: Final grade is based 25% on classroom participation and attendance, and 75% on Final Exam and Quiz grades.

NOTES: Recording devices are not permitted during class lecture sessions.

Rev. 07.01.20

Table of Contents

Preface

An important part of a real estate agent's job is understanding the specifics of real estate appraisal. Whether your specialty is residential or commercial real estate, buyers will count on you to know the basics of appraising property. You will need to understand the need for an appraisal, the appraisal process, and how an appraisal may affect or influence the process of selling and buying properties.

Real estate is a growing field. The Bureau of Labor Statistics Occupational Outlook Handbook, 2018 edition, lists the median yearly income for residential real estate professionals as approximately $50,000. The attractive salary combined with the ability to be your own boss, make it easy to see why the industry continues to expand. In addition, the rate of home ownership continues to grow in the U.S.—and that means the job outlook for real estate agents is promising.

As a real estate professional, you will help clients make their dreams and financial goals come true. Whether helping a newly married couple acquire their first home or an investor purchase rental property, you will evaluate property, determine a fair sale or purchase price, and work through the details of contracts and negotiations. An appraisal is an important component of the listing, offering, negotiations, and financial process of buying a home, which is the reason for this textbook.

HOW TO USE THIS TEXT

This textbook is designed to give you the information you need to understand the complex and objective world of real estate appraisal. You will learn the fundamentals of real estate appraisal, including different types of valuation approaches, housing cycles, appraisal standards, residential construction, and more.

Whether in the classroom or studying on your own, you will find the information presented in a clear and concise manner. The text provides **key terms**, **examples**, **chapter summaries**, **chapter quizzes**, and a thorough **glossary** to reinforce the concepts presented throughout.

To get the most out of your coursework, read each chapter in its entirety, paying close attention to key terms. After reading, be sure to take the chapter quizzes because they will help prepare you for the licensing exam. And, once you have completed your course of study, keep this book handy as a valuable reference tool as you begin your real estate career.

HONDROS LEARNING ™

Hondros Learning is the leading provider of classroom materials for real estate prelicensing and continuing education. Together with Hondros College of Business, we have provided training and educational products to more than one million students.

Successful completion of this course is essential to your career. To help you with that—and passing your licensing exam the first time— these additional real estate products are available from Hondros Learning:

Ohio Real Estate Salesperson CompuCram® Online Exam Prep

Real Estate Vocab Crammer™ Flashcards

Real Estate Principles & Practices textbook

Ohio Real Estate Finance textbook

Ohio Real Estate Law textbook

Ohio Real Estate State-Specific Sales Review Crammer textbook

Real Estate National Sales Review Crammer™ textbook

Real Estate Sales Review Crammer™ Course: National (text included)

Real Estate Sales Review Crammer™ Course: Ohio State Specific (text included)

Recognitions: Reviewer Acknowledgments

Hondros Learning™ would like to thank the following expert reviewers for their comments and suggestions:

Al Batteiger

Al Rosser

Introduction to Appraisal

Appraisal is an area of study within the field of real estate. Many individuals entering the real estate profession question the necessity and resulting benefit of studying and becoming familiar with appraisal. In addition to acquiring knowledge necessary to be successful with valuation topics on the state real estate examination, there are numerous other reasons why real estate licensees must be familiar with what appraisers do and how they do it.

Possessing a keen eye for value and value elements is important to the success of a real estate professional:

- Real estate professionals assist with pricing most listings realistically. A successful real estate professional is able to recognize value elements of a particular property and, on the listing side of the transaction, can assist sellers with proper pricing and using those key elements as highlights in their marketing.

- From the perspective of professionals assisting buyers, counseling buyers as to the value that should be found with a particular property is also important. Appraisals performed by an appraiser are an important element in nearly every real estate transaction. Real estate professionals should have at least a fundamental understanding of how an appraiser will consider a property. Sometimes, real estate professionals must explain the appraisal process to the parties they are working with or within the course of their duties.

This chapter will examine the origins of real estate appraisal as a profession. The standards of professional practice, known as USPAP, will also be discussed as it relates to ensuring the integrity of the appraisal profession and process. Finally, this chapter will look at real estate appraisers and appraisal work, appraiser qualifications, licensing and certification, and designations of appraisers.

Key Terms

Appraisal The act or process of developing an opinion of value; an opinion of value.

Appraisal Foundation A nonprofit organization, created by the leading appraisal organizations, which is recognized as the authority for professional appraisal standards.

Appraisal Institute (AI) Professional organization for appraisers; created in 1990 by the merger of the American Institute of Real Estate Appraisers and Society of Residential Appraisers.

Appraisal Review The act or process of developing and communicating an opinion about the quality of another appraiser's work that was performed as part of an appraisal or appraisal review assignment.

Appraiser One who is expected to perform valuation services competently and in a manner that is independent, impartial, and objective.

FIRREA (Financial Institutions Reform, Recovery, and Enforcement Act) An act passed in 1989 as a comprehensive savings and loan bailout and preventive measure against future savings and loan insolvency. This Act of Congress recognizes USPAP as the current industry standard for appraisal, and identifies the Appraisal Foundation as the authority for professional appraisal standards.

Uniform Standards of Professional Appraisal Practice (USPAP) Professional appraisal standards promulgated by the Appraisal Foundation.

Real Estate Appraisal

Appraisal is *the act or process of developing an opinion of value; an opinion of value.* There are many concepts involved in appraisal. First, it's important to realize that an appraisal is an opinion. It is not a guarantee of value or a precise determination. It's also important that the opinion of value be supportable and based on evidence—even though appraisers use their experience and judgment for interpretation of the evidence. Learning about appraisal includes how appraisers gather and analyze data as evidence and apply their findings to develop an opinion of property value.

The other equally important point is that the opinion of value is as of a certain date—known as the effective date. The **effective date** of the appraisal establishes terms, conditions, and economic circumstances upon which the value is estimated. The appraisal is actually valid for only one day: The effective date of the appraisal. But sometimes, the client may choose to honor the value opinion for certain periods of time after the effective date, such as six months or one year. Of course, this will usually occur only when market conditions are stable or becoming stronger.

Historical Background of Appraisal

Appraisal as a discipline and a profession originated in the 1930s. About that time, lenders began to make more and more mortgage loans to people trying to buy homes. It became necessary to create a more organized process of determining value so lenders could make consistent and informed decisions with regard to these loans.

To meet the needs of lenders, the American Institute of Real Estate Appraisers was formed in 1932, and the Society of Residential Appraisers was formed in 1935. These two organizations merged in 1990 to create the **Appraisal Institute** (*a professional organization for appraisers*). They, along with other leading appraisal organizations in the U.S. and Canada, formed an Ad Hoc Committee to bring their common standards of practice together into what would later be known as the **Uniform Standards of Professional Appraisal Practice (USPAP)**.

Appraisal licensing and certification came about in the early 1990s. Prior to credentialing by individual states, the only obligation of appraisers to comply with USPAP, or any other particular standards, was through an appraiser's membership obligation to the organization to which they belonged. Prior to licensing or certification, if an appraiser was not a member of an appraisal organization, compliance with USPAP was purely voluntary. Today, state licensed and certified appraisers must comply with USPAP as a requirement of their credential.

Uniform Standards of Professional Appraisal Practice

USPAP *are professional standards accepted and copyrighted in 1987 by the Appraisal Foundation.* The **Appraisal Foundation** is *a nonprofit organization, created by leading appraisal organizations, which is recognized as the authority for professional appraisal standards.* The Appraisal Foundation has an **Appraisal Standards Board** which develops, interprets, amends, and publishes USPAP and other publications and communication related to USPAP. Revisions to USPAP occur every two years. In addition, The Appraisal Foundation has an **Appraiser Qualifications Board**. This board establishes the minimum education and experience requirements for appraisers and develops the National Uniform Appraiser Examination.

As previously mentioned, **USPAP** is recognized throughout the United States as the accepted standards of appraisal practice. In fact, the **Financial Institutions Reform, Recovery, and Enforcement Act (FIRREA)**, *passed in 1989 as a comprehensive savings and loan bailout and preventive measure against future S&L insolvency, recognizes USPAP as the current industry standard for appraisals and identifies the Appraisal Foundation as the authority for professional appraisal standards.* Furthermore, through FIRREA, Congress has required that all appraisals in excess of $250,000 in value and all appraisals that will be used in connection with any federally-related transaction through a federally-regulated financial institution be performed only by real estate appraisers who are licensed or certified by the state in which the real estate is located. FIRREA mandates that each state's appraisal licensing and certification standards meet or exceed those established by the Appraiser Qualifications Board.

USPAP Rules

USPAP contains special obligations for appraisers in the form of Rules—the Ethics Rule, the Competency Rule, the Scope of Work Rule, and the Jurisdictional Exception Rule. There are also 10 standards that apply to the particular appraisal function or asset type that appraisers deal with. We will discuss these briefly here.

The **Ethics Rule** includes personal obligations and responsibilities of the individual appraiser, as well as practices that are unacceptable or could be considered misleading or fraudulent. One section of the rule details an appraiser's obligation to perform assignments with impartiality, objectivity, independence, and without bias.

For Example

An appraiser should **not** be biased by the value that a client desires or needs.

Other sections of the Ethics Rule deal with management issues regarding accepting an appraisal assignment where the appraiser's fee is contingent upon certain outcomes or value conclusions, as well as confidentiality obligations and record keeping requirements.

The **Competency Rule** requires appraisers to have the knowledge and experience necessary to complete assignments competently, and also contains specific requirements and procedures for appraisers who don't have sufficient competence at the beginning of an assignment.

The appraiser must look at the whole picture and consider competency. Does the appraiser possess, or is he willing and/or able to acquire the knowledge and experience necessary to complete the assignment? If not, the appraiser must not accept or must withdraw from the assignment.

The **Scope of Work Rule** contains obligations of an appraiser in determining the extent and level of research and analysis that must be performed in a particular assignment in order to achieve credible results.

The appraiser's scope of work can differ in each appraisal. One of the important points for real estate professionals regarding the Scope of Work Rule is that the scope of work determined by an appraiser is specific to each client and for the intended use of the appraisal (e.g., mortgage finance, estate planning, marketing). This is the primary reason why *an appraisal performed for one use cannot be used for other uses*. In addition, *appraisals cannot be reassigned from one client (such as a lender) to another*. An appraiser is in violation of USPAP if he readdresses or assigns an appraisal from one client to another.

The **Jurisdictional Exception Rule** provides guidance and obligations for appraisers when law or public policy contradicts an obligation or prohibition of USPAP.

USPAP Standards

USPAP Standards can be thought of as checklists of personal responsibilities and obligations of the individual appraiser. Appraisers value real and personal property as well as business or intangible assets. Appraisers also perform appraisals and appraisal reviews. Let's look at the 10 USPAP standards:

- **Standards 1 and 2** focus on the development and reporting (respectively) of a real property appraisal.

- **Standards 3 and 4** detail the proper procedure for reviewing an appraisal prepared by another appraiser and reporting the results of that review.

- **Standards 5 and 6** are concerned with developing and reporting for mass appraisals, often for tax purposes.

- **Standards 7 and 8** deal with personal property.

- **Standards 9 and 10** deal with business appraisals.

Appraisal Work

Appraisers (*those expected to perform valuation services competently and in a manner that is independent, impartial, and objective*) work for many types of clients that have different uses for an appraisal report. Appraisers are hired by lenders to develop opinions of property values for mortgages or investments. Appraisers may also be hired by buyers or sellers before they buy, sell, or exchange property. Appraisers may also work on their own for, or be employed by, appraisal companies, developers, property managers, or other companies. Appraisers may also work for governments.

Real property appraisers are used any time a client needs to have a credible value opinion for a property; for example:

- Civil lawsuits
- Divorces
- Bankruptcies
- Estates
- Trusts
- Zoning changes
- Tax matters (donations or property exchanges)

- Eminent domain valuations
- Feasibility studies
- Insurance claims
- Dispute resolution
- Impact studies
- Consulting
- Determining construction or remodeling costs

 This list is not all-inclusive.

Sometimes, appraisers may also be hired for a short period of time to do a large specific appraisal project. Some examples in the private sector include financial audits, or if a company wants to do an acquisition that includes many parcels of real estate. Additional appraisers may be added by a government agency to perform large **ad valorem tax appraisals** (sometimes referred to as **auditor's appraisals**). When more than one property is the subject of an appraisal, the practice is called **mass appraisal**.

For Example

Ohio law requires all county auditors to reassess property values every six years for ad valorem tax purposes using mass appraisal techniques.

Let's discuss what may happen in an assignment in which the power of eminent domain is an element. **Eminent domain** is the government's constitutional power (right) to take private property for public use, as long as the owner is paid just compensation. The process of government taking private land is called **condemnation**. In condemnation actions, a government employed (or retained) appraiser may be called upon to develop an opinion of value of the property in question. The property owner may not agree with the government's valuation, so the owner hires an independent appraiser to arrive at a value.

This type of dispute may end up in arbitration or court as two different appraisers can come up with differing yet well supported opinions of value for the same property. The appraiser's role is to develop opinions that assist the court in determining just compensation in a condemnation action.

 Remember: **Eminent domain** is the *"right"*; **condemnation** is the *"action".*

The judge and jury decide the just compensation, but appraisers may defend their conclusions in court. Since appraisals are an opinion of value, one isn't right and the other one wrong. But a third party may be called upon to look at the objective evidence that the appraisers used in arriving at their conclusions of value (an *appraisal review*). This is why using recognized methods and techniques are important. These topics will be discussed in greater depth as the fundamentals of real estate appraisal are explored in this textbook.

Appraisal Review

An **appraisal review** is *the act or process of developing and communicating an opinion about the quality of another appraiser's work that was performed as part of an appraisal or appraisal review assignment.* An appraisal review takes into account the market data available as of the effective date of the appraisal being reviewed.

An appraisal review may be done for any number of reasons. The lender or client may feel uncertain about the value conclusion in the original appraisal, or the lender/client may simply have policies that dictate that a review appraisal must be performed above a certain loan-to-value ratio or mortgage amount, or for routine quality assurance purposes.

USPAP states that in reviewing an appraisal and reporting the results of the review, an appraiser must form an opinion as to the adequacy and appropriateness of the report being reviewed and must clearly disclose the nature of the review process undertaken.

 When a review assignment includes both an opinion of the quality of another appraiser's work and the reviewer's opinion of the original appraiser's value opinion, the assignment is both a **review** and an **appraisal**.

Appraiser Qualifications

Appraisers need a good understanding of real estate theory and appraisal methods, as well as the education and experience necessary to carry out assignments competently. Appraisal education is offered by many accredited institutions of higher learning as well as professional appraisal organizations. Appraisers must spend considerable time working with an experienced appraiser, gaining knowledge and experience.

Although certification or licensing is voluntary in Ohio, most individuals and entities that hire appraisers require that the appraiser be state licensed or certified. Also, under FIRREA, all appraisals in excess of $250,000 in transaction value that will be used in connection with any federally-related transaction **must** be performed by state licensed or certified appraisers.

To become a licensed appraiser, one has to:

- Be at least 18 years of age.

- Acquire 30 semester credit hours of college level education from an accredited college, junior college, community college, or university OR an Associate's degree or higher (in any field). Certification requires a Bachelor's degree or higher (in any field) from an accredited college or university.

- Take the necessary prelicensing courses (including passing written exams at the end of each course).

- Obtain extensive training through an apprenticeship of two or more years depending on the credential.

- Pass a rigorous licensing/certification exam (after requirements have been met).

 The courses and hours of training/experience are subject to change.

Following licensure/certification, an appraiser must still complete a certain number of hours of continuing education on an annual basis. An appraiser's credential must be renewed each year.

Appraiser Certifications

Through additional education and training/experience, appraisers may obtain different levels of licensing or certifications:

- **Licensed Residential Appraisers**—May appraise residential land, single-family homes, and 2- to 4-unit residential properties valued up to $1 million that are non-complex in nature. May also appraise residential land or single-family or 2- to 4-unit residential properties with a transaction value of up to $250,000 that are complex in nature.

- **Certified Residential Appraisers**—Have no limit on value or complexity of land, single-family homes, or 2- to 4-unit residential properties they may appraise

- **Certified General Appraisers**—May appraise any type of property (e.g., residential, investment, commercial) with no limits on value

Professional Organizations and Designations

Although membership in professional organizations for appraisers is not required, many appraisers belong to one or more professional organizations for the benefits they offer such as continued educational offerings and the ability to obtain professional designations in recognition of their education, experience, and competence.

No doubt, real estate professionals will frequently encounter appraisers who have one or more acronyms related to an earned appraiser designation following their names. Therefore, to assist in recognizing some of these credentials and the organization or society that award them, we will overview them below.

Appraisal Institute®

The Appraisal Institute® (AI®) produces three publications, as well as other special reports and books. Seminars, course work, and other educational opportunities are also offered. The Appraisal Institute® was formed by the merger of the American Institute of Real Estate Appraisers and the Society of Residential Appraisers. Although some people may still hold older designations, three that survived the merger and are still offered by AI® are:

- **MAI®**
- **SRA®**
- **SRPA®**

National Association of Realtors®

The National Association of REALTORS® (NAR®) produces several publications of general interest to those involved in the real estate profession. Seminars, course work, and other educational opportunities are also offered. The professional designations offered by NAR® are:

- **Residential Accredited Appraiser (RAA)**
- **General Accredited Appraiser (GAA)**

American Society of Appraisers®

The American Society of Appraisers® (ASA®) publishes a professional journal (*Technical Valuation*) and the *Appraisal and Valuation Manual*. The professional designations offered by ASA are:

- **Accredited Member (AM)**
- **Accredited Senior Member (ASA)**

National Association of Independent Fee Appraisers

The National Association of Independent Fee Appraisers (NAIFA) publishes *The Appraisal Review*. The professional designations offered by NAIFA are:

- **IFA—Member Designation**
- **IFAA—Agriculture Designation**
- **IFAS—Senior Designation**
- **IFAC—Appraiser Counselor Designation**

Summary

1. An **appraisal** is the act or process of developing an opinion of value. An appraisal is merely an opinion of value, not a guarantee or determination. The appraisal is valid only as of the effective date of the appraisal—not future value.

2. Appraisal as a profession originated in the 1930s, when lenders began to make large numbers of mortgage loans. The **Appraisal Foundation** was formed as a nonprofit corporation with an Appraisal Standards Board to develop, interpret, amend, and publish the **Uniform Standards of Professional Appraisal Practice (USPAP)**. USPAP is recognized throughout the U.S. as the accepted standards of appraisal practice. **FIRREA** recognizes USPAP as the current industry standard for appraisal and identifies the Appraisal Foundation as the authority for professional appraisal standards.

3. USPAP contains four special rules: **Ethics Rule** (includes personal obligations and responsibilities of the individual appraiser, as well as practices that are unacceptable or could be considered misleading or fraudulent); **Competency Rule** (requires appraisers to have the necessary knowledge and experience, or follow requirements and procedures when he doesn't); **Scope of Work Rule** (contains obligations of an appraiser in determining the extent and level of research and analysis that must be performed in a particular assignment in order to achieve credible results); and **Jurisdictional Exception Rule** (provides guidance and obligations for appraisers when law or public policy contradicts an obligation or prohibition of USPAP).

4. USPAP has 10 standards: **1** and **2**. The development and reporting (respectively) of a real property appraisal, **3** and **4**. Appraisal review procedures and reporting the results, **5** and **6**. Development and reporting for mass appraisals, **7** and **8**. Personal property, and **9** and **10**. Business appraisals.

5. An **appraiser** is a person who is expected to perform valuation services competently and in a manner that is independent, impartial, and objective. Appraisers may work for many types of clients that have different uses for an appraisal report.

6. To become a licensed appraiser, one must be at least 18 years of age, 30 semester credit hours of college level education from an accredited college, junior college, community college, or university OR an Associate's degree or higher (in any field), and the necessary prelicensing courses (including passing written exams at the end of each course) are required. One also has to obtain extensive training through an apprenticeship of two or more years (depending on credential). After all requirements have been met, the student must pass the licensing exam. Following licensure, a certain number of hours of continuing education must be completed annually, as well as annual license renewal.

Quiz

1. **An appraisal is a(n)**
   a. determination of value.
   b. guarantee of value.
   c. opinion of value.
   d. projection of future value.

2. **Which is recognized throughout the U.S. as the accepted standards of appraisal practice?**
   a. Appraisal Foundation
   b. Appraisal Institute
   c. FIRREA
   d. USPAP

3. **The primary purpose for the passage of FIRREA was to**
   a. bailout the savings and loan industry and try to prevent future insolvency.
   b. develop, interpret, amend, and publish the Uniform Standards.
   c. establish the Appraisal Foundation.
   d. establish professional standards in real estate appraisal.

4. **An appraiser develops an opinion of value of a property**
   a. based on an assessment of future events.
   b. based on calculated assumptions.
   c. based on the gathering and analysis of objective facts and data.
   d. consistent with the value needed by a client.

5. **Which USPAP Rule contains obligations of an appraiser in determining the extent and level of research and analysis that must be performed in a particular assignment in order to achieve credible results?**
   a. Competency Rule
   b. Ethics Rule
   c. Jurisdictional Exception Rule
   d. Scope of Work Rule

6. **Which USPAP Rule requires appraisers to avoid actions that could be considered misleading or fraudulent?**
   a. Competency Rule
   b. Ethics Rule
   c. Jurisdictional Exception Rule
   d. Scope of Work Rule

7. **Which USPAP Rule provides guidance and obligations for appraisers when law or public policy contradicts an obligation or prohibition of USPAP?**
   a. Competency Rule
   b. Ethics Rule
   c. Jurisdictional Exception Rule
   d. Scope of Work Rule

8. **Which USPAP Rule requires appraisers to have the knowledge and experience necessary to complete an assignment?**
   a. Competency Rule
   b. Ethics Rule
   c. Jurisdictional Exception Rule
   d. Scope of Work Rule

9. **Which statement about appraiser licensing in Ohio is FALSE?**
   a. It is voluntary but may be required for some assignments.
   b. It requires prelicensing education and passing written exams.
   c. It requires a minimum two years of apprenticeship.
   d. It allows an appraiser to take on any type of assignment.

Real Estate and Appraisal

2

This chapter will introduce some concepts that will be important throughout the remainder of this course. The differences between real property and personal property, including legal considerations in making this determination, will be examined. Real estate versus real property, and the bundle of rights that go along with real property ownership, will also be reviewed. Finally, the effect that improvements have on an appraisal will be examined with respect to land, site, fixtures, and improvements.

Key Terms

Annexer A person who owns an item of personal property and brings it onto real property, making it a part of the real property.

Appurtenance A right that goes with ownership of real property. It is usually transferred with the property, but may be sold separately. This is a legal term referring to both physical and non-physical appurtenances.

Bundle of Rights All real property rights conferred with ownership, including (but not limited to) the right of use, right of enjoyment, and right of disposal.

Deed Restriction Limitations on real property use, imposed by a former owner through language included in the deed. Deed restrictions can be in the form of **Restrictive Covenants** or **Restrictive Conditions.**

Fee Simple The greatest estate (ownership) one can have in real property; it is freely transferable and inheritable, and of indefinite duration, with no conditions on title. Also called **Fee Simple Absolute** or **Fee Title.**

Fixture A man-made attachment; an item of personal property that has been attached or annexed to real property in such a way that it legally becomes part of the real property. Major fixtures are called **Improvements**.

Personal Property 1. Tangible items not permanently attached to or part of real estate. 2. Any property that is not real property. 3. Movable property not affixed to land. Also called **Chattel** or **Personalty.**

Police Power The constitutional power of state and local governments to enact and enforce laws that protect the public's health, safety, morals, and general welfare.

(continued on page 12)

Key Terms (cont.)

Property 1. The rights of ownership in an object, such as the right to use, possess, transfer, or encumber real estate. 2. Something that is owned, real or personal.

Real Estate The actual physical land and everything, both natural and man-made, attached to it.

Real Property Not only the physical land and everything attached to it, but also the rights of ownership (**Bundle of Rights**) in the real estate.

Site A parcel of land with enhancements that make it ready for a building or structure.

Trade Fixture Personal property that a tenant or current owner installs for use in his trade or business and that can be removed by the tenant before the lease expires or that the owner can remove prior to transfer.

Zoning Laws Local ordinances dividing a city, county, etc., into zones, specifying different types of land use and requirements in different areas. This is a type of government restriction via police power.

What is an Appraisal?

As discussed in the last chapter, an **appraisal** is an opinion of the value of property as of a certain date that is supportable by objective evidence. But what is meant by property? What is included in an opinion of value? Let's look at the distinction between different types of property, and how they can affect value.

Real Property vs. Personal Property

Before conducting an appraisal, the first thing the appraiser must do is determine exactly what property is being appraised. Following are definitions of different types of property:

- **Property** is defined as the right of ownership in an object, such as the right to use, posses, transfer, or encumber it. Thus, property can be anything that is owned, either real or personal.

- **Real property** is defined not only as the physical land and everything attached to it, but also the rights of ownership (**bundle of rights**) in real estate.

- **Personal property** is defined as tangible items (usually) not permanently attached to or part of the real estate—or any property that is not real property. Personal property is also called **chattel** or **personalty**.

The distinction between real property and personal property becomes important when the possession of land is transferred because the law holds that, unless otherwise agreed to in advance, all real property is included in the transfer, but personal property that happens to be on the land is not included. *Any property that is not real property is considered personal property.* Generally speaking, if property is moveable and not affixed to land, it's usually considered personal property. The words "generally" and "usually" are used here because determining what is personal property and what is real property can sometimes lead to serious disputes and court battles.

For Example

A built-in dishwasher would be considered part of the real property; a refrigerator would most likely be considered personal property. Built-in bookcases are considered real property; a sofa is personal property. Here are some less clear-cut examples: Wall-to-wall carpeting would be considered real property, whereas an oriental rug in the foyer would likely be considered personal property; an in-ground pool is real property, but an above-ground pool is personal property. Disputes often arise over things like storage sheds, satellite dishes, and chandeliers.

Legal Considerations

The legal aspects of what makes something real property versus personal property are detailed in the *Ohio Real Estate Law* textbook. For our purposes here, the discussion of real versus personal property will be boiled down to the two basic issues the Ohio State Supreme Court says are the most important to look at:

1. What was the intention of the annexer?

2. What was the purpose of the annexation?

The **annexer** is *the person who owned the item as personal property and brought it onto the real property, making it part of the real property.*

*   Did the annexer intend for the disputed item to become part of the real property, or to remain personal property?

*   Did the annexer acquire the item to improve the real property, or just for his own use?

In answering these questions, the court will look for objective evidence of the annexer's intention. It's not enough for the annexer to claim that he always intended to remove the item. The court looks at the nature of the item and the manner of annexation as objective evidence of intent.

Actual annexation is *when a fixture is physically attached to the real property. On the other hand, an item may be considered a fixture without being physically attached to the property in any way.* It is called **constructive annexation** *when personal property is associated with real property in such a way that the law treats it as a fixture, even though it is not physically attached to the real property.* In other words, any item that is essential to the use of the real property (e.g., the key to the front door of a house) is a fixture. Items specially designed or adapted for the property are also likely to be considered fixtures (e.g., wall-to-wall carpeting installed over ply-wood sub-flooring and cut to fit a particular room—even if not tacked down, a set of storm windows made for a particular building even if they are being stored in the basement). Even items that have been temporarily removed from the real property for servicing (e.g., built-in dishwasher at the repair shop on the day of closing) can still be fixtures.

For Example

Embedding a birdbath in concrete shows intent to make it a fixture; simply setting one out on the lawn does not.

The original rule was *if the item was securely attached to the real property* (e.g., nailed down), it was considered a **fixture.** If it wasn't securely attached, it wasn't a fixture. This test isn't rigidly applied today. Physical attachment is still taken into account, but isn't decisive.

For Example

Remember the oriental rug in the foyer discussed earlier? Even if the owner tacked it down to keep it from sliding, it could still be considered personal property if the owner never meant for it to stay with the house.

At the other end of the spectrum are personal property items that are so closely associated with the house that they become real property items, even though they may not be physically attached to the house.

For Example

Keys to the house and remote control openers for garage doors are considered real property items. A built-in appliance at the repair shop on the day of closing becomes the possession of the buyer, even if it's not physically in the house at the time of closing.

When disputes arise, the courts also take into account the relationship of the parties involved. Buyers are generally favored over sellers (because the item may have induced the buyer to make the purchase), lenders over borrowers (so as not to diminish the value of the lender's collateral), but tenants over landlords (because courts recognize that personal property items are installed for personal use rather than for the benefit of the property). In fact, specific terminology and laws apply to business tenants. A **trade fixture** is *equipment a tenant installs for use in his trade or business and that can be removed by the tenant before the lease expires* (unless a document forbids it).

Again, these are generalizations, and courts will still look at a number of criteria in arriving at a decision to settle disputes. One criterion that is rarely considered, though, is the value of the item. Furthermore, a written agreement between the parties will always be enforced by the courts. Thus, an agent should always get things in writing to avoid disputes between buyer and seller. If an item is to be excluded, that fact should be clearly stated in the purchase contract. If separate items of personal property are to be included in the sale of real property, it's best to get a separate **bill of sale** detailing those items.

From the appraiser's point of view, it is important that she knows what items are part of the sale so that this can be noted in the appraisal. While the inclusion of personal property items (e.g., appliances) often do not increase the value of real property, any items (real or personal) that are being excluded may have a negative impact on valuation.

For Example

Built-in bookcases that will be removed by the seller could affect the value of the property.

What is Being Transferred?

When an appraiser is determining exactly what is being appraised, there are more considerations. In the last section, the simple distinction between real property and personal property was made, but it can really become more complicated than that. Property was defined as the right of ownership in a thing, such as the right to use, possess, transfer, or encumber it. With real property, it's possible for someone to have only some of these rights. Let's first take a brief look at the technical difference between the terms **real estate** and **real property**, and then examine the important concept of the **bundle of rights** that go with real property ownership.

Real Estate vs. Real Property

Although these two terms are often used interchangeably, it's important to know that there is a technical distinction between them. **Real estate** refers to *the actual physical land and everything, both natural and man-made, which is attached to it*. As previously defined, **real property** refers to *not only the physical land and everything attached to it, but also the rights of ownership* (**bundle of rights**) *in the real estate*.

Bundle of Rights

Bundle of rights are *all real property rights that are conferred with ownership, including (but not limited to) the right of use, the right of enjoyment, and the right of disposal.* Think of the bundle of rights as a bundle of sticks, with each stick representing a different right. If one secures the entire bundle of rights, then that person is said to be the owner. This type of ownership is called a fee simple. **Fee simple** is *the greatest estate one can have in real property. It is freely transferable and inheritable, and of indefinite duration, with no conditions on the title.*

It's possible, though, for the owner to transfer only some of the rights of ownership to another person. Fee simple ownership includes such other items as access rights, surface rights, subsurface rights, mineral rights, some water rights, and limited air rights. The legal term for these rights that go along with ownership of real property is **appurtenances.** *They are usually transferred with the property, but may be sold separately.* This is a legal term referring to both physical and non-physical appurtenances. They may also be limited by past transactions.

For Example

A property owner may sell the mineral rights to property to a mining company, but keep ownership of the farm. Later, when the land is sold, the mineral rights will most likely stay with the mining company (depending on the verbiage of the contract involved), even though the rest of the bundle of rights in the land are transferred to the new owner. The new owner is limited by the past transaction of the previous owner, and may not sell these mineral rights to another party, nor transfer them in a future sale of the land.

The appraiser must know if the entire bundle of rights is being transferred (fee simple) or if there are restrictions or past transactions that may limit the current transfer of ownership in any way. This is important because the value of the real property may be greatly affected. Transfer of access rights to a power company so that they can repair lines, if necessary, generally would not have a significant impact on the value of land. Transfer of mineral rights to a mining company, as in the previous example, likely would impact the value.

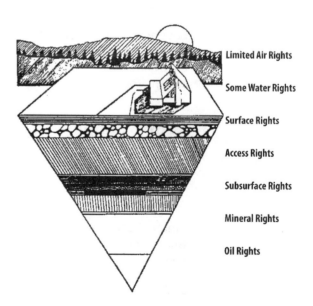

One way to understand the rights that accompany real property is to imagine the property as an inverted pyramid, with its tip at the center of the earth and its base extending out into the sky. An owner has rights to the surface of the land within the property's boundaries, plus everything under or over the surface within the pyramid. This includes oil and mineral rights below the surface, and certain air and water rights.

Deed Restrictions

Deed restrictions *are limitations on real property use, imposed by a former owner through language included in the deed.* These may also be called **restrictive covenants** or **restrictive conditions.** Usually they involve an owner's promise not to use property in a particular way. Deed restrictions are often placed in the deed by the original subdivider of land, although they can also be added later. They must "touch and concern" the land in order to be legal and binding on future transfers.

For Example

A deed restriction may set a minimum size of house that must be built on the land or prohibitions against certain types of fences.

Deed restrictions may also grant the previous owner or other parties access across the land being transferred. Generally, deed restrictions do not have a significant negative impact on the value of real estate unless they are severe.

Government Restrictions

Government restrictions on land can have a more serious impact on its value. The main restriction that government can place on land is referred to as *police power*. **Police power** is *the constitutional power of state (and local) governments to enact and enforce laws that protect the public's health, safety, morals and general welfare.* Police power can take the form of **land use controls** (primarily **zoning laws**), **environmental protection laws**, **eminent domain**, and **escheat.** These are detailed in the *Ohio Real Estate Law* and *Ohio Real Estate Principles and Practices* textbooks. From an appraisal standpoint, the most important government restrictions that will be discussed are **zoning laws**, **environmental protection laws**, and **eminent domain**.

Zoning Laws

Zoning laws are *local ordinances dividing a city, county, etc. into zones, specifying different types of land use in different areas.* Zoning and other laws restricting land usage (e.g., building codes) are passed to protect the health, safety, and welfare of the community. Land use controls impact real estate since they may limit development and thus, affect property values. Land may be more valuable with an office building instead of a house, but zoning laws may not permit that land usage.

Environmental Protection Laws

Land use controls at state and federal levels are increasing in an effort to protect the environment. Regulations can involve blocking or restricting the use of land where there are environmental concerns. Sometimes, this conflicts with land owners' usage of land.

For Example

Land can't be used for a hazardous waste site (or some industrial uses) without government approval. The government also controls land use in protecting wildlife, endangered species, and wetlands. Federal agencies may deem land a safe haven or protected area that can't be developed.

Eminent Domain

Eminent domain is the government's constitutional power (right) to take (or appropriate or condemn) private property for public use, as long as the owner is paid just compensation. Eminent domain affects real estate because of government involvement in fair market pricing, and by making adjacent land more or less valuable depending on the proposed use (e.g., freeway interchange versus a landfill).

 Remember: Eminent domain is the *"right"*; **condemnation** is the *"action"*.

How Do Improvements Affect an Appraisal?

Improvements are additions to real property. These improvements can be natural (e.g., trees, lot feature) or they can be man-made. Usually, improvements refer to man-made additions. There are really two types of man-made improvements:

- **To** the land (such as site improvements that provide water, sewer, etc.)
- **On** the land (major improvements that are buildings or structures)

Improvements to the Land: Land vs. Site

This is another important distinction that is important when dealing with real estate and real estate appraisals. **Land** refers to the surface of the earth: Actual dirt on the ground, part of a waterway that is owned, or even a swampy marsh. From a legal standpoint, land also refers to everything under the ground to the center of the earth, and everything over the land into the air (within limits to allow for air traffic). **Site** refers to *a parcel of land with enhancements that make it ready for a building or structure.* Thus, when we talk about site "improvements" to land, we mean objects like the addition of water service or a well, sewer lines, or septic system, or any other services that are typical for an area.

When vacant land is being appraised, site improvements can add value. Compared with raw land, a buyer, lender, or other person would probably agree that the land is worth more if it's ready to be built on right away either because there's a well and septic system already in place or because public utilities are ready to be hooked up.

When homes or other buildings are part of the appraisal, however, site improvements often do not add measurable value. This is because it's expected that a house would have running water and indoor plumbing. In fact, a lack of site improvements in line with the rest of the homes in the area could significantly detract from the value of a house. A lone house with a septic system could be less attractive (and worth less) than other houses in the area that have public sewer hookups. When certain site improvements aren't the norm for a neighborhood, a home with such improvements will benefit.

For Example

A subject property is located in a neighborhood where most of the houses have well water, but the house being appraised has city water. This feature could add value.

Improvements on the Land: Fixtures vs. Improvements

Fixtures (*man-made attachments to real property*) are items of personal property that have been attached to, or closely associated with, real property in such a way that they legally become part of the real property. **Improvements** are also man-made attachments to real property, but generally refer to major fixtures (e.g., a building). Thus, "improvements" to real property mean objects or structures, like a house.

When describing real property in a legal description, however, only the surface is detailed, and often only boundaries of the property are mentioned. The law implies inclusion of all of the appurtenances (e.g., water rights) that we discussed, as well as all attachments and improvements that have legally become part of the real property by virtue of their attachment or close association with it. In fact, when real property is being appraised, fixtures and improvements are often a substantial part of the value. This is why the distinction between personal property and real property is so important. The appraiser must be careful to include everything that is part of the real property, and exclude everything that is personal property.

Assuming that there is an improvement on the real property, this becomes the focal point of the appraisal. Specific fixtures (e.g., a swimming pool) or site features (e.g., a ravine) can also affect value. Of course, only features that are considered to be desirable to and recognized by the market add value, while undesirable features can detract from the value. Just because one person likes a particular feature does not mean that it automatically adds value to a property or that the market would recognize value in the feature. The feature must be something that most people would pay for, as determined by an analysis of market patterns. Bad features that most people would not want (or worse, would want to pay to have removed) can subtract from the value. These desires may even change over time, such as with swimming pools which go in and out of vogue. This is where an appraiser's experience comes in. This will be discussed more in Chapter 3 as part of the concepts of value.

Summary

1. **Property** is defined as the right of ownership in an object, such as the right to use, possess, transfer, or encumber it. **Real property** is the land and everything attached (appurtenant) to it, plus rights of ownership in real estate. **Personal property** is all tangible items not permanently attached to or annexed as part of real estate (also known as **personalty** or **chattels**). When land is transferred, the law says that, unless otherwise agreed in advance, all the real property is included in the transfer, but personal property that happens to be on the land is not included. Usually, if property is moveable and not fixed to the land, it's personal property.

2. When courts look at real versus personal property disputes, there are two main questions: 1. What was the intention of the annexer? and 2. What was the purpose of the annexation? Nature of the item and manner of annexation are viewed as objective evidence of intent. Physical attachment is considered, but not decisive. The value of the item is rarely considered. The relationship of parties is considered. Courts favor buyers over sellers, lenders over borrowers, and tenants over landlords. Trade fixtures can be removed by business tenants. Written agreements are always enforced.

3. **Real estate** refers to actual physical land and all things attached (appurtenant) to it. **Real property** is land and rights of ownership in real estate (bundle of rights). **Bundle of rights** are all real property rights that are conferred with ownership, including right of use, right of enjoyment, and right of disposal. One who secures the entire bundle of rights is the owner in fee simple. **Fee simple** is the greatest ownership: Freely transferable, inheritable, indefinite duration, with no conditions on title.

4. **Appurtenances** are legal rights that go along with ownership (e.g., access, surface, mineral, water, air). These are usually transferred with the property, but can be sold separately, and may be limited by past transactions. Other limits on ownership are **deed restrictions/restrictive covenants and conditions**. Often used by original subdivider, but can be added later. Must touch and concern the land to be legal (e.g., minimum house size). Government restrictions via **police power** that can impact land value include **zoning**, **environmental laws**, and **eminent domain**.

5. Improvements are additions to property—usually man-made. Land is the surface of the earth (dirt, water, etc.), and legally, everything under the ground to the center of the earth and everything over the land into the air (with limits for air traffic). **Site** refers to land with enhancements that make it ready for a building. Site improvements include such objects as a well, septic tank, or public utilities.

6. **Fixtures** are man-made attachments to real property. They are items of personal property that have been attached to, or so closely associated with, real property in such a way that they legally become part of the real property. Improvements are natural or man-made attachments to real property and usually refer to major fixtures (e.g., a building). When describing real property in a legal description, only the surface is detailed, and often only boundaries of the property are mentioned. The law implies inclusion of all of appurtenant rights (air, mineral, etc.), as well as all attachments and improvements that have legally become part of the real property by virtue of their attachment to it. Assuming there's an improvement on the real property, this becomes the focal point of the appraisal.

Quiz

1. *Which would most likely be considered personal property?*
   a. barbecue grill
   b. deck at the back of a house
   c. patio
   d. porch

2. *Which would most likely be considered real property?*
   a. lawn furniture
   b. roll-away bed
   c. sleeper sofa
   d. window seat

3. *Which question is NOT considered by the court when deciding if something is real property or personal property?*
   a. Is the item securely attached to the property?
   b. What was the intention of the annexer?
   c. What was the purpose of the annexation?
   d. What was the cost of the annexed property?

4. *Which is NOT considered part of the bundle of rights that are transferred with real property ownership?*
   a. right of disposal
   b. right of enjoyment
   c. right of use
   d. right of litigation

5. *Assuming that they are not limited by past transactions, all are legal appurtenances that go along with the transfer of real estate, EXCEPT unlimited _____ rights.*
   a. air
   b. mineral
   c. subsurface
   d. surface

6. *Which government restriction/police power could have the most direct impact on the value of property?*
   a. deed restrictions
   b. eminent domain
   c. restrictive covenants
   d. zoning

7. *Which would more likely be considered a fixture than an improvement?*
   a. stand-alone garage
   b. septic system in place
   c. buried utility line
   d. above-ground pool

Value and the Real Estate Market

This chapter will discuss the concept of value by looking at value characteristics, physical characteristics, and then the four broad forces that affect value. Specific factors that affect value will also be examined, as well as types of value.

Key Terms

Arm's Length Transaction A transaction that occurred under typical conditions in the marketplace, with each of the parties acting in their own best interests.

Buyer's Market A situation in the real estate market in which buyers have a large selection of properties from which to choose (advantage to the buyer).

Cost The dollars needed to develop, produce, or build something.

Economic Base The main business or industry in an area that a community uses to support and sustain itself.

Law of Diminishing Returns An economic principle that says beyond a certain point, the added value of an additional feature, addition, repair, etc., is less than the actual cost of the item. Also called the **Law of Decreasing Returns**.

Law of Increasing Returns An economic principle that says the added value of an additional feature, addition, repair, etc., is more than the actual cost of the item.

Market Price The price property sold for in an actual transaction.

Market Value The most probable price that a property should bring in a competitive and open market.

Progression A principle that says the value of a home is positively affected by the other homes in an area. Usually said about the "worst" home in the "best" area.

Regression A principle that says the value of a home is negatively affected by the other homes in an area. Usually said about the "best" home in the "worst" area.

Seller's Market A situation in the real estate market where property offerings are scarce and buyers have fewer properties being offered on the market to choose from (advantage to the seller).

Supply and Demand A law of economics that says, for all products, goods, and services, when supply exceeds demand, prices will fall and when demand exceeds supply, prices will rise.

Value The amount of goods or services offered in the marketplace in exchange for something else.

The Concept of Value

Value is *the amount of goods or services offered in the marketplace in exchange for something else*. But value does not always equal price. Price is what a particular person feels something is worth—and hence the price she is willing to pay for something. Value is what a typical person would pay for something as determined by an examination of the marketplace. The problem is that there are many factors that can influence value. As such, it is important to understand these factors in order for an appraisal to be as accurate as possible. These factors include great forces that affect many aspects of the economy and the entire real estate market in a given region, all the way down to very specific factors that affect only one individual property.

Before anything can have value, though, there are certain things that an item must possess. Value is really a two-way street. If a person has something that no one else wants, value is diminished (except maybe to that person). In order to get the maximum value for property, there must be a realization of certain **value characteristics** by the user and other potential users of the property. Value characteristics, together with physical characteristics, make up the characteristics of real estate.

Value Characteristics

There are four value characteristics of real estate: **Demand**, **Utility**, **Scarcity**, and **Transferability** (remembered easily as the acronym **D-U-S-T**).

Demand

Demand is the need or desire for a specific good or service by others. Demand is an essential ingredient in creating value. Without demand, any amount of supply is meaningless. But when there are purchasers who want what the seller has, the seller can command value. Everyone needs real estate; it's a matter of whether they want to satisfy that need through buying or renting. That's where desire comes into play. Home buyers typically look to satisfy basic needs or individual wants beyond life's essentials. When an individual has something people desire, he is able to maximize value even more (but not outside the bounds of reason—or what the market will bear—taking into account everything we have learned to this point).

Utility

Utility is the ability of a good or service to satisfy human wants, needs, or desires. Utility is the degree of usefulness to a prospective buyer. In addition to demand for housing, the home must be perceived as useful (e.g., enough bedrooms) for the home to have value to a potential buyer.

Scarcity

Scarcity is the perceived supply of a good or service relative to the demand for the item. Real estate is generally perceived to be a valuable commodity because there is a limited supply. This notion feeds buyers' anticipation that they are buying a house as an investment that, generally, will increase in value as time goes by. Value is also derived from the fact that there's only one of a particular house in a given location. If potential buyers desire a specific home, more value is created.

Transferability

Transferability is the ability to freely buy, sell, encumber, or dispose of property in any way that the owner sees fit—and the fewer the restrictions on real estate, the higher the perceived value. When there are conditions on title to land which restrict its future transfer, it's likely that a buyer would not pay as much for this type of property (given that ready substitutes exist in the market). Value is derived from freedom to transfer title readily from one person to another.

Another consideration most often associated with transferability is **effective demand**, or effective purchasing power. Effective demand considers the ability of a particular market to afford a property.

For Example

When a multi-million dollar home is offered for sale in a market where there is significant poverty or unemployment, there may not be a presence of effective demand.

Physical Characteristics

There are three physical characteristics of real estate: **Immobility**, **Indestructibility**, and **Uniqueness**.

Immobility

Immobility refers to the fact that it can't be moved from one place to another. This is an equal benefit, or detriment, to all real estate in the same general area.

Indestructibility

Indestructibility refers to the fact that it can't be destroyed or consumed like other products. Thus, real estate will always have some minimum value by virtue of its existence.

Uniqueness

Uniqueness refers to the fact that each parcel of land, each building, and each house are said to be different. No two are exactly the same; this is also called **non-homogeneity**.

Broad Forces That Affect Value

There are four broad forces that affect all aspects of life and the economy. As such, they also have a significant impact on value in the real estate market. These broad forces are: **Physical**, **Economic**, **Governmental**, and **Social** (remembered easily as the acronym **P-E-G-S**).

Economic Forces

Economic forces that can affect value in the real estate market include things like **business cycles**, **economic base**, **supply and demand**, **inflation**, and the **cost of money (interest rates)**. Each of these economic forces affects all businesses. But in the real estate market, there are additional realities which must be taken into account. Let's briefly look at each of these with respect to real estate.

Business Cycles

Business cycles are general swings in business activity, resulting in expanding and contracting activity at different phases of the cycle. Real estate cycles typically trail behind business cycles because they depend on many elements of business cycles (e.g., steady jobs) to be in full swing before they respond.

Economic Base

The **economic base** of an area is *the main business or industry which a community uses to support and sustain itself*. While the presence of a healthy economic base is important for all businesses, it's critical for the real estate market. Other business can "export" their products or services outside the area or simply move to a new location, but real estate cannot be moved.

Supply and Demand

The law of **supply and demand** *says that for all products, goods, and services, when supply exceeds demand, prices will fall and when demand exceeds supply, prices will rise.* Real estate markets also respond to the laws of supply and demand, but there's a lag time for market forces to respond. This lag time is the result of the time it takes for a house to be bought, sold, or built. If an individual loses his job today, he can't expect to sell his home tomorrow. Or if construction companies see a need for housing, it takes time for them to build houses; when they see that there's no longer a need for housing, they may have some houses started which must be finished.

When the real estate market is in **balance**, there will be slightly more properties available than there are buyers. Later in this chapter, we'll discuss supply and demand as it relates to value of individual properties.

Inflation

Inflation is an increase in the cost of goods or services. This is also called **cost inflation**, which mostly affects new home prices as builders pass on increased costs of labor and building materials. **Inflation** is defined as too much money chasing too few goods. This is also called **demand inflation**, which mostly affects existing home prices, as too many people seek to live in an area with too few houses. High inflation hits real estate harder than many other businesses because actual prices are much higher.

For Example

A 10% increase on a $100,000 home (a $10,000 increase) would make a buyer think harder about his purchase than a 10% increase on a $50 pair of shoes (a $5 increase).

Cost of Money (Interest Rates)

Cost of money is the interest rate people or businesses must pay to use another person's money for their own purposes. Inflation can be one factor that pushes interest rates higher or lower. And while high interest rates affect most big ticket items, high interest rates hinder real estate more than other goods since mortgages are long-term commitments.

Governmental Forces

Governmental forces that can affect value in the real estate market include **revenue generating laws (taxes)**, **right to regulate laws (police power)**, **fiscal and monetary policy**, **secondary mortgage markets**, and **government programs**. Some of these forces impact all businesses; others are directed specifically at real estate.

Revenue Generating Laws

Revenue generating laws consist of taxation and specific tax policies. **Taxation** is the governmental process of levying a charge upon people or things; specifically property taxes. Low taxes might encourage residential or commercial real estate activity in a certain area, whereas high taxes could have the opposite effect. **Specific tax policies** are tax laws enacted to encourage or discourage certain behaviors or activities. Just like property taxes, federal taxes can affect behavior.

For Example

The federal income tax deduction for home mortgage interest is designed specifically to encourage home ownership and stimulate housing activity.

Right to Regulate Laws

The right to regulate laws deals with the **police power** that governments reserve for themselves. We discussed the government's police power under "government restrictions" in the last chapter. Just remember that zoning laws, environmental protection laws, and eminent domain can affect real estate markets by limiting the types of real estate activity that occur in a certain area.

Fiscal and Monetary Policy

Fiscal policy is the government's plan for spending, taxation, and debt management. We just saw how taxation and specific tax policies can influence real estate markets. **Monetary policy** is the means by which government can exert control over the supply and cost of money. Through monetary policy, the Federal Reserve can make more or less money available to banks for lending; in effect, raising or lowering interest rates.

We know that interest rates can influence the real estate market. The government uses monetary policy to try and influence real estate cycles, heating up demand to spur economic activity, or cooling off demand to control inflation. These concepts are dealt with more thoroughly in the Ohio Real Estate Finance and Ohio Real Estate Principles and Practices textbooks.

Secondary Mortgage Markets

Secondary mortgage markets include private and government-sponsored enterprises that buy and sell real estate mortgages. Since mortgages are bought and sold from all over the country, there are three important influences on real estate markets:

1. When secondary mortgage markets buy up mortgages from local banks, those banks then have more money to lend out again in the local market.

2. By selling mortgages from all over the country to local banks, those banks then have a diversified portfolio of loans, which helps to moderate their local real estate cycles.

3. Standardization of loan criteria across the country improves the overall quality of loans.

Government Programs

Government programs are assistance mechanisms enacted by legislation and administered by the executive branch of government. The two main federal government housing programs are the **FHA (Federal Housing Administration)** and the **VA (Department of Veterans Affairs)**. The FHA provides insurance and the VA offers loan guarantees to lenders, allowing lenders to loan money to people who might otherwise have trouble qualifying. These programs affect real estate markets by making housing more (or less) accessible, depending on the current status of the programs, rules, and legislation.

Social Forces

Social forces that can affect value in real estate markets include **demographic changes**, **migrations of the population**, **social trends**, and **buyer tastes and standards**. Again, some of these forces have a more pronounced affect on real estate.

Demographic Changes

Demographic changes have to do with changes in the general population. These changes include such things as overall population growth and growth rates, population age, and size of families. As populations change, so do their housing needs. Growing populations need more housing; however, changes in family size may dictate that new housing should be downsized. An aging population may call for more residences geared to the lifestyle needs of older home buyers and senior citizens.

Migrations of the Population

Migrations of the population involve general trends toward, for example, one city over another or one area of town over another. Migrations do affect all business, but migrations have a more significant impact on the real estate market because land cannot be moved or created to fill demand.

Social Trends

Social trends encompass many aspects of the previous two categories, as well as such things as single parent households, people buying houses later in life, and the growing number of empty nest households. Each of these trends has the potential to affect the value of certain types of real estate (e.g., large houses may become less desirable as some of these social trends continue).

Buyer Tastes and Standards

Buyer tastes and **standards** can include everything from specific features of a property to overall attitudes evident in the real estate market.

For Example

The number of condominium communities increases as people seek more active lifestyles with less maintenance responsibilities, and living space that is typically nicer (though smaller) than a home of equal cost.

Physical Forces

Physical forces that can affect value in the real estate market include things on a property (e.g., **topography**, **water**), external to a property (e.g., **location**, **popularity**), or both (e.g., **environment**, environmental issues).

Topography

Topography is the contour of the land. This can affect the value of a particular parcel of real estate, as well as all land in an area. Land that's too hilly may not permit desired building; land that's flat may be deemed not to have character.

Water

Water can encompass a number of desirable or undesirable features which can affect real estate values. Waterfront property is usually more valuable; swamps or areas prone to flooding are less valuable. Lack of city water can also make real estate less desirable because wells can be expensive (they must be deep and may go through rock).

Location

Location is the exact position of real estate. Real estate in a growing neighborhood, city, or region is more valuable than in a declining area.

Popularity

Popularity can impact real estate value as areas go in and out of favor with the public because of location, jobs, climate, or for other reasons.

Environment

Environment includes not only things on a property or external to a property, but also natural or man-made phenomena. Natural **soil composition** that makes ground unsuitable for building can have a negative impact on value; so can the presence of underground storage tanks. Positive value attributes could be a natural waterway or man-made lake. External factors can affect the entire area.

Specific Factors That Affect Value

One of the most important factors that affects value is also the most simple to understand: Change. **Change** is constantly occurring, such that none of the great forces or property specific factors remain constant. Thus, value is also subject to constant change. This is why an appraisal is valid only as of its effective date. The changes may be subtle or drastic, but it is the appraiser's responsibility to ensure that all changeable factors affecting property value are taken into account in an appraisal.

While the principle of change as it relates to the four great forces has an equivalent impact on all real estate in a given area, this is not the case with property-specific factors. Change affects property-specific factors differently for each property. Likewise, the principles of value affect all properties, but have a slightly different effect on the value of an individual property in regard to other competing real estate in the marketplace. These specific factors that affect value can be subdivided into **economic (broad market) factors** and **physical (property specific) factors**.

Economic (Broad Market) Factors

Earlier, we discussed economic forces as one of the great market forces that affected value in the real estate market as a whole. Now, let's look at the most important economic factors that can also have a specific effect on an individual piece of property:

- Supply and demand
- Uniqueness and scarcity

Supply and Demand

The law of **supply and demand** says that for all products, goods, and services, when supply exceeds demand, prices will fall and when demand exceeds supply, prices will rise. This principle plays a very important role in real estate because of the inherent difficulties in adjusting supply and demand. Because of the lag time for market forces (e.g., construction companies) to respond to supply and demand situations, there are often **buyer's markets** and **seller's markets**.

Buyer's Markets

A **buyer's market** is *a situation in the real estate market in which buyers have a large selection of properties from which to choose.* This situation (which creates an advantage to the buyer) may be due to population shifts away from an area, overbuilding by construction companies, or bad economic conditions (e.g., a plant closing). A buyer's market can be neutralized if some sellers pull their homes off the market, but a glut is a glut and usually there's downward pressure on real estate values. When more homes are available, the increased supply tends to keep home values lower. Often, in this situation, a buyer is in a position to negotiate for a lower price or more favorable terms of sale.

Seller's Markets

A **seller's market** is *a situation in the real estate market where property offerings are scarce and buyers have fewer properties being offered on the market to choose from.* This situation (which creates an advantage to the seller) may be due to people moving into an area, little building by the construction industry in response to a prior glut, high construction costs for labor or materials, good economic conditions (e.g., a new plant opening), or lower interest rates. When fewer properties are available, the decreased supply (relative to the demand) tends to keep home values higher. Often, in this situation, a seller is in a position to stay closer to the original asking price or negotiate favorable terms.

During the lag time for market forces to respond, the imbalance of supply and demand can have a real impact on the value of a house; positive or negative. This may be noted in an appraisal if the subject home's value is higher than expected because there is a housing shortage in the area. Conversely, an appraiser may have to justify lowering a home's appraisal value because there is a temporary glut in the market due to the closing of a major company that hurt the economic base of an area.

 Remember: The real estate market is said to be in **balance** when there are slightly more homes available than buyers. This keeps real estate prices in check, and curtails the impact of people who put their homes for sale at a higher price to test the market. In fact, the market will determine if their price is too high.

Uniqueness and Scarcity

Other factors which can influence a specific piece of real estate are uniqueness and scarcity. **Scarcity** is tied to the supply and demand model, and specifically relates to the fact that there is a limited amount of real estate within a geographical region. When people want to live in a certain area, they must compete with others who want to live there for the limited supply of land in that area.

For Example

Scarcity may be noted in an appraisal if the subject is the last vacant lot in a desirable neighborhood, perhaps justifying a slightly higher value.

Uniqueness goes to the very heart of real estate ownership—no two properties are exactly alike. Uniqueness, though, can be good or bad. A "unique" feature of a house could actually make it less desirable and hurt its value if the owner of a home included features which other people don't want. Of course, a unique feature that adds character to a home can make it more desirable and add to its value.

Physical (Property Specific) Factors

Physical characteristics of a specific property are important factors that contribute to its ultimate value. These property specific factors go beyond the obvious quality and condition of the improvements on the land; instead, these principles of value go directly to the very nature of the land itself and its usage. These property-specific factors must also be considered when valuing a piece of property:

- Highest and best use
- Location
- Substitution
- Conformity
- Contribution

Highest and Best Use

Highest and best use is the most profitable, legally permitted, feasible, and physically possible use of a property. This is the most important property-specific factor that an appraiser considers before making a determination of value. As can be seen from the comprehensive definition, a number of factors go into making this determination. With most houses, this is not a significant analysis; for example, a property in the middle of a residential neighborhood, which is restricted to residential houses. Highest and best use becomes a vital consideration, though, when examining vacant land or land that has different zoning now than it did when the original structure on it was built.

If a house sits on a widened street, surrounded by commercial buildings, it's very likely that the land would be more valuable if it also were put to a commercial use. However, doing so must be legally permitted (by zoning laws) and the owner must be able to build the proposed structure on the land. All of these factors must be considered when an appraiser is valuing real estate.

Determining highest and best use is a very important step in the appraisal process, and will be discussed again in detail in Chapter 4.

Location

Location is the exact position of a parcel of real estate. Location can be talked about with respect to a given neighborhood, and even within the neighborhood itself. It's easy to understand that homes in a growing, popular, and prosperous neighborhood are more highly sought after and valued than those in other neighborhoods. It's also important to recognize, though, that each individual home's location within that neighborhood affects its value.

For Example

A home on a corner lot, next to the park, or in a cul-de-sac would likely have a higher value than a home next to a railroad track.

Situs is a term used to describe the place where something exists, an area of preference, or preference by people for a certain location. Remember, in real estate the three most important aspects of a house (or land) are location, location, location.

"Best" and "Worst" Homes

An important corollary to the concept of location is the effect of surrounding homes on valuation. The principle of **progression** (usually said about the "worst" home in the "best" area) says the value of a home is positively affected by the other homes in an area.

For Example

The value of a home that is run-down can benefit from being in a good area among other homes that are well-kept. The value of this theoretical "worst" home can only go so low because the desirability of the other homes in the neighborhood will keep its value from falling too far. People will pay more for the run-down home, anticipating that they can recoup their investment by fixing it up.

Conversely, the principle of **regression** (usually said about the "best" home in the "worst" area) says the value of a home is negatively affected by other homes in an area.

For Example

The value of a luxurious home in an average area can be hurt by the fact that people may not want to pay too much for a home that's not surrounded by comparably priced homes, and they may fear a lower resale value. The value of this theoretical "best" home can only go so high because people who can afford this "best" home will be attracted to other neighborhoods.

Substitution

Substitution says an informed buyer will not pay more for a home than a comparable substitute. Although each home is said to be unique, there's a point beyond which a buyer won't go for a particular home. Of course, one really doesn't know where that point is until he tries to sell his home for too much and no one buys it. The theory of substitution can also be applied to items within a home.

For Example

When an appraiser determines the value of a fireplace in an area where most homes don't have one, the appraiser must take into account that a buyer is not going to pay more for that home than he would for a similar home plus the cost of adding a fireplace to it. In other words, if a fireplace costs $2,500 to add to a typical home in the area, an appraiser can't justify adding much more than that to the value of a home.

Conformity

Conformity says that a particular home achieves its maximum value when it is surrounded by homes that are similar in style and function. This actually goes for neighborhoods as well. Neighborhoods are more desirable when there's a general similarity in utility and value for all homes in a particular area.

The best/worst home scenario and principles of **progression** and **regression** also come into play here. The appraiser's job is to see how well the property conforms to the neighborhood, and to see if the home's features and improvements are typical for the neighborhood. Most people want to live in areas with similar homes. A home that stands out as being too different from the rest may be worth less than that same home would be if it were in another more homogeneous neighborhood. Also, if too many homes stand out as different, the neighborhood's overall desirability may be affected.

Contribution

Contribution says that a particular item or feature of a property is worth only what it actually contributes in value to that piece of real estate.

For Example

Mary owns a four-bedroom home in a neighborhood of three- to four-bedroom homes. She plans on building an addition to her home to accommodate a fifth bedroom. However, since five-bedroom homes are not desirable in her neighborhood, she should not expect her home's value to be increased by the same amount as the cost of the addition when or if she sells it.

The theory of contribution is trickier when it comes to repairs. Necessary repairs may or may not add value to a property, depending on where the value started. Just because a $100,000 house needs a new $5,000 roof does not mean the value of the house automatically increases to $105,000. The new roof may be a nice feature that helps to sell the home, but it isn't necessarily worth $5,000 more.

On the other hand, if a home is in serious need of repair, the $4,000 spent on new siding could add significantly more value than just $4,000. This is especially true in a **progression** situation. Of course, not every repair will have this effect.

Law of Diminishing Returns

The **law of diminishing returns** *says that beyond a certain point, the added value of an additional feature, addition, repair, etc., is less than the actual cost of that item*. This is also called the **law of decreasing returns**. In other words, a homeowner can add too much to a property such that she cannot increase the price enough to recoup the money that she has invested. Homeowners may still want or need to do something to their property, but they shouldn't expect to get the full cost of the labor and materials back when they go to sell.

For Example

A homeowner spends $50,000 for kitchen cabinets in a neighborhood where the high-end value of homes is $75,000. The expenditure for kitchen cabinets is no doubt an over-improvement and is a prime example of the effects of the law of diminishing returns. Conformity and regression are at work here, too. Does the typical buyer in this price range want, need, or maybe most importantly, expect this level of cabinetry? It may influence the buyer's opinion of quality of the property, but almost certainly not dollar-for-dollar.

Let's look at another example.

For Example

A property owner has been in his home for just over a year. During that time, he spent $3,000 converting the previous three bedrooms into one large bedroom, replaced the five-year-old roof (with a different shade/pattern), spent over $12,000 repainting walls and replacing floor coverings (to shades of purple to match his furniture), replaced the nearly new 95% efficiency heating system (with a $10,000 98% efficiency system), and spent $5,000 converting half of the two-car garage into an office.

Strange and unlikely, you say? Not necessarily. In such a scenario, it is very likely the property owner will add the costs of these items to the initial property price paid, and probably apply some factor of appreciation. This process won't likely yield a reliable indication of market value because, in essence, the property may be worth less than what the owner paid for it.

For Example (cont.)

The question is, will the expenditures be perceived to hold contribution value by the typical buyer? If three bedrooms is the norm for the market, the conversion of three to one creates a functional obsolescence—conformity and regression once again.

The same would be true of the garage conversion if a two-car garage mostly conforms to the market. In such a case, the costs incurred would be lost, in addition to the loss of value due to the decrease in functional utility. Unless the roof was aesthetically unpleasant before it was replaced, the only advantage may be the five-year extension of the roof's life, certainly not the cost of replacement. And, yes, certain buyers like purple walls and flooring, but would that buyer represent the typical buyer, and how long would it take for that party to surface? Even if this buyer is recognized as "the market" for the property, the anticipated marketing time may increase. The benefit of the slight increase in efficiency of the heating system might not be fully recognized by market participants and probably not to the extent of the replacement cost.

The previous example helps to answer the question, "How much will replacing or updating an item increase the (market) value?" The logical response might be to consider how unacceptable that item is to the market currently.

Law of Increasing Returns

The **law of increasing returns** *says that the added value of an additional feature, repair, etc., is more than the actual cost of that item*. This goes back to the progression example where the house was in such need of repair that making any improvement (e.g., installing new siding) would have a dramatic increase in its value. Of course, one can go too far, and beyond a certain point, the law of diminishing returns will come into effect.

 Remember: The value of an item or improvement is equal only to what the market determines a typical buyer is willing to pay for it, not what it actually cost.

Types of Value

So far, we have talked about maximizing value. That's fine in theory but, in reality, there are many different kinds of value which produce very different value opinions. In fact, a property can have many different values at the same time. The type and definition of value in an appraisal should always be appropriate for its intended use.

For Example

A seller wants market value, the bank is interested in **loan value**, and an insurance company is concerned with **insurance value**.

Let's look at these and other types of value.

Market Value

Market value is *the most probable price that a property should bring in a competitive and open market* (e.g., a typical transaction). This value conclusion is the most frequently specified in an appraisal and, therefore, is likely to be the most common type of value used in typical real estate transactions in which real estate agents take part.

A typical transaction, also called an **arm's length transaction**, means that *the transaction occurred under typical conditions in the marketplace, with each of the parties acting in their own best interests*, where the:

- Buyer pays cash for the property at closing or obtains a mortgage through a lender so as to pay the seller the agreed-upon price at closing.

- Seller does not grant any unusual payment concessions, such as owner financing or other payment terms.

- Buyer and seller are not related in any way.

- Buyer and seller are both acting in their own best interests.

- Buyer and seller are not acting out of undue haste or duress.

- Buyer and seller are both reasonably informed about all aspects of the property, its potential uses, market value, and market conditions.

- Property has been available on the market for a reasonable period of time.

All of these factors should be taken into consideration when determining a property's value by comparing different sales to arrive at an estimate of value. These points affect the sale price of a property and, therefore, its perceived value. The appraiser's analysis includes determining whether any of these conditions affected the buyer's actions. If, in fact, the buyer was influenced by any of these atypical conditions, the transaction would not be considered arm's length.

For Example

If the seller was forced to sell because of a lost job, this would tend to lower the selling price of the subject home. If the seller agreed to some type of owner financing, this would allow the selling price to be higher. Again, an appraiser takes all of these things into account.

Market Value and the Secondary Market

Market value is now seen as the most probable selling price for real estate, according to the secondary mortgage market participants Federal Home Loan Mortgage Corporation (Freddie Mac) and Federal National Mortgage Association (Fannie Mae), as well as by the Uniform Standards of Professional Appraisal Practice (USPAP) guidelines.

Here is Fannie Mae's specific definition:

Market value is the most probable price a property should bring in a competitive and open market under all conditions requisite to a fair sale, the buyer and seller, each acting prudently, knowledgeably, and assuming the price is not affected by undue stimulus. Implicit in this definition is the consummation of a sale as of a specified date and the passing of title from seller to buyer under conditions whereby:

(1.) Buyer and seller are typically motivated;

(2.) Both parties are well informed or well advised, and each is acting in what he considers his own best interest;

(3.) A reasonable time is allowed for exposure in the open market;

(4.) Payment is made in terms of cash in U.S. dollars or in terms of financial arrangements comparable thereto; and

(5.) The price represents the normal consideration for the property sold unaffected by special or creative financing or sales concessions granted by anyone associated with the sale.

Loan Value

Loan value is the amount of money a lender is willing to let someone borrow to finance a property. Usually, this figure is a percentage of appraised value, known as a **loan-to-value ratio (LTV)**. This is explained in more detail in the Ohio Real Estate Finance textbook.

For Example

A lender may agree to let a person borrow 90% (LTV) of the appraised value. So if a house appraises for $100,000, then the loan value would be $90,000.

Insurance Value

Insurance value is the amount the property can be insured for, usually representing only the replacement costs of the structure and disregarding any value for the land (because land can't be "lost," and only the building needs to be replaced if it is destroyed). Insurance normally covers only **replacement cost**—the cost of building a functional equivalent of the original building, usually one that is the same size and utility as the original, but with modern materials. A different policy at a higher premium is needed to cover **reproduction cost**—which is the cost of building an exact replica of the original building, giving a new structure the same look and feel as the original.

Assessed Value

Assessed value is the amount of value used to calculate taxes due, and usually represents a percentage of the market value.

For Example

If the market value of a house is $100,000 with an assessment level of 35%, $100,000 x 35% would result in an assessed value of $35,000. This figure is then used along with the millage for a given area to determine tax due. Millage calculations are explained in the Math Appendix in the Ohio Real Estate Principles and Practices textbook.

Other Types of Value

Other types of value real estate agents may encounter include **asset value** (the value of property based on specific investment criteria), **book value** (the value of property as capital based on accounting methods), **liquidation value** (the value a property could get if sold under the duress of a must-sell situation with less than typical market exposure), and **salvage value** (the value of property in a distress situation).

For Example

A lawyer (the appraiser's client) specifies the appraisal's intended use is for settlement of a legal matter, with the appraisal's purpose being to determine the value of the property for a "quick sale." The term "quick sale" most likely infers *liquidation value* as the type of value desired in the assignment. Of course, before coming to this conclusion, the appraiser should confirm the client is suggesting the property must be sold in a less-than-typical marketing period, with less-than-typical market exposure.

Value vs. Price vs. Cost

Although, at times, the term "value" seems to be synonymous with "price," they really aren't. **Value** is what a typical buyer would pay for something; **price** is what one buyer paid; and **cost** is the dollars needed to develop, produce, or build something. **Market value** (as previously defined) is the most probable price that a property should bring in a competitive and open market (e.g., a typical transaction). But, the value of a property should not be confused with its price. **Market value** is what the property is *expected* to sell for; **market price** is *what the property actually sold for in a transaction.*

While the market price represents the final selling price, it is highly likely this is different from the **asking price** (*amount the seller asked for the property when it was first put on the market*) or the **offering price** (*amount the buyer first proposed to buy the property for*).

Of course, both value and price may have nothing to do with what the property actually cost to build. The value or price of the property is not necessarily related to what the person paid for the property—the price may have been more or less at that time. The current **market value**, as determined by a qualified appraiser, may or may not equal what someone will pay for it now.

Summary

1. Value is the amount of goods or services offered in the marketplace in exchange for something. Maximizing value requires four value characteristics **(D-U-S-T)**: Demand, Utility, Scarcity, and Transferability; and three physical characteristics: Immobility, Indestructibility, and Uniqueness. Buyers must want the home, feel it's useful to satisfy their needs, perceive a limited supply, and be free to transfer the home later.

2. Four broad forces that affect value are **(P-E-G-S)**: **Physical** (topography, water, location, popularity, and environment), **Economic** (business cycles, economic base, supply and demand, inflation, and cost of money), **Governmental** (revenue generating laws/taxes, right to regulate laws/police power, fiscal and monetary policy, secondary mortgage markets, and government programs—FHA/VA), and **Social** (demographics, migrations, trends, and tastes/standards).

3. Specific factors affecting value are economic or physical. **Change** is constantly occurring, so value is also subject to constant change (why appraisal is good for only one day). Economic (broad market) factors are supply and demand, and uniqueness and scarcity. **Supply and demand** create buyer's and seller's markets due to lag time for market forces to respond (although **balance** occurs when slightly more homes are available than buyers). **Uniqueness** can help or hurt a property and **scarcity** is due to limited land. Physical (property specific) factors are highest and best use, location, substitution, conformity, and contribution. **Highest and best use** is the most profitable, legal, feasible, and physically possible use of land. **Location** is the exact position of land. Progression occurs when the "worst" home's value is positively affected by others; regression occurs when the "best" home's value is negatively affected by others. **Substitution** is the theory that an informed buyer won't pay more for a home/feature than a comparable substitute. **Conformity** is the theory that a home achieves maximum value when surrounded by like homes. **Contribution** is the theory that an item is worth only what it contributes in value to real estate. The **law of diminishing returns** says that, beyond a certain point, added value of item is less than its actual cost.

4. Types of value include: **Market value**—the theoretical price real estate is most likely to bring in a typical transaction; **loan value**—the amount a lender is willing to let someone borrow for a property; **insurance value**—the amount property can be insured for (usually replacement cost of building, with no value for land); and **assessed value**—the amount used to calculate taxes due (usually a percentage of market value).

5. **Market value** is seen as the most probable price by Freddie Mac, Fannie Mae, and USPAP. A typical transaction is an **arm's length transaction**—a transaction that occurred under typical conditions in the marketplace where each party was acting in their own best interests. "Typical" conditions include: 1. Paid cash or mortgage through lender, 2. No owner financing or unusual payment terms, 3. Buyer and seller not related, 4. Buyer and seller acting in own best interests, 5. No undue haste or duress, 6. Parties are reasonably informed about property and market, and 7. Property has been on the market for a reasonable period of time.

6. **Value** and **price** aren't always equal. **Value** is what a typical person would pay; **price** is what one specific person paid; and **cost** is the dollars needed to build. **Market value** is what the property is expected to sell for; **market price** is what the property actually sold for. Both value and price may have nothing to do with what a property actually cost to buy or build.

Quiz

1. **The real estate market is said to be in balance when there are more**
   a. buyers than houses for sale.
   b. buyers than sellers.
   c. houses for sale than buyers.
   d. houses than apartments.

2. **The influence of the cost of money on real estate is**
   a. irrelevant because interest rates are not important to real estate.
   b. less than other big ticket items because mortgages have adjustable rates.
   c. more than other big ticket items because mortgages are long term.
   d. negligible because people are not always rational.

3. **How do the government programs administered by the FHA and VA affect the real estate market?**
   a. They build additional low-income housing.
   b. They make fewer houses available for the general public.
   c. They provide insurance or make loan guarantees to lenders.
   d. They service only veterans.

4. **The physical forces affecting real estate contribute to its value because**
   a. economies of scale will help those who buy more.
   b. people can just move to a new area anytime they want.
   c. a popular area will always remain popular and desired.
   d. there is a limited supply that cannot be moved, destroyed, or created.

5. **Uniqueness and scarcity help the value of real estate because**
   a. it's impossible to find exactly what you want in a house.
   b. no two properties are exactly the same.
   c. real estate is difficult to find.
   d. real estate is unlimited.

6. **ABC Company just opened in a new suburb of Pittsburgh. Potential workers are hoping to move into the area but there are limited houses for sale and no new construction underway. What type of market has been created?**
   a. a balanced market
   b. a buyer's market
   c. a seller's market
   d. a trader's market

7. **A new company that moves to an area helps the local real estate market by helping maintain a healthy**
   a. balance.
   b. economic base.
   c. economy of scale.
   d. environment.

8. **A nice, well-kept house located in the heart of an all-residential area, surrounded by other well-kept houses of similar style and value, is an example of**
   a. conformity.
   b. highest and best use.
   c. both conformity and highest and best use.
   d. neither conformity nor highest and best use.

9. **A run-down house in a good neighborhood**
   a. benefits from the principle of progression.
   b. benefits from the principle of regression.
   c. is hurt by the principle of progression.
   d. is hurt by the principle of regression.

10. **When the value of an additional feature is worth more than the actual cost of the item, this is an example of the law of**
    a. decreasing returns.
    b. diminishing returns.
    c. increasing returns.
    d. progressive returns.

11. *Maximum value for a property can be achieved only when*

    a. demand, utility, scarcity, transferability, and purchase ability are present.

    b. the market is in balance.

    c. supply outweighs demand.

    d. there is a buyer's market.

12. *Market value is the*

    a. dollars needed to rebuild the property.

    b. price determined by Freddie Mac, Fannie Mae, and/or USPAP.

    c. price a property actually sold for.

    d. theoretical price that real estate is most likely to bring in a typical transaction.

13. *Which is NOT part of an arm's length transaction?*

    a. buyer and seller are acting in their own best interest

    b. buyer and seller are not related

    c. buyer and seller are reasonably informed about the property and its uses

    d. buyer and seller have agreed upon payment terms for a land contract

The Appraisal Process

T his chapter briefly discusses the three appraisal approaches—sales comparison, cost approach, and income approach—before going into a detailed description of the steps in the appraisal process. The steps are similar regardless of the approach(es) relied upon for the appraiser's opinion of value. The steps are explained as they relate to the overall gathering and analysis of data. The approaches to value developed by the appraiser are reconciled to reach a conclusion of value, which is reported in written or oral fashion using one of three appraisal report types.

Key Terms

Change A principle affecting value in real estate that says all factors that influence real estate—physical, economic, governmental, and social—are constantly changing and thus, the property value itself is subject to constant change.

Cost Approach An appraisal method that develops an indication of the value of real property by figuring the cost of building the house or other improvement on the land, minus (-) depreciation, plus (+) the value of the vacant land.

Income Approach An appraisal method that develops an indication of the value of real property by analyzing the amount of income the property could generate using market data.

Lease A contract for which one party pays the other rent in exchange for possession of real estate.

Life Estate A freehold estate that lasts only as long as a specified person lives. That person is referred to as the **life tenant** or the **measuring life**.

Partial Interest Any interest in real property which one may have, other than the full bundle of rights.

Sales Comparison Approach An appraisal method that develops an indication of the value of real property by comparing the property being appraised with other recently sold properties. Data are collected and adjustments made for differences. Also called **Market Approach**.

Site A parcel of land with enhancements that make it ready for a building or structure.

Subject Property Property for which a value opinion is sought.

Property Valuation

For those unfamiliar with appraisal, the consensus might be that an appraiser gathers and looks at data about the property being appraised and then starts crunching numbers. Others are under the impression that the appraiser looks at, or considers, a property and then forms an immediate opinion about its value—the "crystal ball" misconception. Appraisal opinions are developed *objectively*. There is no place in professional appraisal practice for unsupported or "off the top of the head" subjectivity.

The Appraisal Process

When an appraisal is performed, there is a specific step-by-step procedure that must be followed. The purpose of this process is to ensure the process is orderly. By using the same logical progression of analysis in a thorough, comprehensive, and accurate manner, appraisals become a valuable tool lenders and others can rely on when making assessments and decisions with regard to a specific property.

The steps that must be performed for all appraisals include:

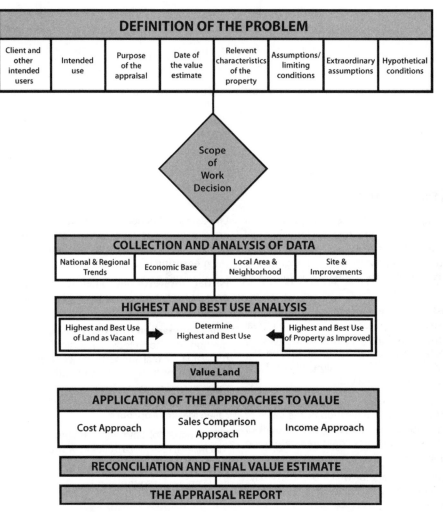

Let's examine each step in depth and discuss how an appraiser would accomplish each to arrive at a final opinion of property value.

Defining the Problem

Defining the problem consists of *identifying information the appraiser uses to determine the scope of work in an assignment*. Here, the appraiser identifies these elements:

- Client and intended users
- Intended use
- Purpose of the appraisal
- Date of value opinion
- Relevant property characteristics
- Other assignment conditions

Identify the Client and Other Intended Users

The **client** is the *party who engages the appraiser in an appraisal assignment, and with whom the appraiser has an appraiser-client relationship*. An **intended user** is a party *identified by the client* at the time of the assignment. The *client is always an intended user* in an assignment. Additional intended users may be specified by the client; and may or may not have the same need or use as the client. Therefore, additional intended users in an appraisal assignment might require additional steps or a different process for the appraiser than if the client was the only intended user.

In a mortgage transaction, it is important for real estate professionals to understand that the borrower, the property owner, and/or the real estate agent are not intended users in an assignment unless specified by the client at the onset. Thus, an appraiser cannot, without such specification or later consent, discuss the appraisal or the appraised value, or provide a copy of an appraisal report to any of these parties. Also, per USPAP, paying for an appraisal does not make that party the client or an intended user. This often becomes a topic that must be addressed by real estate professionals.

Identify the Intended Use of the Appraisal

An appraisal is the basis for a decision regarding real property. What that decision will be, or the **use of the appraisal**, is a *key determinant* of the research and analysis performed during the appraisal's development. Similar to intended users, different intended *uses* might require different research and/or analysis, or at different levels.

Identify the Purpose of the Appraisal

The **purpose of an appraisal** is always to *determine a value opinion for a defined type of value* and is very different from the intended use of the appraisal.

Market value is the value conclusion *most frequently specified* in an appraisal. However, other types of value can be derived, based on the appraisal's use. The type and definition of value should always be appropriate for its intended use.

Identify the Date of the Value Estimate

Two dates are required for every appraisal—the *effective date* and the *date of the report*. The **effective date** *establishes the context for the value opinion;* the **date of the report** is *an indication of the perspective from which the appraiser is examining the market*.

Because real estate markets are in constant change, the *effective date* of the value opinion must be determined and clearly stated in the appraisal report. Once again, intended use often dictates the date of relevance to a value opinion. The **effective date** can be a *current date, a retrospective date*, or a *prospective date*.

Usually, appraisals are performed with a *current effective date*. A **retrospective appraisal** uses an *effective date in the past*. Retrospective appraisals are performed for a variety of intended uses when a prior value opinion is needed, including estates, insurance claims, litigation, tax matters, etc.

An intended use calling for a *prospective* value opinion is usually a rare instance. In a **prospective appraisal,** the appraiser is *determining an opinion of a property's value on the date of the report as of a date in the future* (effective date) utilizing anticipated market conditions.

Identify the Relevant Characteristics of the Property

The list of property characteristics is endless: Single-family residence, multi-unit apartment building, manufactured home, vacant land, factory, commercial building, leasehold interest, etc. **Relevant property characteristics** have significant influence on the extent to which the property is identified and/or inspected, data that will be researched and analyzed, valuation methods employed, and the final reconciliation of value.

Relevant property characteristics include both the **physical** and **legal specifics** of the real estate and the **rights** being considered in the assignment.

Type of Property

An appraiser will likely approach assignments quite differently (e.g., single-family residential property vs. residential apartment, proposed improvements vs. existing structure). For example:

* Identification of proposed improvements requires extensive analysis of construction documents.

* An existing structure usually entails a completely different identification process.

* A drive-by inspection may not be sufficient if the property being appraised is not visible from the road.

* Appraising a fractional interest in real property is technically different, depending on type and definition of value and the property's characteristics.

Location

Properties can be *specific* or *general* in use. Sometimes, the property design determines its use. In other cases, zoning and deed restrictions play a key role, as these relate directly to the property's locational characteristics.

For Example

A single-family home, limited by regulation to a single residential use, is *specific* in use. But when regulations allow, for example, residential *or* commercial use, the diligence imposed on the appraiser becomes greater and the residential property's use could become *general*. Another example is a retail building in a mixed retail/office location.

Another relevant property characteristic inherent to location is *economic considerations*.

For Example

A property lacks demand due to a depressed economy. Consider a very developable parcel of land situated between two recently completed residential subdivisions. Most residents in adjoining subdivisions work at a local primary industry, or at a secondary employer whose business depends on the primary. The parcel has great potential to accommodate future residential development and, considering conformity, this use seems most logical. However, the primary industry eliminated one entire shift in the factory, and laid-off one-half of its workforce. Economically, the physical characteristics of the land parcel are challenged, especially if regulations limit its use to residential development.

A circumstance related to economics and physical characteristics is *supply and demand*. In the previous example, the physical characteristics of the property limit the use and the market segment for that use is out of balance, with a far greater supply of that particular property type in relation to demand.

Interest to be Appraised

In most cases, an appraisal is performed for an opinion of value for the *fee simple interest,* or entire physical property including the bundle of rights. However, a *partial interest* including a lease or life estate, fractional interest, or even a physical segment of the property is sometimes the subject of an appraisal. Additionally, the appraiser must identify any personal property being considered in the assignment.

When an appraisal is performed for something less than a complete transfer of rights in a fee simple transaction, the appraisal is said to be an *appraisal of partial interests.* A **partial interest** is *any interest in real estate which one may have, other than the full bundle of rights.*

For Example

An individual may have only *mineral rights,* a *lease,* or a *life estate.*

Mineral rights could be sold off separately so the value of these rights could be the subject of an appraisal. When the land is later sold, the fact that some of these rights were sold off separately would impact the value of the property. An appraisal must take this into account.

A **lease** is *a contract for which one party pays the other rent in exchange for possession of real estate.* A lease is an encumbrance that affects value. It can be a positive influence (e.g., when an office building is fully leased) or a negative influence (e.g., when an old building can't be torn down because of a lease with a tenant). A leasehold estate can also have value if it is a long-term lease at a lower price than current market rental rates in the area (providing the lease can be transferred).

A **life estate** is *a freehold estate that lasts only as long as a specified person lives. That person is referred to as the life tenant or* **measuring life**. The life tenant could live in the house, but once he dies, the house reverts back to the owner so it won't go through the life tenant's estate and probate court. Parents could actually sell off their interest in a property creating a **life estate pur autre vie** (life estate for the life of another). When the parents die, their children still get the property back from whomever they sold it to. Obviously, this type of partial interest would be of considerably less value than a **fee simple estate**. But it is possible to sell off partial interests in real estate in this manner, and an appraisal must take this into account.

Thus, the purpose of an appraisal may be a valuation for purposes of selling the entire bundle of rights, or for selling off some of the rights separately. There are also other reasons to value property.

For Example

An insurance appraisal has different goals and requires different criteria and data than a loan appraisal.

Each type of appraisal requires different skills and experience to arrive at an accurate estimate of value.

Identify Other Assignment Conditions

There are many assignment conditions the appraiser considers. Most importantly, for our discussion here, the appraiser considers laws, regulations, and guidelines that apply in an assignment. Government agencies like HUD, the FHA, and the VA have certain property identification (inspection), analysis, and reporting requirements. Others, such as Fannie Mae, Freddie Mac, and Ginnie Mae, have their own regulations. It is fairly safe to say that, in all appraisals performed for most mortgage transactions, there will be certain regulations necessary for the appraiser to comply with. Here are a few common examples:

- The FHA requires the appraiser to view the crawl space and attic, and observe the operation of mechanical systems of the subject property (as applicable).

- Fannie Mae does *not* allow for the appraisal of a physical segment (or part) of a property.

- Fannie Mae (and others) requires the use of the standardized residential reporting forms.

- Fannie Mae (and others) requires that the interior of a manufactured dwelling be inspected, as well as the exterior.

- Fannie Mae (and others) requires a *minimum of three* comparable sales when developing the sales comparison approach.

The importance of competently recognizing laws and regulations prevailing in an assignment during problem identification, especially in many appraisal assignments for use in residential lending, is that ethically, the appraiser cannot disregard them.

Scope of Work

After the appraiser properly considers all information obtained during problem identification, the next step in the process is to determine the **scope of work**. The scope of work includes the appropriate development elements for the remainder of the assignment.

It may be helpful to think of *scope of work* as an appraisal plan—an outline identifying the work needed to complete the appraisal. The "plan" can be used as a guide for all who will participate in the appraisal, as well as a basis for the appraiser to establish an appropriate fee for the assignment.

Appraisals are not "one size fits all." The *scope of work* determines the steps going forward including, but certainly not limited to:

- Extent to which the property is identified

- Extent to which the property is inspected

- Type and extent of data researched

- Type and extent of analysis applied

The decisions made here must lead to credible assignment results. In other words, the *scope of work* determination must be logical and reliable for the intended user and intended use, and will depend greatly on the relevant property characteristics.

Collection and Analysis of Data

In addition to collecting and analyzing data, a real estate appraiser must verify the data. It's important for the appraiser to ensure that all data and facts relied upon in performing the appraisal are the most current and complete available. In Chapter 5, we'll talk about sources of appraisal data that an appraiser typically uses. Two types of appraisal data are *general data* and *specific data*.

General Data

Appraisers should have ready access to typical general data information required for an appraisal, since most appraisers work within a given region or area. This general data will cover some of the broad forces that we talked about which affect value: **P-E-G-S—P**hysical, **E**conomic, **G**overnmental, and **S**ocial. Appraisers must be current regarding interest rate trends, on a national level, and business conditions affecting the economic base of an area. Changes in federal laws are as important as changes in local laws, particularly zoning. Demographic changes, population shifts, and buyer tastes on the national and local level are all important. Physical and environmental changes and trends all come into play.

General data sources typically include:

- Government records

- Public records and filings

- Magazines, newsletters, and trade publications

- Other sources the appraiser has come to rely upon because of their timeliness and accuracy

Most professional appraisers keep up-to-date files with the latest information on economic trends in an area, as well as changes in laws and other aspects affecting real estate markets.

Specific Data

Specific data that's collected, verified, and analyzed can be further divided into two categories:

- Data about the subject property

- Data for comparative purposes

Subject Property Data

Specific subject property data includes information on a subject's site and improvements. Each must be described in detail. A site's legal description is often found in title work or public records, and verified by personal observation. Description of improvements is acquired through personal observation of the interior and exterior of the structure. USPAP rules state that an appraiser must also analyze any current sales contract, option, or property listing, if available to the appraiser, and analyze any prior sales of the property occurring within the past three years.

Comparative Purposes Data

Specific data for comparative purposes requires that data be obtained for each of the approaches to value being developed:

Approach	Obtained From
Sales Comparison	• Buyers, sellers, real estate agents, multiple listing services, and public records
Cost	• Cost manuals detailing building and construction costs in a given area • Good relationships with builders and developers
Income	• Sellers, investors, accountants, and others • Internet-based sources, from public records to cost information

Determine the Highest and Best Use

Determining the highest and best use for the subject property is *one of the most important steps in the appraisal process in a market value assignment*. In fact, highest and best use is at the heart of the valuation process. The appraiser must look at the use of the land which supports the highest value for the property as of the effective date of the appraisal.

The goal of determining highest and best use is to determine whether or not the property is being used for its most profitable permitted use. Of course, with homes in a residential neighborhood, this is not usually an issue. What about a house in a commercial district? Usually, the property would be more profitable if it were generating income from a commercial use (as opposed to being rented as a residence).

With vacant land in an area that's changing, growing, or expanding, highest and best use can be a significant point that needs to be addressed. As mentioned, sometimes a change of structure is best to maximize the value of the land. In fact, razing one type of structure in favor of another is also a consideration. To determine the highest and best use for a property, the appraiser performs three steps:

1. Estimates value as if the land were vacant

2. Estimates value as the land is currently improved

3. Compares the values derived from each of the first two steps to determine the highest and best use

Tests of Highest and Best Use

When evaluating the highest and best use of a property, the appraiser looks at four tests for highest and best use:

Is the ideal improvement....	Evaluation Based Upon	Questions
Legally permitted?	Government restrictions, as well as deed or other restrictions	• Is the ideal type of building permitted with the existing zoning on the property? • What is the chance of a zoning change? A zoning change must be shown to be reasonable or probable—not speculative.
Physically possible?	Physical limitations of the land	• Is the lot big enough to allow for the building and required setbacks? • Does the topography of the land allow the ideal type of building? • Will the ground support the weight of a large building?
Economically feasible?	If there is a market for the improvement	• Can the market support another improvement of this type in its supply/demand model? • Are the other principles of value conducive to this type of improvement?
The most profitable?	The economic advantage that would be produced	• Would other types of improvements bring greater value to the land?

Keep in mind that an appraiser may actually look at several different options before arriving at a conclusion of highest and best use, but only the option that provides the greatest economic advantage is selected and ultimately determined to be the highest and best use. However, the final determination of highest and best use (like all values derived in appraisal) is the appraiser's opinion. The appraiser's opinion must always be supported by objective data and facts that have been thoroughly analyzed. The appraiser's experience, knowledge, and skill are very important.

Other Points about Highest and Best Use

For appraisal purposes, market value of property is always considered as if the land is vacant and available for development to its highest and best use. The appraiser must perform careful analysis of all alternative uses for the property before arriving at a conclusion. If certain uses are not possible, the appraiser should note this in the appraisal report, along with the appropriate reasons.

 If the determination is that a property would be more valuable if the current structure were torn down and replaced with a new type of building, the cost of razing the building must be subtracted from the value figure.

A valid analysis of highest and best use translates into the most profitable use of the land, which in turn determines the most probable (and highest) price the property can command in the open market.

As a final note, it is important to understand that there are certain assumptions made when discussing the determination of highest and best use:

- There is only one highest and best use for land at a given point in time.

- Highest and best use implies the right mix of capital improvements and land.

- Land not devoted to highest and best use results in a loss of income.

- Highest and best use gives the owner maximum economic advantage.

- Highest and best use allocates land resources efficiently; maximizing economic return.

- Highest and best use gives economic benefits to surrounding land (conformity).

- Highest and best use gives economic benefits to community (conserves a scarce resource—land).

Determine the Value of the Land

In many appraisals, the scope of work will include an analysis of land, or site value as vacant. A **site** is *a parcel of land with enhancements that make it ready for a building or structure*. These enhancements include elements such as sewer, septic system, well, water, or other utility hookups. Land must be valued separately for the cost approach method of appraisal, since a separate site value is added to the cost of replacing the building to arrive at a total value. A separate site value is also used for the building residual income technique (an income approach appraisal method). Another use for a separate value of land is an insurance appraisal, where a value is sought for a building without regard for the land. Here, the total value of the property, minus the value of the land, is one way to derive the value of the building by itself.

There are five popular methods to derive a value for land apart from any structures on it:

- Sales comparison
- Allocation
- Subdivision analysis
- Land residual
- Ground rent capitalization

Each of these methods will be fully discussed in Chapter 8.

Application of the Approaches of Value

The value opinion for the subject property should be developed using the applicable approach(es) to value (e.g., sales comparison approach, cost approach, income approach). In some cases, all of the approaches to value could be applicable and be developed. In other circumstances, only one or two of the approaches to value will be developed.

Here is a sampling of questions that come to mind when determining the applicability of the approaches to value:

- How can the sales comparison approach be used if there aren't enough (or any) recent comparable sales in the area for an uncommon building that's being sold (e.g., school, church, library)?

- How can the cost approach be used to arrive at an accurate cost for an old building, a unique building (e.g., museum), or a large structure that would be subject to future inflationary pressure to rebuild and prone to cost overruns (e.g., arena)?

- How useful is the income approach for residential properties in an area that is almost exclusively owner-occupied and there is little or no data on rent or income figures for homes in the area?

Sometimes, one valuation approach can be used to support the conclusions reached in another valuation approach. The three appraisal approaches—**sales comparison approach, cost approach,** and **income approach**—will be discussed in detail in Chapters 9, 10, and 11.

Reconciliation and Final Value Estimate

Indications of value from the approaches that have been developed are reconciled to arrive at a final value conclusion. Rarely, if ever, are the value indications from different approaches equal. This is where the appraiser's knowledge and experience are invaluable. Reconciliation involves giving each approach to value an appropriate weight, depending on the type of property being analyzed and the amount and quality of data available.

For Example

If the appraisal is for a single-family home, the appraiser would likely give the most weight to the sales comparison approach. This is not only because it would provide the most recent information, but also because the appraiser knows this approach typically provides the most reliable information and the most accurate indicator of a property's market value.

If the appraisal were for an income-producing property, the appraiser would likely give the most weight to the income approach; and so on.

The indications from each of the three approaches are **never** mathematically averaged. Opinions are not developed by using mechanical techniques, but rather sound judgment. This is where the appraiser's experience contributes as he decides the importance of the results and conclusions of the overall appraisal effort. It's important to remember that even with all of the appraiser's extensive knowledge and experience, and the extensive research and calculations that go into an appraisal, the appraiser is able only to form an opinion of the value of a property. Only the marketplace can truly determine the value of a property.

Report Conclusions

The final step of the valuation process is to prepare and submit a report of the conclusions. The report should include all data gathered and analyzed, including specific references where appropriate to support conclusions, and a final value estimate for the subject property.

USPAP has specific standards and guidelines that apply to each type of written or oral report. These specific guidelines for appraisal reports will be examined in greater detail in Chapter 12.

There are three important requirements for all reports, written or oral, from which USPAP does not allow deviation:

Each written or oral property appraisal report must:

(a) clearly and accurately set forth the appraisal in a manner that will not be misleading;

(b) contain sufficient information to enable the intended users of the appraisal to understand the report properly; and

(c) clearly and accurately disclose all assumptions, extraordinary assumptions, hypothetical conditions, and limiting conditions used in the assignment

Report Types

USPAP allows an appraisal to be *oral* or *written*. However, oral reports are rare for most appraisals, and have special USPAP requirements. In most cases, the appraisal report will be written.

The appraisal report is the primary means of communicating the appraisal results to the client. The appraisal report not only reports a final opinion of value for the subject property, but also explains the appraiser's reasoning to the client and anyone else authorized to use the appraisal.

The appraiser may choose, based upon the intended use and the intended user(s) of the appraisal, various levels of reporting as allowed by USPAP. In addition, the appraiser may choose, or be directed by the client, to report the appraisal by using a narrative format, which is somewhat like a thesis, or a reporting form. *Most residential appraisals for use in financing utilize standardized mortgage industry forms.*

Uniform Residential Appraisal Report (URAR)

The **Uniform Residential Appraisal Report (URAR)** form is a standard industry appraisal report form used by lenders and appraisers. It was developed and approved by the secondary mortgage market participants Fannie Mae and Freddie Mac. As the name implies, it is used for residential appraisals and is preferred by lenders because it is standardized; allowing residential properties to be compared in a consistent manner. Real estate agents will likely see this form throughout their career.

 The entire, completed URAR appraisal report form appears in Chapter 12.

Summary

1. Value opinions for a property can be developed using the **sales comparison approach** (value opinion by performing market analysis of area where subject property is located), **cost approach** (value opinion by figuring cost of building, minus depreciation, plus site value), or **income approach** (value opinion by analyzing income a property could potentially generate).

2. The first step in the appraisal process is to **define the problem**. This includes identifying the client and any other intended users, the intended use, the type of value to be determined in the assignment, and the effective date of the appraisal. **Effective date** is important because of the principle of **change**—all factors influencing real estate (economic, physical, etc.) constantly change; so do property values. Relevant property characteristics must be identified, and so must the rights being appraised. A **partial interest** is any interest one may have in real estate other than full bundle of rights (e.g., mineral rights or lease). Finally, any assignment conditions, such as FHA or Fannie Mae regulations must be identified.

3. The next step of the appraisal process is to determine the **scope of work** to be performed in the assignment. The scope of work includes the appropriate development elements for the remainder of the assignment. Then, the appraiser needs to collect and analyze the relevant **general data** and **specific data**. Specific data includes data on the subject property and data for comparative purposes.

4. Determining **highest and best use** is one of most important appraisal steps. The goal is to determine if property is used for its most profitable permitted use. There are three steps. **Step 1**: Estimate value as if land were vacant (Is ideal improvement legally permitted? Can it be physically built? Is it economically feasible? Is it most profitable?). **Step 2**: Estimate value as land is currently improved. **Step 3**: Final determination of highest and best use by comparing conclusions derived from Steps 1 and 2. Other points on highest and best use: Only one highest and best use at a time; implies right mix of capital and land; land not used for highest and best use equals loss of income; highest and best use gives owner economic advantage; allocates resources efficiently; gives economic benefit to nearby land (conformity); gives economic benefit to community (conserves scarce resource—land).

5. Value of land or site is often derived separately (mostly for cost approach). There are four methods—**sales comparison, allocation, extraction,** or **capitalization of ground rents**. Next, property is appraised using one or more of the three approaches to value—**sales comparison approach**, **cost approach**, and **income approach**.

6. Value indications from the three approaches are reconciled, **never** mathematically averaged. The appraiser's judgment and experience decide which approach is given most weight. Report conclusions of value estimates should include references to data used. USPAP says report must be clear, accurate, and not misleading; have enough information so it can be understood; and must disclose assumptions or conditions. Appraisal reports may be **written** or **oral**, and must provide detail sufficient for the intended use and the intended user(s). Also, reports can be provided in a narrative format or by a standardized industry form.

Quiz

1. **Which is NOT an approach to value?**
   a. comparative market analysis
   b. cost approach
   c. income approach
   d. sales comparison approach

2. **As an appraiser defines the appraisal problem, he would NOT identify the**
   a. effective date of the appraisal.
   b. purpose of the appraisal (type of value).
   c. relevant characteristics of the property being appraised.
   d. racial makeup of a neighborhood.

3. **A partial interest in real estate is**
   a. also known as fee simple interest.
   b. an interest that is the entire bundle of rights, plus some additional rights.
   c. any interest in real estate that is less than the entire bundle of rights.
   d. an interest that is held by more than one co-owner.

4. **The principle of change says**
   a. all factors that influence real estate are constantly changing and, thus, the property value itself is subject to constant change.
   b. the property value itself should only increase.
   c. some factors that influence real estate are subject to change and, thus, the property value itself may change from time to time.
   d. the appraiser and the method used will affect the market value of real estate.

5. **Why is the effective date important in an appraisal?**
   a. The appraisal is valid for one year from the date of the appraisal.
   b. The appraisal is valid for six months from the date of the appraisal.
   c. The appraisal is valid only as of the effective date on the appraisal.
   d. The date is not important because of the principle of change.

6. **Appraiser J is completing an appraisal assignment for a 15-year-old house. Which type of data would be LEAST relevant to the appraisal?**
   a. general data covering the great forces in the marketplace
   b. specific data for comparative purposes (such as other sales or cost information)
   c. specific data on the subject property (such as legal description)
   d. specific data on the transfer history of the property going back to the original deed

7. **When looking at highest and best use, what is the primary question the appraiser must answer?**
   a. Can the client afford to have existing improvements razed?
   b. What is the best way to ensure value without tearing down the existing structure(s), if at all possible?
   c. What is the ideal improvement for each possible zoning type?
   d. What is the ideal improvement for the land if it were vacant?

8. **Which is NOT an important assumption of highest and best use?**
   a. Highest and best use gives maximum economic advantage to the owner.
   b. Highest and best use implies the right mix of capital improvements and land.
   c. Land devoted to highest and best use will always result in a loss of income.
   d. There is only one highest and best use for land at a given point in time.

9. **When reconciling indications of value, an appraiser _____ mathematically averages them.**
   a. always
   b. never
   c. rarely
   d. sometimes

10. **According to USPAP, appraisal reports must**
    a. be prepared on an industry form.
    b. be provided to the client in written form only.
    c. be provided to the property owner, even if he is not the client.
    d. clearly and accurately set forth the appraisal in a manner that will not be misleading.

Appraisal Data

The collection and analysis of appraisal data is an important part of the appraisal process. Without accurate and reliable information, an appraisal lacks credibility. This chapter will detail some of the sources that appraisers use to obtain and verify data used in an appraisal. It will also look at final product of an appraisal: The appraisal report. This analysis will include a review of some of the sections that appear in the Uniform Residential Appraisal Report (URAR) form used by lenders and appraisers for residential properties.

Key Terms

Cost Manuals Books, electronic media, and online sources that give estimated construction costs for various types of buildings in different areas of the country.

General Data Information that covers the forces that affect property values, but are not directly related to a particular piece of property. General data covers **p**hysical, **e**conomic, **g**overnmental, and **s**ocial factors (P-E-G-S) and can be local or national.

Multiple Listing Services (MLS°) A listing service whereby local member brokers agree to share listings and commissions on properties sold jointly.

Specific Data Information that is relevant to the subject property itself or specific comparable properties. There are two types of specific data: **Subject Property Data** (information on the subject property site and improvements) and **Comparative Purpose Data** (information about comparable sale properties, as well as income and cost information).

Uniform Residential Appraisal Report (URAR) A standard appraisal report form used by lenders and appraisers; developed and approved by secondary mortgage market participants Fannie Mae and Freddie Mac.

Types of Appraisal Data

As discussed in the last chapter on the appraisal process, there are two categories that appraisal data can fall into:

- General data
- Specific data

General Data

General data *covers forces that affect a property's value, but are not directly related to a particular piece of property.* General data encompasses all information that affects a particular area or region, including the four great forces that affect real estate (**P-E-G-S**): **P**hysical features, **E**conomic trends, **G**overnment policies, and **S**ocial trends. It also covers information relevant to business and the housing market both nationally and locally.

Specific Data

Specific data *covers all information relevant to the subject property itself or specific comparable properties.* Specific data includes such things as features of the site and improvements, as well as information that is collected for comparative purposes (e.g., comparable sales, cost data, income information). There are two types of specific data:

- **Subject Property Data**—Includes information on the subject property site and improvements.
- **Comparative Purpose Data**—Includes information about comparable sale properties, as well as income and cost information.

Before looking at examples of appraisal data, let's look at the data resources that appraisers use as the source of the data they need.

Appraisal Data Resources

Appraisers use a number of data resources in their data collection process. Some of these sources should already be familiar to real estate agents; others may not be as they are more closely associated with the appraisal profession. These resources can be divided into the categories of general data resources and specific data resources.

General Data Resources

General data resources can be divided into sources on the national and local level. Depending on the appraisal, further clarification may be needed on a regional, state-wide, or city level. Typically, when looking at general data resources, the appraiser is interested in trends:

- Is the economy (or perception of the economy) generally favorable and, thus, conducive to more people seeking homeownership?
- What about interest rates?
- Are any new government regulations coming that may impact homeownership?
- What demographic changes are taking place (e.g., changes in family size)?
- Is the population of the city/region growing or declining?

More information regarding the local economy and government may be required:

- Is a local business looking to expand and add more jobs, or are layoffs coming?
- How stable is the economic base? Is it dependent on one primary industry or are many sectors contributing to stability?
- Are there any growth plans for the city? If so, in what direction?
- Are any zoning changes likely to take place in the near future?

An appraiser who actively practices in a particular area may not have to do this general assessment each time an appraisal is done. Rather, an appraiser reviews general data on a regular basis and often keeps updated files which contain facts and information relevant to the real estate markets where he practices appraisal most often. These files are the appraiser's best resource.

A list of general data resources appears in the following chart. Each resource is constantly monitored for relevancy, accuracy, and reliability of information. Unreliable sources are discarded or not relied on heavily, while new sources are continually added.

General Data Resources *		
Government Repositories	**Professional Repositories**	**Other Resources**
Government census data	Trade publications or newsletters	Magazines and newspapers
Government publications	Professional magazines, journals	Maps and reports
Government records	REALTOR® boards	Lenders and mortgage companies
Courthouse and registrars	Multiple listing services (MLS)	Property managers and rental companies
Public records and filings	Internet resources	Moving and storage companies
U.S. Department of Commerce or local chamber of commerce	Home builder associations or other professional associations	Employment agencies or labor groups
Planning, highway, county commissioner's offices	Accountants, lawyers, engineers, and other business people	Builders, contractors, and architects
FHA or other government agencies	Specialized research companies	Colleagues and other contacts

Note that these lists are not all inclusive. Some of these sources may also be used as specific data.

Notice that *multiple listing services (MLS)* is a general data resource (also included on the next page as a specific data resource). A **multiple listing service (MLS)** is *a listing service whereby local member brokers agree to share listings and commissions on properties sold jointly.* This is a good resource for appraisers because it usually contains detailed sales and feature information about properties in a given area, but must be verified. The main drawback is that it doesn't cover all properties sold, particularly those sold by owners.

Specific Data Resources

Specific data resources can be subdivided into sources that provide specific data or information about the *subject property* and sources that provide specific data or information for *comparative purposes*. Here, the appraiser is interested in very specific facts, numbers, and data that are relevant to the property being appraised. Research must be done to obtain this information.

For Example

The appraiser will often rely on courthouse records or other public records as the starting point for compiling information on the subject property. But appraisers must always check the accuracy of the information obtained from other sources. One of the most important ways to do this is with a thorough personal inspection of the subject property. In fact, much of the information an appraiser needs is obtained by a simple personal inspection. The appraiser will measure the outside walls of a property to determine square footage and make other observations that are noted in the appraisal report. These observations will range from general impressions of the property's appearance all the way down to specific details about materials used in the bathroom.

Sources that provide specific data or information for comparative purposes will vary depending upon the approach(es) to value that will be developed by the appraiser. Like the personal inspection of the subject property noted above, the most reliable data obtained for comparative purposes is also of a personal nature. Previous buyers or sellers, as well as real estate agents or other professionals involved in a transaction, are often the appraiser's best source of information. It is hard to know the reasons, motivations, concessions, or other special circumstances that may have influenced a transaction unless one talks to the parties involved. In fact, sometimes this is the only way to make sure that a sale was an arm's length transaction and that there was no undue pressure on either of the parties to act.

Unlike general data resources, specific data resources must be consulted *every time* an appraisal is done. Appraisers can't make assumptions based on previous appraisals, nor can old data be used. Comparable sales are considered most reliable if they have transacted during similar market conditions. Other data should be the most relevant to the assignment.

A list of specific data resources appears in the following chart. Note that there is some overlap between the different types of specific data, as well as some overlap with general data resources. For all specific property information, the most reliable sources are personal inspection and conversations with the parties involved. As with general data resources, specific data resources must also be verified for accuracy. This will be discussed more in the next section on data collection.

Specific Data Resources*		
PROPERTY SPECIFIC		
Personal inspection	County records: deed, mortgage, taxes	Multiple listing services (MLS)
Buyer, seller, broker, and agent	Internet resources	Published, recorded information
COMPARATIVE		
Sales Comparison Data	**Cost Approach Data**	**Income/Expense Data**
Personal inspection (condition)	Personal inspection (depreciation)	Personal inspection (vacancy)
Buyer, seller, broker, and agent	Cost manuals (books, electronic, Internet)	Seller, broker, and agent
County records: deed, mortgage, taxes	Supply houses and labor pools	Property managers and rental companies
Multiple listing services (MLS)	Architects, contractors, and engineers	Accountants and other professionals
Computer databases and Internet	Internet resources	Financial statements
Published, recorded information	Professional magazines, journals, and organizations	Professional journals and organizations

Note that these lists are not all inclusive.

Data Collection

Data collection is an important part of the appraisal process. Just as important is the verification and analysis of the data. In fact, verification is the most important aspect of an appraisal. All data collected should first be verified for relevancy, accuracy, and reliability. The appraiser must also consider the relevance of the data.

 Remember: Ideal sales comparison data should reflect market conditions similar to those on the effective date of the appraisal.

Cost approach data should be from the most recent *cost sources*. **Cost sources** include *printed manuals, electronic media, and online sources that give estimated construction costs for various types of buildings in different areas of the country.* Income and expense data should be relevant and representative to the type of value in the assignment (e.g., market level income and expenses are used when appraising for market value).

Efficient Data Collection

Technology has assisted to streamline the appraisal process. From cross-checking and cross-referencing sources to gathering data and completing appraisal reports, technology has made data collection more efficient. Numerous appraisal software programs are available to help the appraiser perform routine tasks and process reports and paperwork more efficiently. In most areas, courthouse records and other public information can be obtained online, and still more information on building costs, economic trends, and real estate in general can be found on the Internet. And of course, there are the multiple listing services which are available online in most areas.

As more and more information can be accessed online, it's important for the appraiser to take steps to verify the accuracy of the information being used as the basis of the appraisal by cross-checking with other sources. One of the best means for verifying much of the data about the subject property is still a personal inspection. This may slow the appraisal process somewhat (and may be one of the reasons that the appraisal is perceived as a bottleneck in real estate closings), but the methodical verification of all relevant data is necessary to arrive at conclusions that can be relied upon by lending institutions, and others who may never see the subject property and rely on the experience and expertise of the appraiser to make an informed decision.

General and Specific Data Sections—URAR Form

The **Uniform Residential Appraisal Report (URAR)** is *a standard appraisal report form used by lenders and appraisers. It has been developed and approved by secondary mortgage market participants Fannie Mae and Freddie Mac.* Our discussion focuses on the Uniform Residential Appraisal Report form, since it is likely that real estate agents will come in contact with this form most often in their careers. There are certainly other reporting forms that may be used for different property types and in different circumstances than will be presented here—both less and more detailed. For most residential appraisals, though, it's usually adequate for an appraiser to address those areas covered by the URAR.

We'll look at the URAR as a basis for compiling data, as we discuss some of the data and sources needed to complete each section. It is likely that information is first recorded elsewhere by the appraiser on some other data gathering form(s) before being transcribed to a URAR. We'll discuss the content on the first page of the URAR form. The second page contains sections for reporting the analysis of the cost approach, sales comparison approach, and income approach, along with sections for comments and reconciliation. This portion of the URAR will be discussed in later chapters.

Uniform Residential Appraisal Report   File # 18988

The purpose of this summary appraisal report is to provide the lender/client with an accurate, and adequately supported, opinion of the market value of the subject property.

Property Address 22 OAKWOOD DRIVE	City WESTERVILLE State OH Zip Code 43081
Borrower CHRISTOPHER S. JONES Owner of Public Record JAMES R. & MARIA S. HOLDER	County FRANKLIN

Legal Description LOT #27, PHASE II, LAKE RIDGE SUBDIVISION

Assessor's Parcel # 62-42316000   Tax Year 2004   R.E. Taxes $ 4,397.00

Neighborhood Name LAKE RIDGE SUBDIVISION   Map Reference 45 P40   Census Tract 0071.93

Occupant ☒ Owner ☐ Tenant ☐ Vacant   Special Assessments $ ☐ PUD   HOA $ N/A ☐ per year ☐ per month

Property Rights Appraised ☒ Fee Simple ☐ Leasehold ☐ Other (describe)

Assignment Type ☒ Purchase Transaction ☐ Refinance Transaction ☐ Other (describe)

Lender/Client SECOND FEDERAL MORTGAGE   Address 2723 NORTH MAIN STREET, HILLIARD, OHIO

Is the subject property currently offered for sale or has it been offered for sale in the twelve months prior to the effective date of this appraisal? ☒ Yes ☐ No

Report data source(s) used, offering price(s), and date(s). THE SUBJECT HAS BEEN LISTED THROUGH THE COLUMBUS MULTIPLE LISTING SERVICE FOR $179,900. THE PROPERTY HAS BEEN LISTED APPROXIMATELY 35 +/- DAYS.

I ☒ did ☐ did not analyze the contract for sale for the subject purchase transaction. Explain the results of the analysis of the contract for sale or why the analysis was not performed. THE CURRENT AGREEMENT TO PURCHASE INCLUDES THE FOLLOWING PERSONALTIES: RANGE, REFRIGERATOR AND MISCELLANEOUS WINDOW COVERINGS. NONE ARE CONSIDERED TO CONTRIBUTE SIGNIFICANT VALUE TO THE TRANSACTION.

Contract Price $ 178,000   Date of Contract 6/1/2005   Is the property seller the owner of public record? ☒ Yes ☐ No Data Source(s) FRANKLIN CO. REC.

Is there any financial assistance (loan charges, sale concessions, gift or downpayment assistance, etc.) to be paid by any party on behalf of the borrower? ☒ Yes ☐ No

If Yes, report the total dollar amount and describe the items to be paid. $3,000.00   THE SELLER IS PAYING UP TO $3,000 TOWARD THE PURCHASER'S POINTS AND/OR CLOSING COSTS.

Note: Race and the racial composition of the neighborhood are not appraisal factors.

Neighborhood Characteristics	One-Unit Housing Trends	One-Unit Housing		Present Land Use %	
		PRICE	AGE		
Location ☐ Urban ☒ Suburban ☐ Rural	Property Values ☒ Increasing ☐ Stable ☐ Declining	$ (000)	(yrs)	One-Unit	90 %
Built-Up ☐ Over 75% ☒ 25-75% ☐ Under 25%	Demand/Supply ☐ Shortage ☒ In Balance ☐ Over Supply	155 Low	2	2-4 Unit	%
Growth ☒ Rapid ☐ Stable ☐ Slow	Marketing Time ☒ Under 3 mths ☐ 3-6 mths ☐ Over 6 mths	279 High	9	Multi-Family	%
Neighborhood Boundaries SPRINGHILL DRIVE TO THE NORTH, STONERIDGE DRIVE TO THE EAST,		180 Pred.	5	Commercial	%
FLOWER AVENUE TO THE SOUTH, CUSTER DRIVE TO THE WEST.				Other	10 %

Neighborhood Description THE IMMEDIATE MARKET AREA IS PREDOMINATELY SINGLE-FAMILY HOUSING OF VARIOUS STYLES WITH SCATTERED UPPER-MID RANGE CUSTOM CONSTRUCTION. PROXIMITY TO SERVICES, EMPLOYMENT, AND RECREATION IS CONSIDERED AVERAGE. OTHER LAND USE IS THE INFLUENCE OF A PUBLIC PARK WITHIN THE DEFINED NEIGHBORHOOD.

Market Conditions (including support for the above conclusions) INTEREST RATES APPEAR TO BE STABLE AND REMAIN FAVORABLE, WITH MANY FINANCING AVENUES AVAILABLE. ONGOING NEW CONSTRUCTION SUPPORTS STEADY TO RAPID GROWTH PATTERN OF THE OVERALL MARKET. EXISTING HOUSING RESALES COUPLED WITH NEW CONSTRUCTION MAINTAIN SUPPLY/DEMAND IN BALANCE.

Dimensions 110' X 150'   Area 16,500 SQ.FT.   Shape RECTANGULAR   View RESID. HOUSING

Specific Zoning Classification R-4   Zoning Description LOW DENSITY RESIDENTIAL DISTRICT

Zoning Compliance ☒ Legal ☐ Legal Nonconforming (Grandfathered Use) ☐ No Zoning ☐ Illegal (describe)

Is the highest and best use of subject property as improved (or as proposed per plans and specifications) the present use? ☒ Yes ☐ No If No, describe

Utilities	Public	Other (describe)		Public	Other (describe)	Off-site improvements - Type	Public	Private
Electricity	☒		Water	☒		Street ASPHALT	☒	☐
Gas	☒		Sanitary Sewer	☒		Alley NONE	☒	☐

FEMA Special Flood Hazard Area ☐ Yes ☒ No   FEMA Flood Zone X   FEMA Map # 39049C0069H   FEMA Map Date 4/21/1999

Are the utilities and off-site improvements typical for the market area? ☒ Yes ☐ No If No, describe

Are there any adverse site conditions or external factors (easements, encroachments, environmental conditions, land uses, etc.)? ☐ Yes ☒ No If Yes, describe

NO ADVERSE SITE CONDITIONS OR ENCROACHMENTS HAVE BEEN NOTED. FLOOD INFORMATION IS PER FLOODSOURCE FLOOD MAPPING SERVICE, AND IS NOT TO BE RELIED UPON FOR FLOOD INSURANCE DETERMINATION. THE CLIENT SHOULD RELY UPON THEIR FLOOD CERTIFICATION SOURCE FOR FINAL DETERMINATION.

General Description	Foundation	Exterior Description materials/condition	Interior materials/condition
Units ☒ One ☐ One with Accessory Unit	☐ Concrete Slab ☒ Crawl Space	Foundation Walls POURED CONC.	Floors WOOD/CRPT/CER
# of Stories 2	☐ Full Basement ☒ Partial Basement	Exterior Walls VINYL/BRICK	Walls DRYWALL
Type ☒ Det. ☐ Att. ☐ S-Det./End Unit	Basement Area 642 sq.ft.	Roof Surface DIM. SHINGLE	Trim/Finish STND. OAK
☒ Existing ☐ Proposed ☐ Under Const.	Basement Finish 75 %	Gutters & Downspouts ALUMINUM	Bath Floor CERAMIC
Design (Style) 2 STORY	☐ Outside Entry/Exit ☒ Sump Pump	Window Type DOUBLE HUNG	Bath Wainscot CERAMIC
Year Built 1999	Evidence of ☐ Infestation	Storm Sash/Insulated INSULATED	Car Storage ☐ None
Effective Age (Yrs) 3 YEARS	☐ Dampness ☐ Settlement	Screens YES	☒ Driveway # of Cars 2
Attic ☐ None	Heating ☒ FWA ☐ HWBB ☐ Radiant	Amenities ☐ Woodstove(s) #	Driveway Surface CONCRETE
☐ Drop Stair ☐ Stairs	☐ Other Fuel NAT. GAS	☒ Fireplace(s) # 1 ☒ Fence WD. PRIV.	☒ Garage # of Cars 2
☐ Floor ☒ Scuttle	Cooling ☒ Central Air Conditioning	☒ Patio/Deck REAR ☒ Porch FRONT	☐ Carport # of Cars
☐ Finished ☐ Heated	☐ Individual ☐ Other	☐ Pool ☒ Other B-I SPA	☒ Att. ☐ Det. ☐ Built-in

Appliances ☒ Refrigerator ☒ Range/Oven ☒ Dishwasher ☒ Disposal ☒ Microwave ☐ Washer/Dryer ☒ Other (describe) TRASH COMPACTOR

Finished area above grade contains: 7 Rooms   3 Bedrooms   2.1 Bath(s)   1,952 Square Feet of Gross Living Area Above Grade

Additional features (special energy efficient items, etc.). MONITORED SECURITY AND FIRE ALARM SYSTEM. GARAGE HAS FINISHED INTERIOR, 2 ELECTRIC DOOR OPENERS AND BUILT-IN STORAGE AREA.

Describe the condition of the property (including needed repairs, deterioration, renovations, remodeling, etc.). THE SUBJECT WAS FOUND TO BE IN OVERALL ABOVE AVERAGE CONDITION AND REASONABLY MAINTAINED. THE EFFECTIVE AGE IS SLIGHTLY LESS THAN ACTUAL DUE TO OVERALL CONDITION.

Are there any physical deficiencies or adverse conditions that affect the livability, soundness, or structural integrity of the property? ☐ Yes ☒ No If Yes, describe

Does the property generally conform to the neighborhood (functional utility, style, condition, use, construction, etc.)? ☒ Yes ☐ No If No, describe

An appraiser may complete additional addenda pages to further explain or comment on any area of the information and/or analysis used in the appraisal. Subsequent chapters of this text will discuss additional content and exhibits that an appraiser may include in a typical appraisal report.

 A complete Uniform Residential Appraisal Report form can be found at the end of Chapter 12.

Subject Data

This first section on the URAR form deals with data on the subject property. Most of the data requested is straightforward and can be gathered from public records, or other sources that contain public records (e.g., legal description, assessor's parcel number, taxes, current owner). Neighborhood, map reference, and census tract may take a little more research, but are easily attainable. The balance of the information is supplied by the lender or available from the purchase contract.

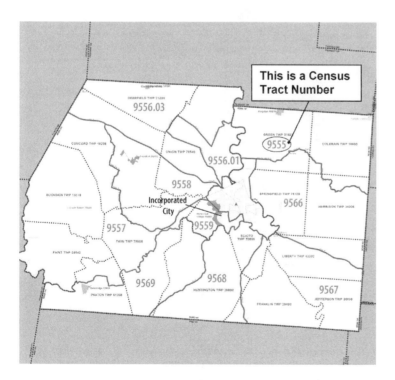

Census Tract Map

The numbers represent census tracts. The darker lines represent each census tract's boundaries.

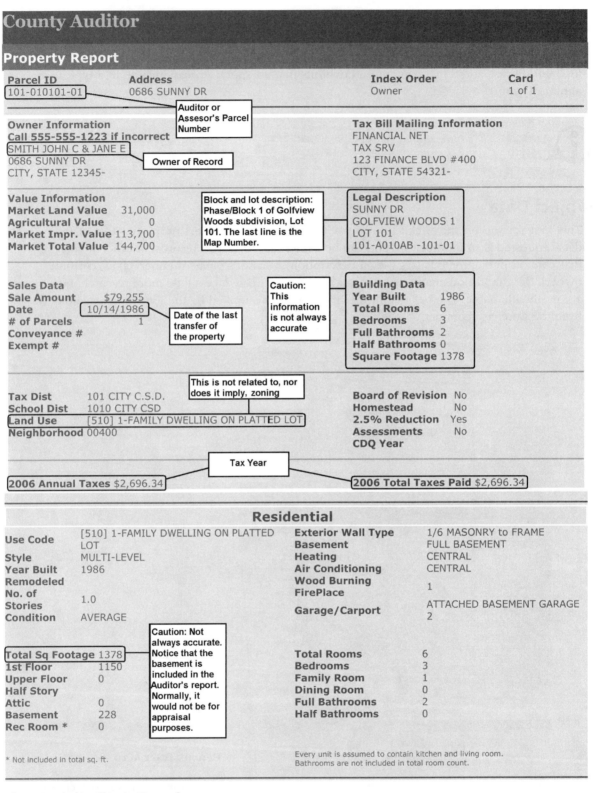

Assessor's/Auditor's Record

The Assessor's or Auditor's property (or tax) record contains myriad data and information an appraiser uses in an appraisal. While property or tax records may look and be organized differently in various jurisdictions, this illustration highlights several information points that are commonly found in most records.

Improvements

Type	Improvement	Dimensions	Measurements	Year Built
No Records Found				

Sketch/Photo

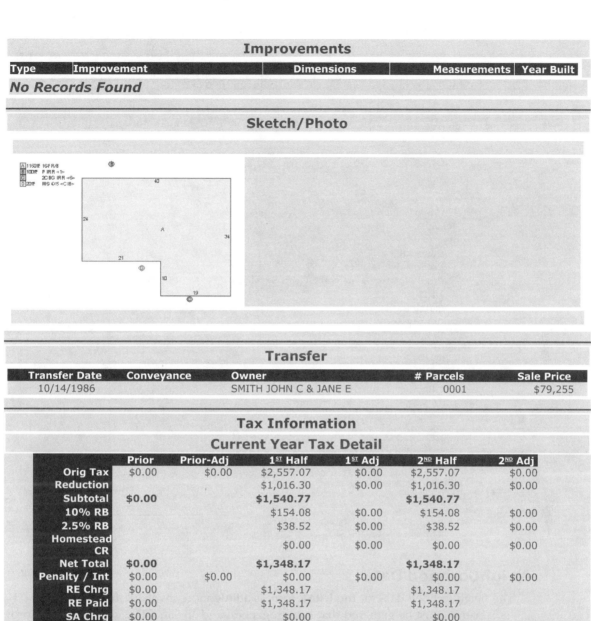

Transfer

Transfer Date	Conveyance	Owner	# Parcels	Sale Price
10/14/1986		SMITH JOHN C & JANE E	0001	$79,255

Tax Information

Current Year Tax Detail

	Prior	Prior-Adj	1ST Half	1ST Adj	2ND Half	2ND Adj
Orig Tax	$0.00	$0.00	$2,557.07	$0.00	$2,557.07	$0.00
Reduction		$1,016.30	$0.00	$1,016.30	$0.00	
Subtotal	$0.00		$1,540.77		$1,540.77	
10% RB			$154.08	$0.00	$154.08	$0.00
2.5% RB			$38.52	$0.00	$38.52	$0.00
Homestead CR			$0.00	$0.00	$0.00	$0.00
Net Total	$0.00		$1,348.17		$1,348.17	
Penalty / Int	$0.00	$0.00	$0.00	$0.00	$0.00	$0.00
RE Chrg	$0.00		$1,348.17		$1,348.17	
RE Paid	$0.00		$1,348.17		$1,348.17	
SA Chrg	$0.00		$0.00		$0.00	
SA Paid	$0.00		$0.00		$0.00	
Total Owed	$0.00		$1,348.17		$1,348.17	
Total Paid	$0.00		$1,348.17		$1,348.17	$2,696.34
Balance Due	$0.00		$0.00		$0.00	
Future Charge		$0.00		$0.00		$0.00
Future Paid		$0.00		$0.00		$0.00

Detail of Special Assessment

	Prior	Prior-Adj	1ST Half	1ST Adj	2ND Half	2ND Adj
			No Records Found			

Payment Information

Date	Half	Proj	Prior	1ST Half	2ND Half	Surplus
06/14/07	2-06		$0.00	$0.00	$1,348.17	$0.00
01/19/07	1-06		$0.00	$1,348.17	$0.00	$0.00
06/16/06	2-05		$0.00	$0.00	$1,253.38	$0.00
01/18/06	1-05		$0.00	$1,253.38	$0.00	$0.00
06/16/05	2-04		$0.00	$0.00	$1,189.86	$0.00
01/14/05	1-04		$0.00	$1,189.86	$0.00	$0.00

Levy Info

Proposed Levies for August 7, 2007 election	Mills	Current Monthly Tax	Estimated Monthly Tax	Note

Levies Passed or Commencing in Tax Year 2007	Mills	Current Monthly Tax	Estimated Monthly Tax	Note

Tax Distribution

Current Owner (s)	SMITH JOHN C & JANE E		Tax District	101 - CITY C.S.D.
			School District	1010 - CITY CSD
County				
General Fund				$65.13
Children's Services				$160.66
Alcohol, Drug & Mental Health Services				$97.30
MRDD				$202.01
Metro Parks				$18.44
County Zoo				$28.30
Senior Options				$28.02
School Dist	CITY			$1,866.45
Township				
Vocational School	CENTRAL STATE			$57.61
City / Village	CITY			$139.16
Library / Other				$33.26
Total				$2,696.34

Tax Year 2006
The above distribution was updated on 5/8/2007

Neighborhood Data

The neighborhood data for the URAR form is a little more involved than subject data. Here, information must be gathered that is both general and specific. The appraiser must provide a true picture of the subject's area and specific neighborhood where the property is located.

All of the factual, objective data can be obtained from sources discussed earlier. Note that some of the items needed rely on the appraiser's knowledge and experience. Gathering and evaluating neighborhood data is an important part of a normal appraisal. In fact, much emphasis is placed on this section. This will be detailed in Chapter 6, which discusses appraisal externalities.

Neighborhood Boundary Map

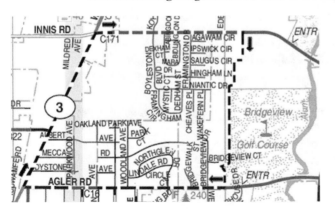

The neighborhood boundary map serves to illustrate what the appraiser has defined as the subject's immediate neighborhood. The description for the map to the left would be Innis Road to the north, Bridgeview Golf Course to the east, Agler Road to the south, and Route 3 to the west.

One of the frequent points of discussion between lenders and appraisers is also contained in the neighborhood data section: *Is the neighborhood (or subject market) considered to be urban, suburban, or rural?* Unfortunately, there is no common or standardized definition that can be applied to these terms:

- **Urban** is most often thought of as an area within a town or city that has full availability to all services common to that setting.

- **Suburban** is most often associated with an area adjacent to an urban area, but may enjoy some or all of the common services as do urban residents.

- **Rural** is most often thought of as an area disassociated with an urban or suburban setting, usually not having access to common services with the urban area.

Many lenders and mortgage investors perceive more risk associated with lending for properties the appraiser has specified as rural (or sometimes suburban). In some cases, this caution may be warranted, while in others it may not. Appraisers must present an honest interpretation of the property setting. Real estate professionals should be aware that, in some cases, if a property is deemed to be "rural," the property *may* have fewer financing avenues.

Site Data

Site data is recorded in detail in the URAR form and is a combination of researched facts and personal observations. The main information needed includes a legal description, zoning information, and a map. Most data items can be obtained from public records. Zoning information is important for determining highest and best use.

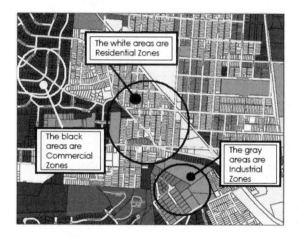

Zoning Map

This zoning map example demonstrates several zoning classifications. An appraiser can locate the subject property in one of the zones, then find the zoning regulations for that particular area.

County plat maps show the position, boundaries, easements, and other details of a site. The appraiser is not required to do a survey to determine encroachments (a separate person or company may need to be hired), but the appraiser must still use judgment in determining if the site has any adverse restrictions, encroachments, or easements. The appraiser's initial research or personal observations may necessitate more research be done in this area.

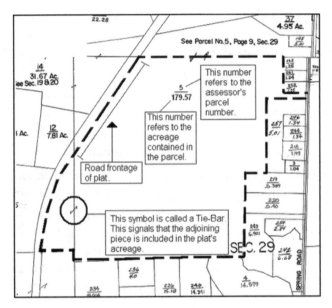

Plat Map

This is an assessor's, or tax, map and is available from local authorities. Its appearance can vary from area to area. It is used by the appraiser to obtain various elements of data, some of which is labeled.

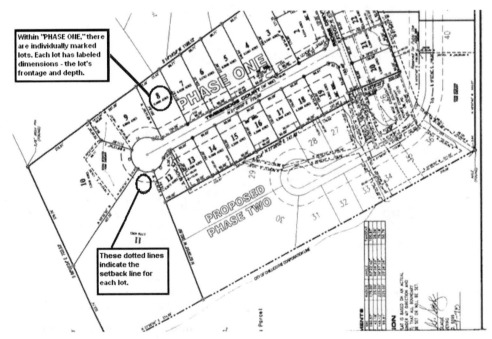

Subdivision Plat Map

Here we see a typical subdivision plat that is put on record when the subdivision is dedicated. This particular map represents one phase in a subdivision. Notice that the dimensions of each numbered lot are on the plat, as are the building set-back boundaries, utility easements, etc. For a lot and block description, the appraiser may need to refer to a subdivision plat map.

SUBDIVISION COVENANTS AND RESTRICTIONS

1. APPROVAL

No building shall be erected, placed, or altered until the building plans, specifications, and elevations have been approved by the developer in writing.

Quality of materials, workmanship, and harmony of exterior design with existing structures must also be approved by the developer in writing.

2. USE

Each and every lot will be used for residential purposes only.

Each lot must be improved with a residential structure not to exceed two and one-half stories and must have an attached garage of not less than two cars and not more than four cars.

No temporary structure, trailer, basement, tent, shack, garage, barn, or other outbuilding shall be used at any time as a residence either temporarily or permanently.

No lot may be split to create another building lot.

No animals, livestock, or poultry of any kind shall be raised, bred, or kept on any lot, except that dogs, cats, or other household pets may be kept provided they are not bred or maintained for commercial purposes.

No noxious or offensive activity shall be carried on upon any lot, nor shall anything be done thereon which may become an annoyance of nuisance to the neighborhood.

No commercial vehicles, recreational vehicles, boats, trailers, construction equipment, or trucks over ¾ ton capacity shall be on any lot or street, except if in a garage; completely enclosed.

3. BUILDING REQUIREMENTS

The ground floor of any dwelling shall have a minimum living area of:

> one-story – 1,400 square feet
>
> one and one-half story - 1,200 square feet
>
> two story – 900 square feet
>
> split - level and tri – level – 1,100 square feet on the upper floor
>
> bi-level – 1,300 square feet on the upper floor

All dwellings must be constructed of brick, stone, or cedar siding with the color approved by the developer in writing.

No building materials may be on-site for more than 60 days prior to construction or 15 days after completion, and construction must be completed within 6 months after commencement.

No outside sheds shall be erected.

4. LANDSCAPING

All lots shall be kept mowed and free from obnoxious weeds and grasses.

Shrubs, trees, bushes, and plantings of any kind shall be kept well maintained and free of unsightly material.

Initial landscaping design must be approved by the developer.

5. MAINTENANCE

No lot, building, or other improvement shall be permitted to become overgrown, unsightly, or fall into disrepair. All improvements shall be kept in good condition at all times.

6. SWIMMING POOLS

Above-ground pools are prohibited.

7. FENCES

No fence, wall, or barrier of any kind (including shrubbery or hedges) may be erected, except underground dog fences, which are subject to the approval of the developer.

8. ANTENNA

No antenna or dish for transmission or reception of television signals, radio signals shall be erected on any lot.

9. FUEL TANKS

No above-ground fuel tanks shall be permitted.

10. SIGNS

No sign of any kind shall be displayed to the public view on any lot, except one sign of not more than 6 square feet to advertise the sale of the property.

11. LIGHTING

No house may be erected on any lot unless there is an outdoor post yard light of either gas or electric power. The owner shall keep said light in good working order and properly maintained.

12. MAILBOXES

To insure conformity with the subdivision, all mail boxes shall be of a construction compatible with the subdivision, and is subject to the approval of the developer.

13. LIMIT OF RESTRICTIONS

These covenants are to run with the land and shall be binding for a period of thirty days from the date of these covenants, and shall be extended for successive periods of 10 years unless the majority of the owners of the lots file an instrument with the recorder agreeing to change the covenants in whole or in part.

14. ENFORCEMENT

In the event of a violation of any of the covenants or restrictions, it shall be lawful for any owner of any of the lots to prosecute any proceedings of law or in equity against the person or persons violating or attempting to violate any of these covenants or restrictions and either prevent such violations or recover damages for such violations.

Subdivision Regulations

The subdivision regulations are placed on record at a subdivision's dedication along with the subdivision plat. Here, we see examples of typical restrictive covenants in this sample subdivision covenants and restrictions.

Often times, an appraiser will make a simple site sketch for inclusion with the site data form and to be kept with the file on the property. In this sketch, the appraiser will note shape and dimensions, as well as encroachments, easements, or physical features of the site that prevent building upon a portion of it. This sketch may or may not be included with the appraisal, depending on any present points of significance. At the very least, the appraiser must alert a client to any points that seem special or unusual and may impact the value of the property. A street map showing the exact location of the property and the comparable sales used for the sales comparison approach is usually included as part of the appraisal report.

Site Sketch

This site sketch indicates the primary dwelling, the barn, the pond, and the driveway. Notice that it also illustrates the location of the driveway easement running through this property to access the property next door.

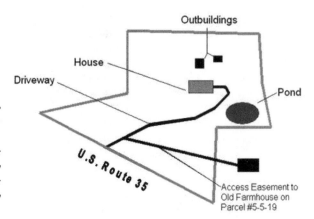

Most of the other site data items that are part of the appraisal report are simply personal observations made by the appraiser as he inspects the site. The presence of public utilities and off-site improvements can affect the value of a site. The appraiser must note the topography, drainage, landscaping, and even the view of the site. All of these factors may or may not be important, depending on the particular site.

For Example

Topography usually comes into play in the value of a site only if it prevents certain types of buildings or precludes building in certain areas of the property—conditions affecting marketability. Drainage and landscaping are usually considerations only when they are not adequate. The view can add or subtract value from a site if it is at one extreme or the other—for example, breathtaking mountains or an unsightly landfill.

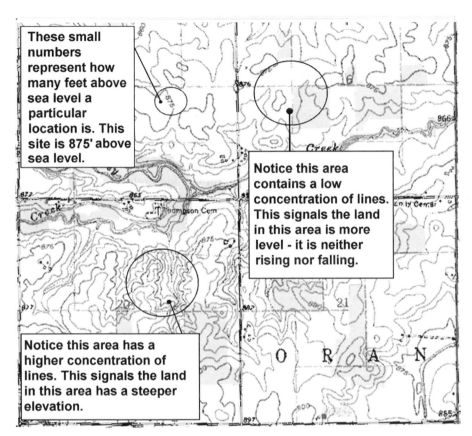

These small numbers represent how many feet above sea level a particular location is. This site is 875' above sea level.

Notice this area contains a low concentration of lines. This signals the land in this area is more level - it is neither rising nor falling.

Notice this area has a higher concentration of lines. This signals the land in this area has a steeper elevation.

Topography Map

This map is available from local and national sources. The topography map details the contour of the land. Notice that as the topography lines are closer together (or more dense), the steeper the elevation is at that point. More space between the topography lines indicates a level, or gentle slope. Periodically throughout the map, the topography lines will indicate the number of feet above sea level. Local information is available to assist with determining how many feet above flood plain the land parcel must be so as not be in a flood plain.

FEMA Flood Map

The FEMA flood panel (map) is available from www.fema.gov. The appraiser can use it to locate the subject property and recognize a flood hazard area. Flood hazard areas on the Flood Insurance Rate Map (FIRM) are identified as a Special Flood Hazard Area (SFHA). SFHA is defined as the area that will be inundated by a flood event having a 1% chance of being equaled or exceeded in any given year. This is also referred to as the base flood or 100-year flood.

SFHAs are labeled Zone A, Zone AO, Zone AH, Zones A1-A30, Zone AE, Zone A99, Zone AR, Zone AR/AE, Zone AR/AO, Zone AR/A1-A30, Zone AR/A, Zone V,

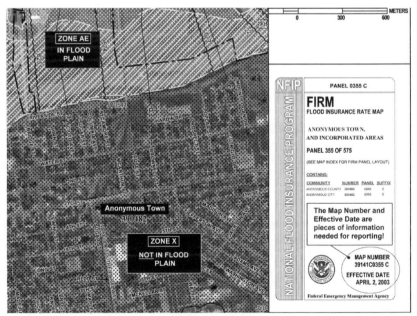

Zone VE, and Zones V1-V30. Moderate flood hazard areas, labeled Zone B or Zone X (shaded) are also shown on the FIRM, and are the areas between the limits of the base flood and the 0.2% annual-chance (or 500-year) flood. The areas of minimal flood hazard, which are the areas outside the SFHA and higher than the elevation of the 0.2% annual-chance flood, are labeled Zone C or Zone X (unshaded).

The flood panel number and date of FEMA's flood determination should also be included in the appraisal report.

Description of Improvements

The description of improvements in the URAR form contains some of the information found in the building data form used by most appraisers. In fact, some of the information requested is quite detailed.

Almost all of this information can be obtained from personal observation. Another source may be the seller, real estate agent, or other person who has knowledge of the property. Nevertheless, it is important for the appraiser to verify as much of this information as possible. If an appraiser is provided with information that cannot personally be verified, it's important that the source of that information be noted in the appraisal file and appraisal report. Some of these items may affect the value of the subject property. This concept will be discussed in greater detail in Chapter 9, which covers the sales comparison approach.

Summary

1. Appraisal data can be either general or specific. **General data** covers forces that affect a property's value but are not directly related to a particular piece of property. General data covers physical, economic, governmental, and social forces, and can be local or national in nature. Two types of specific data are **subject property data** (data on the site and improvements) and **comparative data** (data about comparable sale properties and income and cost information).

2. With general data, the appraiser is interested in trends and other information that affects the subject property, but is not limited to only the subject. An appraiser regularly practicing in a particular area may not have to do this general assessment every time, but does check the general data resources on a regular basis and often keeps updated files relevant to where she does most appraisals. General data resources include public records and filings, Internet, government offices, and professional publications.

3. With specific data, appraisers need very specific facts and information. Appraisers always verify the accuracy of sources—often personal inspection is the best source of information or verification. Specific data resources must be consulted each time. Comparable sale data should reflect similar market conditions. Specific data resources include personal inspection, buyer, seller, broker or agent, county records, multiple listing service (MLS), cost services, Internet, contractors, property managers, or accountants.

4. Data collection is an important part of the appraisal process, as is verification and analysis. All data collected must be verified for relevancy, accuracy, and reliability. Relevance must also be considered.

5. The **Uniform Residential Appraisal Report (URAR)** form is the most frequently used form in a residential property appraisal assignment. The information may first be recorded elsewhere before being transcribed to the URAR.

6. The first section of the URAR covers subject data. Subject data information is gathered from public records, participants to a transaction, online sources, the lender, or purchase contract. The neighborhood data section covers general and specific information. Site data section covers legal description, zoning, and appraiser observations such as encroachments, easements, or restrictions on the site. The description of improvements section covers building data. Most of the information can be obtained from personal observation. If another source is used (e.g., the seller), the appraiser should cite the source.

Quiz

1. **When preparing an appraisal, an appraiser would NOT collect**

   a. general data on a national and local level.

   b. specific data about the subject property.

   c. specific data for comparative purposes.

   d. general data on current mortgage interest rates.

2. **A primary purpose of gathering general data is to**

   a. act as a means of verifying and cross-checking specific data.

   b. correlate general data with a specific subject property and its selling price.

   c. look at general trends that may affect value in the real estate market.

   d. make specific predictions about future interest rate levels.

3. **The most reliable resource for gathering specific data about the subject property is**

   a. the FHA or other government agencies.

   b. personal inspection.

   c. professional journals.

   d. the property owner.

4. **Which is important to the data collection process?**

   a. analysis of data only

   b. both analysis of data and verification of data

   c. neither analysis of data nor verification of data

   d. verification of data only

5. **Which data section does NOT appear in the Uniform Residential Appraisal Report?**

   a. neighborhood data

   b. site data

   c. subject data

   d. cost manual data

External and Environmental Influences

6

This chapter discusses external and environmental physical factors that can affect property values. There are many factors outside the boundaries and within a property that can affect its value. Some of these factors have already been discussed—the four great forces that can influence real estate (P-E-G-S). The emphasis of this chapter is the physical influences on real estate.

The primary physical externality that affects real estate is **neighborhood;** this is where our discussion will begin. Neighborhoods, how neighborhood boundaries are determined, neighborhood life cycles, and how the four great forces affect neighborhoods will be discussed in detail.

The physical aspects of real estate are often affected by economic, governmental, and social concerns as well. Other appraisal externalities to be considered are *environmental concerns*, which can influence value directly, and environmental issues. These will be addressed later in this chapter.

Key Terms

Decline The third stage a neighborhood goes through in its life cycle, when property values begin to fall as demand falls.

Environmental Hazard A situation in which there is potential for harm to persons or property from conditions that exist in a property or the surrounding area.

Gentrification The process of rapid revitalization of properties in a neighborhood which causes current residents to be displaced.

Growth The first stage a neighborhood goes through in its life cycle when property values rise as development activity begins and continues.

Neighborhood Any constant, contiguous area that may be identified by similar characteristics or physical boundaries. Also referred to as **Market Area**.

Nuisance Anything outside property boundaries that interferes with the right of quiet enjoyment.

Radon Gas A naturally occurring radioactive gas that emanates from the earth; it is odorless, colorless, and tasteless but has been identified as a cancer-causing agent.

Revitalization The final stage a neighborhood goes through in its life cycle when property values rise again as demand increases, resulting in increased renovation and rehabilitation. (Rapid revitalization is called **Gentrification**.)

Stability The second stage a neighborhood goes through in its life cycle when the area is built up to the point where there is little, if any, vacant property. Also called **Equilibrium**.

Stigmatized Property A property made undesirable to most people by a past event, often a crime or environmental hazard.

Neighborhoods

A **neighborhood** is defined as *any constant, contiguous area that may be identified by similar characteristics or physical boundaries.* This is also referred to as a **market area**. These properties could share physical characteristics (e.g., similar style, age) or physical boundaries (e.g., natural boundaries such as a river or artificial boundaries such as a highway). Neighborhoods can also be defined by other characteristics. Properties that have similar uses or zoning, price ranges or income levels, or that share shopping, social, civic, or recreational facilities may all be considered part of the same neighborhood. In fact, almost anything can define a neighborhood **except** for race, ethnicity, or any other protected classes. A neighborhood is simply a small part of a larger community.

Defining a neighborhood, though, can be more complex than it may seem. An appraiser must define the neighborhood for each appraisal but must be careful not to use superficial boundaries. Time and effort must be taken to ensure the neighborhood is defined correctly so the comparable sales chosen for the appraisal will reflect an accurate comparison of value. In fact, in a normal appraisal, much of the emphasis and energy is placed on performing a neighborhood analysis.

Neighborhood Boundaries

The appraiser will often start to define a neighborhood by looking at the natural and artificial geographic boundaries of an area. Natural boundaries include obvious rivers and lakes, but also less obvious parks, mountains, or valleys. Artificial boundaries include man-made dividing lines such as streets, highways, and railroads and may also be drawn along school, zoning, or political districts.

Next, the appraiser should observe the area to test these boundaries. This personal inspection should look at the preliminary area the appraiser defined to see if there are perceptible changes in neighborhood characteristics at any of the physical boundaries defined. During this personal inspection, the appraiser is also looking for similarity of land usage and types of improvements, as well as consistency of building style and landscaping; even maintenance or upkeep can be evaluated as a means of confirming neighborhood boundaries.

Finally, the appraiser should test his conclusion of neighborhood boundaries by comparing the social and economic characteristics of the area to make sure these are consistent within the defined neighborhood. Census data or other data on age, occupation, income level, etc., should be gathered and compared as a final step in confirming the appraiser has appropriately defined the neighborhood.

Life Cycle of a Neighborhood

If a neighborhood has been defined correctly, there are usually minimal future changes or alterations to the boundaries. Occasionally, a new section may be added to a neighborhood, or a change in a road may exclude some houses that were once considered part of a neighborhood. However, a properly defined neighborhood—taking into account not only physical boundaries, but also style, age, usage, and income levels—will likely continue to age together. A neighborhood's life cycle includes four stages: **Growth**, **stability/equilibrium**, **decline**, and **revitalization**.

Growth

Growth is *the first stage a neighborhood goes through in its life cycle, when property values rise as development activity begins and continues.* Buyers fuel this growth by continuing to purchase property in the area. This demand equals acceptance of the area and of the prices being charged, and allows the area to grow to maturity.

Stability/Equilibrium

Stability or **equilibrium** is *the second stage a neighborhood goes through in its life cycle, when the area is built up to the point where there is little, if any, vacant property*. At this stage in a neighborhood's life cycle, property values are at their highest. Demand typically remains high, as buyers continue to prefer this neighborhood as it enters a mature stage. Prices will rarely drop during this period as the real estate market is near equilibrium. Stability and maturity are characteristics of the equilibrium stage in a neighborhood's life cycle. There are some neighborhoods that never go beyond this stage.

Decline

Decline is *the third stage a neighborhood goes through in its life cycle, when property values begin to fall as demand falls*. Decline in a neighborhood is typically observable through decay or deterioration. This leads to the area becoming even less desirable, and the cycle feeds upon itself. A less desirable area where properties exhibit deferred maintenance translates into lower prices, and lower prices mean that lower-income residents with less money to spend on repairs will be attracted to the homes. As values decline, the problem is compounded by conversion of some properties to rental units (where upkeep is often not as meticulous as by owner-occupants), or to commercial uses. This can, in turn, help accelerate the decline.

Revitalization

Revitalization is *the final stage a neighborhood goes through in its life cycle, when property values rise again as demand increases, resulting in increased renovation and rehabilitation*. After a complete revitalization stage, the neighborhood can return to a stability/equilibrium stage, and the cycle begins again. Revitalization occurs when properties are again seen as attractive for their location, architectural features, or perhaps price. Whatever the reason, people begin to spend money to fix up these homes, and they again become desirable. Revitalization is generally a slow process. *The process of rapid revitalization of properties where current residents are displaced* is called **gentrification**. While this benefits the neighborhood, it can create problems for tenants who are forced from the area due to higher rents or a trend of owner-occupied rather than tenant-occupied homes.

How the Four Broad Forces Affect Neighborhoods

The four broad forces that influence all aspects of the real estate market (P-E-G-S) also influence neighborhoods. Of course, the effects can be positive or negative. Let's look at how these forces can affect the boundaries of neighborhoods as well as the neighborhood's life cycle.

Economic Effects

Economic factors can play a role in determining the boundaries of a neighborhood, primarily through housing prices, the income level of the residents, the level of business development in the area, or even property usage. Economics can also come into play with regard to the construction industry, where increased activity on previously vacant land may result in a redefinition of neighborhood boundaries.

Economic factors can also affect a neighborhood's life cycle. Like all real estate, neighborhoods benefit from a good economic base or suffer from a weak one. A good economic base can help with growth and stability. A bad economic base can accelerate a decline, or may even be the cause of it. While high interest rates can actually hurt all neighborhoods, they hit low income neighborhoods the hardest. Low interest rates spur growth and help with revitalization. Income levels and general business activity can also affect the life cycle of a neighborhood.

Governmental Effects

Government factors often contribute to defining the boundaries of a neighborhood. In fact, city streets and other man-made barriers are often one of the main determinants of a neighborhood's boundaries. Other governmental factors that can contribute to establishing a neighborhood's boundaries include zoning, school or taxing districts, the designation of a historical district, or the boundaries of governmental services (e.g., fire and police departments).

Government factors that affect a neighborhood's life cycle are many of the same factors that influence boundaries. The re-routing or widening of a street can have significant effects on a neighborhood. Growth would be fostered in a commercial neighborhood that had a street widened; decline would be fostered if a street was re-routed or closed off. Widening a residential street can help a neighborhood grow if traffic congestion is eased, but may cause decline in the neighborhood that borders the street. If the government changes zoning on the border streets from residential to commercial, the property values of those neighborhood properties may benefit as well.

Zoning changes can also be a big factor in the cycle of a neighborhood. Increased industrial activity because of a nearby zoning change can severely impact a neighborhood and speed up its decline. Taxes can be another large influence in the life cycle of a neighborhood. Taxes that are frequently increased or are at high levels can cause a neighborhood to become less desirable and lead to decline. Tax breaks and incentives can be used to prompt revitalization in a neighborhood where many properties need renovation or rehabilitation.

Social Effects

Social factors that may help determine the boundaries of a neighborhood include such things as recreational and cultural activities. Accessibility to commercial, retail, and jobs can also play a role in defining boundaries. Additional factors may be the level of education, social status of a given area, or buyer perceptions of a neighborhood's social factors.

For Example

If buyers perceive that there are recreational or cultural opportunities in a neighborhood, this will lead to growth and stability. If the perception is that these opportunities are lacking, this could lead to decline.

Similarly, the perception of convenience is likely to influence a neighborhood's life cycle. Another social factor that can influence a neighborhood's life cycle is demographic trends (e.g., population age, family size). These factors can serve to make a particular neighborhood more or less desirable, and hence grow or decline, based on the characteristics of properties in the neighborhood.

Physical Effects

Physical factors are a major determinant in establishing the boundaries of a neighborhood. Roads and rivers are obvious examples. Other physical boundaries include everything from parks to areas of similar land usage or properties that have comparable maintenance and upkeep.

Physical factors affecting a neighborhood's life cycle can include road or zoning changes, or the maintenance and upkeep of homes in a neighborhood. Conformity of architectural styles of buildings or homes in an area can help a neighborhood; too many homes straying from the norm can hurt a neighborhood's overall appeal. Additional physical factors are nuisances or environmental hazards.

Nuisances and Environmental Hazards

A **nuisance** is *anything outside property boundaries that temporarily interferes with the right of quiet enjoyment.* This, by definition, necessitates that the nuisance originate from another person's property. One cannot be a nuisance to himself—only to neighbors. A nuisance that is more or less permanent is referred to as an **external obsolescence** and can affect property values in a neighborhood.

For Example

An external obsolescence may be noise from an airport, or the stench from a factory farm. Both of these would tend to hurt property values by making property less desirable, and hence contribute to the decline of a neighborhood.

Furthermore, implicit in the definition of a nuisance is that it cannot contribute to a neighborhood or property values in a positive way.

An **environmental hazard** is *a situation in which there is potential for harm to persons or property from conditions that exist in a property or the surrounding area.* Environmental hazards can be either separate from a property or contained within the boundaries of a property. Both scenarios will be considered as we discuss how environmental hazards affect neighborhoods and property values.

External Environmental Concerns

Environmental concerns *outside* the boundaries of a property can have a significant impact on its value. Environmental concerns cover more than just nuisances. Visible signs of environmental concerns may push buyers away for fear of contamination and make a property or neighborhood less valuable.

For Example

An environmental concern may be toxic substances in nearby landfills, waterways with high levels of pollution, or thick smog from nearby factories.

Other less-quantifiable hazards may still pose a problem for a property or neighborhood (e.g., proximity to nuclear power plants, presence of high-tension power lines). Regardless of the fact that scientific research has not produced conclusive evidence of risk, there's a strong perception among some buyers that these environmental factors are, at best, undesirable and, at worst, unsafe. The most difficult part is that property owners often feel helpless, since these hazards are often outside their control and may never be removed or cleaned up.

Stigmatized Properties

A **stigmatized property** is *one made undesirable to most people by a past event; often a crime or environmental hazard.* Although the term is often used to refer to properties where a traumatic act has taken place (e.g., murder, suicide), the term can also refer to properties held to be undesirable because of past environmental hazards where the perception of a problem may linger on. Most times, the agent must disclose this fact to prospective buyers.

 Real estate agents should check their broker's policies when it comes to stigmatized properties.

With some environmental hazards, the fear persists even after the hazard has been removed or neutralized. This is particularly true with toxic waste dumps that have been cleaned up or closed, and nuclear power plants that have been shut down. Fear of contamination may still persist in the minds of many buyers. These fears may or may not be well-founded. A buyer's typical reaction is: "Why take a chance when there are ready substitutes elsewhere?" Thus, once an environmental hazard (or the perception of one) takes hold, it can become extremely difficult for a neighborhood to make the transition from decline to revitalization. In fact, many times, this never occurs and the neighborhood stays in decline.

Environmental Concerns within a Property

In addition to external environmental concerns, other environmental concerns may be present *on* a particular property. These can be as dangerous (or more so) than external hazards, but at least the property owner (or potential buyer) has the ability to rectify these problems impacting the value of the property. Some of the primary environmental concerns include:

- Lead-based paint
- Asbestos
- Urea-formaldehyde foam insulation
- Radon gas
- Underground storage tanks
- Mold
- Methamphetamine labs

 Sellers must disclose the known presence of any of these hazards on the Residential Property Disclosure Form.

Lead-Based Paint

Lead-based paint is also an area of concern. Under the Residential Lead-Based Paint Hazard Reduction Act, sellers and landlords are required to disclose known lead paint hazards for homes built prior to 1978. To implement these lead paint disclosure requirements, the EPA and HUD have issued regulations as follows:

1. Sellers and landlords must disclose any known lead-based paint hazard in homes, and must give buyers and tenants any reports available from prior lead tests.
2. Sellers and landlords must give buyers and renters a pamphlet about how to protect families from lead in homes.
3. Home buyers have a 10-day period (or other mutually agreed upon time) to conduct a lead paint inspection or risk assessment at their own expense, if desired.
4. Sellers, landlords, and real estate agents must include certain language in sales contracts and/or leasing agreements to ensure that disclosure and notification actually take place. (This has been included in most board real estate contracts.)

Sellers, landlords, and real estate agents all share responsibility for ensuring compliance with these rules. Sellers aren't required to remove lead paint, correct hazards, nor do any testing. Certain properties are exempt from these lead paint requirements. For more information, refer to the *Ohio Real Estate Principles and Practices* textbook.

From a property value standpoint, lead-based paint is not always a major issue since it is seen as a correctable condition. Contingency language in a purchase contract should spell out what happens if lead paint hazards are found.

Lead-Based Paint Disclosure
Housing Sales

Property Address _____

LEAD WARNING STATEMENT

Every buyer of any interest in residential real property on which a residential dwelling unit was built prior to 1978 is notified that such property may present exposure to lead from lead-based paint that may place young children at risk of developing lead poisoning. Lead poisoning in young children may produce permanent neurological damage, including learning disabilities, reduced intelligence quotient, behavioral problems, and impaired memory. Lead poisoning also poses a particular risk to pregnant women. The seller of any interest in residential real property is required to provide the buyer with any information on lead-based paint hazards from risk assessments or inspections in the seller's possession and notify the buyer of any known lead-based paint hazards. A risk assessment or inspection for possible lead-based paint hazards is recommended prior to purchase.

Intact lead-based paint that is in good condition is not necessarily a hazard. See the EPA pamphlet **"Protect Your Family From Lead in Your Home"** *for more information.*

Seller's Disclosure (Please initial where indicated):

☐☐ **(a) Presence of lead-based paint and/or lead-based paint hazards** (check one):

☐ Known lead-based paint and/or lead-based paint hazards are present in the housing. (explain)

☐ Seller has no knowledge of lead-based paint and/or lead-based paint hazards in the housing.

☐☐ **(b) Records and reports available to the seller** (check one):

☐ Seller has provided the buyer with all available records and reports pertaining to lead-based paint and/or lead-based paint hazards in the housing (list documents below).

☐ Seller has no reports or records pertaining to lead-based paint and/or lead-based paint hazards in the housing.

Buyer's Acknowledgment (Please initial where indicated):

☐☐ **(c) Buyer has received copies of all information listed in (b) above.**

☐☐ **(d) Buyer has received the pamphlet** *Protect Your Family from Lead in Your Home.*

☐☐ **(e) Buyer has** (check one below):

☐ Received a 10-day opportunity (or mutually agreed upon period) to conduct a risk assessment or inspection for the presence of lead-based paint and/or lead-based paint hazards; or

☐ Waived the opportunity to conduct a risk assessment or inspection for the presence of lead-based paint and/or lead-based paint hazards.

Agent's Acknowledgment (Please initial where indicated):

☐ **(f) Agent has informed the seller of the seller's obligations under 42 U.S.C. 4852d and is aware of his/her responsibility to ensure compliance.**

Certification of Accuracy: The following parties have reviewed the information above and certify, to the best of their knowledge, that the information provided by the signatory is true and accurate.

By: _____ _____   _____ _____
Seller   Date   Buyer   Date

_____ _____   _____ _____
Seller   Date   Buyer   Date

_____ _____   _____ _____
Agent   Date   Agent   Date

For Example

The contract may allow a buyer (tenant) to rescind the contract if unacceptable levels of lead are found, or a seller (landlord) may have the right to remove the lead. Other times, lead hazards are negotiated (perhaps as a price reduction), like any other property defect.

Asbestos

Asbestos is a fibrous material that was once very common in many building materials because of its insulating and heat-resistant value. It was embedded in various construction materials and especially used around furnaces and ductwork. It was also commonly used as a roofing shingle, exterior siding, and floor covering material. However, asbestos is no longer used because if asbestos particles become airborne and get into a person's lungs, they are believed to cause cancer. Asbestos can pose a value problem, since removal is an expensive process that must be done by EPA-licensed contractors.

There is some debate over whether existing asbestos should be removed or left alone. Since it is only thought to be a problem once it becomes airborne, some people believe it best not to disturb it. Others worry, that if left alone, asbestos could become airborne at a future point due to some unforeseen accident or fire. From an appraisal standpoint, it is important to note the presence of asbestos—if found, it can have a significant impact on the value of a property. If there is a suspicion that asbestos is present, an expert should be called.

Urea-formaldehyde Foam Insulation

Urea-formaldehyde foam is a type of insulation that was popular because it could be blown into an existing structure. Recently, safer types of blown insulation have been developed as alternatives. Urea-formaldehyde foam was banned from residential use by the EPA because of potential health risks from toxic fumes the substance can give off when first installed. The presence of urea-formaldehyde can impact the value of a property, so it is important for the appraiser to note its presence. If there is a suspicion that urea-formaldehyde foam is present, an expert should be called.

Radon Gas

Radon gas is *a naturally occurring radioactive gas that emanates from the earth; it is odorless, colorless, and tasteless but has been identified as a cancer-causing agent.* Radon gas is radioactive and, if indoors, can present a problem as it can build up to dangerous levels. Ohio has mid to high levels of radon, according to EPA statistics. Most homes do not have a problem, but radon can vary from one house to the next—even on the same street.

The effect radon has on property values is hard to determine. The actual cost of purging a house of radon gas is relatively inexpensive—often less than the cost of eliminating termites. In fact, with low levels of radon, simply sealing cracks may be enough. With higher levels of radon, it may be necessary to install a remediation system that may include a fan to pull gas from below the basement and vent it to the outside. However, the effects on property value of buyer perceptions of radon gas are hard to determine.

In addition to concerns about cancer, there is also concern about the liability issue. Buyers and sellers need to be concerned about future liability if a home was sold with high amounts of radon. Who must pay for the associated costs of fixing the problem? What about health issues? Presently, sellers are generally not held liable if they, in good faith, did not know of the existence of any adverse conditions.

However, this could change as sellers can now be held liable for other environmental hazards—even if the sellers did not know they existed. Still, sellers must disclose any known radon hazards. Since radon can impact property value, it's important for appraisers to note its presence. If there is a suspicion that radon is present, an expert should be called.

Underground Storage Tanks

The EPA has enacted tougher standards for underground storage tanks by imposing additional steps owners and property managers must take to protect underground storage tanks against corrosion, spills, leaks, and overfills. Steps include installing leak detection, catch basins, and automatic shut-offs. Although tanks that hold less than 100 gallons, fuel tanks used for heating, and certain waste water treatment tanks are exempt, the **Residential Property Disclosure form** requires the seller to disclose the presence of any underground storage tanks or wells. What was once a common practice for the storage of fuel or chemicals in rural areas may now be an expensive process of ensuring tanks don't leak—or digging them up and removing them altogether. This can pose even bigger environmental dilemmas for commercial properties, where costs can be much higher. If underground storage tanks are present, an expert should be called.

Mold

Mold is a fungus that can grow anywhere on any organic material. In order to grow, mold requires three components:

1. Moisture
2. Oxygen
3. Food source

A leaky roof that goes undetected or serious water damage creates a perfect atmosphere for mold growth. New construction, which creates tightly sealed homes, can pose a problem by allowing moisture to remain trapped in the home. If not found in time, mold can actually consume the substance on which it is growing.

Some molds produce *toxic substances* known as **mycotoxins**. One of these types of mold is **stachybotrys**, or **black mold**, *which is greenish-black in color and grows on materials with high cellulose content such as drywall, ceiling tiles, and wood that is chronically moist.* In some situations, mold can even grow behind the surface of walls or wallpaper.

There are many different varieties and types of molds, but not all molds are created equal—some are dangerous to humans; some are not. Mold can produce allergens which can trigger reactions such as wheezing, eye and skin irritation, and a stuffy nose. For some people, mold can cause asthma attacks.

Suspected health issues caused by mold include:

- Chronic fatigue
- Flu-like symptoms
- Digestive problems
- Immune system problems
- Neurological problems

The EPA has not specifically required mold disclosure or set standards to measure contamination. Some states (including California and Texas) have passed their own legislation regarding mold issues, and some states now require real estate agents to conduct a thorough visual inspection of properties for the existence of mold. Regardless of state legislation, it is a good idea for real estate agents to be alert to telltale signs that mold is present.

Some signs indicating a presence of moisture in the home, and thereby increasing the likelihood of finding mold, include:

- Visible mold growth
- Plumbing leaks
- Leaking roofs or windows
- Strong, musty odors
- Water stains on ceilings, walls, or floors
- Warped wood
- Cracked or peeling paint
- Peeling dry-wall tape
- Clogged gutters

Licensees must be careful not to act as experts or make claims they cannot verify. They should merely inform clients of any suspicions and advise them to seek further information from a specialist or home inspector. Sellers should be encouraged to disclose any actual or potential problems. More and more states are implementing new laws regarding mold and real estate, including disclosure statements and requirements for licensees.

Extra steps that may be taken include having homebuyers purchase separate mold protection insurance policies. The property should also be inspected by a specialist for mold and any related problems.

Methamphetamine Labs

Methamphetamine (meth) is an illegal, man-made drug that is extremely addictive. Like cocaine, it is a stimulant. Since the ingredients are not necessarily hard to find, meth labs are found in homes, apartments, motels, wooded areas, and even cars.

Along with a higher risk of fire and explosions from having a meth lab on a property, meth's cooking process creates a dangerous residue, toxic byproducts, and fumes. The residue can contaminate a property by affecting floors, ceiling, walls, carpeting, air-conditioning and heating vents, blinds, and personal property (e.g., clothing, toys).

Since the residue permeates the property, it cannot always be removed. Toxic byproducts poured down the drain or into the soil can create a mini toxic waste site. If a property has been exposed to these conditions and residue remains, anyone living in it can develop health problems, ranging from serious respiratory problems, burning in the hands and feet, nausea, headaches, liver damage, and even death. Some houses have been demolished as a result of the proliferation of chemicals.

Other Environmental Concerns

Property owners are being held to a higher standard than ever before. Continued updates and amendments to the **Comprehensive Environmental Response, Compensation and Liability Act (CERCLA)** have increased the burden on sellers and owners of property. With regard to property contaminated with environmental hazards, not only can past producers and/or dumpers of the contamination be held liable, but so can the current owner and any owners of the property at the time of the contamination. The rationale for increasing the scope of liability to any party having ownership is an attempt to place the burden of identifying hazardous sites on the marketplace. The law specifically includes liability for owners who knew, or should have known, of the contamination. This implies that owners may now have to test not only their own property, but perhaps even surrounding properties before a buying decision is made. Even the lender in a management capacity can be held liable.

This ruling was upheld in *U.S. v. Mirabile*.

Given this climate, it's important for everyone involved in a transaction to take steps to protect themselves. Appraisers must take extra effort to ensure they are aware of any potential environmental hazards as the value of a property, and surrounding properties in the immediate area or an entire neighborhood, can be severely impacted. When in doubt, call an expert.

Summary

1. Factors outside the boundaries of a property that affect its value include **P-E-G-S**. The main physical externality that affects real estate is the neighborhood. Environmental concerns also influence value indirectly (entire neighborhood) or directly (certain property).

2. **Neighborhoods** or **market areas** are groups of homes or properties with common characteristic(s). They share physical traits (e.g., style, age) or boundaries (e.g., rivers, roads). Other characteristics that define neighborhoods include: Similar use, zoning, price range, income level, and shared social, civic, or recreation facilities. Almost anything can define neighborhood (**excluding** race, ethnicity, and other protected classes). A neighborhood/ market area differs from a community, which is a larger area. An appraiser makes his initial neighborhood decision based on physical boundaries, then tests it by physically observing the neighborhood; he confirms his conclusions with socio-economic data.

3. Properly defined neighborhoods generally age together through four phases of a life cycle: Growth, stability/equilibrium, decline, and revitalization. **Growth** is when property values rise as development activity begins and continues. **Stability/equilibrium** is when property values are at their highest level and there is little vacant property. **Decline** is when property values fall as demand falls. Decline is often observable as deferred maintenance. **Revitalization** is when property values rise as demand increases, which leads to renovation and rehabilitation. Rapid revitalization is called **gentrification**.

4. P-E-G-S factors affect a neighborhood. **Physical factors** determine boundaries via roads, rivers, etc. They affect the life cycle based on road/zoning changes, upkeep, nuisances, and hazards. **Economic factors** determine boundaries through price, income level, business development, and property usage. They affect life cycles because of economic base, interest rates, income levels, and general business activity. **Governmental factors** determine boundaries by streets, man-made barriers, zoning, school, taxing, historical district, and boundaries of government services (fire and police departments). They affect life cycles through road/zoning changes and tax rates. **Social factors** determine boundaries by recreation, cultural activities, commercial, retail, job convenience, education level, and social status. They affect the life cycle due to buyer perceptions and demographics.

5. A **nuisance** is anything that interferes with the right of quiet enjoyment (e.g., airport noise, farm stench). A permanent nuisance can be an **external obsolescence**. An environmental hazard is a situation of potential harm to persons or property from conditions that exist in a property or nearby area (e.g., toxic waste dump, nuclear power plant, high-tension power lines). The perception of risk may persist among buyers even after the danger is removed. **Stigmatized properties** are undesirable due to a past event(s), like properties where a crime took place or which had a past environmental hazard (these usually must be disclosed—real estate agents should check their broker's policies).

6. Environmental concerns within a property can be dangerous, but sometimes can be rectified. Seller must disclose known hazards on Residential Property Disclosure Form. For houses built before 1978, the **lead-based paint** brochure must be given to buyers and potential tenants, known lead paint hazards must be disclosed, and buyers must be given a 10-day period to conduct lead tests. **Asbestos** is a heat resistant material once used as insulation but now determined to cause cancer. **Urea-formaldehyde foam** is insulation that was once blown in, but is now banned by the EPA because of toxic fumes. **Radon gas** is a naturally occurring radioactive gas that can get into homes through cracks and build up to dangerous levels if not prevented. **Underground storage tanks** requires steps to stop corrosion, spills, leaks, and overfill (some are exempt). **Mold** is a fungus that can grow anywhere and on any organic material. **Methamphetamine** (meth) is an illegal, man-made drug that is extremely addictive. Along with a higher risk of fire and explosions from having a meth lab on a property, meth's cooking process creates a dangerous residue, toxic byproducts, and fumes.

Quiz

1. *Which CANNOT define a neighborhood's boundaries?*
   a. ethnic origin of residents
   b. income level of residents
   c. natural and artificial boundaries
   d. upkeep and maintenance

2. *The four life cycle stages a neighborhood normally goes through, in order, are*
   a. decline, revitalization, stability/equilibrium, and growth.
   b. growth, stability/equilibrium, decline, and revitalization.
   c. revitalization, growth, decline, and stability/equilibrium.
   d. stability/equilibrium, decline, growth, and revitalization.

3. *Gentrification is the*
   a. aging of a neighborhood.
   b. aging of the population.
   c. rapid deterioration of the neighborhood.
   d. rapid revitalization of the neighborhood.

4. *Which is NOT a way that the government can affect the life cycle of a neighborhood?*
   a. changing tax rates
   b. changing zoning
   c. widening a road
   d. imposing deed restrictions

5. *A nuisance*
   a. affects some of the owner's bundle of rights.
   b. always emanates from within the property's boundaries.
   c. can always be removed.
   d. involves a person trespassing on the property.

6. *A stigmatized property*
   a. is irrationally shunned by an uneducated buyer.
   b. is one that may be undesirable to some people because of a past event.
   c. need not be disclosed to a potential buyer by the real estate agent.
   d. should be avoided at all costs.

7. *What action is NOT necessary to comply with EPA lead-based paint regulations for houses built before 1978?*
   a. Buyers must be given a 10-day period to conduct lead tests.
   b. Known lead paint hazards must be disclosed.
   c. A lead paint brochure must be given to buyers and prospective tenants.
   d. Sellers must hire a contractor to remove any lead-based paint.

8. *Radon gas*
   a. can present a problem indoors if allowed to build up to dangerous levels.
   b. is expensive to remediate.
   c. is a man-made waste byproduct.
   d. makes a house worthless because it must be condemned by the EPA.

Residential Construction and Home Inspection

This chapter aims to familiarize real estate agents with general information regarding the construction of homes. We will look at the basics of residential construction from the process of building a new home to completion, as well as the different styles and layouts of houses. For more detailed information, refer to the Home Inspection Supplement in the Appendix.

Key Terms

Building Codes 1. A means of setting construction standards requiring builders to use particular methods and materials. 2. Regulations establishing minimum standards for construction and materials.

Concrete Footers A base that a foundation sits on. They must be poured on solid ground, below frost depth, and wider at the bottom than the structure to be supported.

Foundation The basic structure on which the rest of the building will sit. A foundation can be **concrete slab, pier and beams, crawl space**, or **basement**.

Framing The basic load bearing skeleton of the house to which interior walls, exterior walls, and roof are attached.

Gross Living Area (GLA) Residential space that is finished, livable, and above grade. Garages, finished basements, and storage areas usually do not count as GLA.

Home Inspection A visual examination of the physical structure and systems of a home.

Permits Official government documents that acknowledge work a person wants to do on a property and allow it to be done.

Pitch A roof's vertical rise in inches, divided by its horizontal span in feet.

Rough-ins Any type of interior work to a house or building that is not part of the finish work (e.g., plumbing, HVAC, electrical).

Why Learn the Basics of Residential Construction?

This chapter begins by looking at the process of having a home built. It is important for real estate agents and residential appraisers to have working knowledge of a home, its construction, and its systems. This knowledge will aid them in having intelligent conversations with others they encounter and demonstrate their professionalism. A professional is defined by knowledge. Whether an agent or appraiser actually deals with newly built homes or only with existing homes, some exposure to the home building process and an understanding of what goes into a home will enhance their stature among the people they interact with on a daily basis.

The Process of Building a New Home

There are several necessary steps in the building process. Some items within the steps may vary depending on which path a person chooses (e.g., an individual may choose a builder's existing house plan or create his own, or may hire sub-contractors himself or hire a builder) and the area a person lives but overall, the process is very similar.

Site Work

The first step in the home building process is **site work**. Here, improvements may have to be made to land to make it viable. If a lot is part of a subdivision, some or all of the site work may already be done. If a lot is raw land, it will be necessary to trench into public water or sewer lines, or dig a well for water and create a leach bed for a septic system. In the latter case, it will be necessary to work closely with the local health department to ensure compliance with all regulations.

Other site work will depend on the house chosen—its style, features, and position.

For Example

Trees may need to be cleared, a basement dug, and a rough driveway put in place.

Of course, first considerations should evolve around these questions:

- Are there deed restrictions which dictate the style or minimum size of house that must be built?
- Are there easements which cannot be built on?
- How far back from the street and how far away from neighboring houses does the law require the house to be built?

In addition to restrictions and local ordinances, the positioning of the house on the lot should take into account aesthetics and energy conservation. Not only can a house be positioned to take advantage of the best view, but other factors can also influence the direction a house faces.

For Example

The south side receives the most winter sun, while facing a house east or west would accent the morning or evening sun.

The Foundation

After site work is finished, next comes the foundation. The **foundation** is *the basic structure on which the rest of the building will sit.* The foundation holds up the rest of the house, so it's important for it to be strong and dry. Usually, a foundation will have *concrete footers.* **Concrete footers** are *the base that a foundation sits on.* A hole is dug so concrete can be poured onto solid ground, such that the footer is wider at the bottom—and wider than the structure it will support. Local building codes will dictate how footers must be built (their size and placement), based on the ground being built upon, the type of foundation to be used, and the frost depth common in the area (footers go below the freeze line—the deepest that ground freezes in winter). Typical residential foundation types are **concrete slabs**, **piers and beams**, **crawl spaces**, and **basements**.

Concrete Slabs

A **concrete slab** is a foundation made from a layer of poured concrete reinforced with steel rods (called **rebar**). This type of foundation sits directly on the ground, with only a thin layer of sand or gravel, perhaps with a mesh, waterproofing membrane and/or Styrofoam sheeting to act as insulation. With concrete slab foundations, concrete footers may or may not be used (as a separate piece). When concrete footers are not used, additional holes are dug deep into the ground so the continuous pour of concrete produces piers that are connected as one piece with the concrete slab.

Piers and Beams

A **pier and beam** foundation has columns of concrete, wood, or steel (the **piers**) resting on footers or another type of reinforced base, with supports of wood or steel (the **beams**) that span the columns to provide support for the floors, roof, etc. The lower beams that span the piers are called the **floor joists**. The floor and framing support for the walls and ceiling are nailed to the floor joists. The piers can be almost flush with the ground or extend into the air. Typically, building codes will limit the height of the piers to discourage using this as a way to build a house onto the side of a hill.

Crawl Spaces

A **crawl space** is the unfinished space below the first floor of a house or other structure, but space that is less than a full story in height. A crawl space is technically not a foundation, but rather a part of another foundation type.

For Example

Most crawl spaces are the result of a pier and beam foundation where the piers stick out of the ground less than a full story in height. The resulting space between the ground and first floor of a house is a crawl space.

A crawl space can also be created where only a partial basement is dug below a house.

Basements

A **basement** is part of a house or building which is partially or entirely below grade (ground level), and used to support the rest of the structure. Basements are typically at least one full story in height. A basement is formed as a result of space that is dug first before a house or building is erected. The walls of the basement can be poured concrete, or built from concrete blocks or stone. The basement walls sit on concrete footers and serve as the foundation for the house.

One end of the floor joists sit on the ledges or sills of the basement walls around the perimeter of the house. The other end of floor joists (in the middle of the house) sit on some type of support column, or beam which sits on the support column. Support columns may be concrete piers, wood or block pillars, or metal floor jacks, and sit on a slab or footer.

Framing

The **framing** is *the basic load bearing skeleton of the house to which interior walls, exterior walls, and roof are attached.* Framing also includes the solid support structure surrounding window and door openings. When framing is complete, a person can actually walk around the floor plan of the home, from room to room, to see how the layout feels. The final step in framing is the roof sheathing.

Although houses may sometimes be built of concrete blocks (particularly one-floor ranches), blocks are usually reserved for commercial buildings. The typical house is wood framed (although metal studs that are used for commercial buildings are being used by some builders). The three basic types of wood frame houses are **platform**, **post and beam**, and **balloon frame**.

Platform

In **platform** framing, the house or building is constructed one story at a time, with each story serving as a platform upon which to build the next story. Wood studs are cut to the height of each story, with horizontal flooring and support across the top of the studs. The studs for the next story are then cut and attached to the flooring.

 This is the most common type of framing.

Post and Beam

In **post and beam** framing, the floor for higher stories (and the roof) is supported by beams that sit on top of posts and the outside wall perimeter. This is similar to the way a post and beam foundation is constructed. With post supports, not as many interior walls are needed, allowing for larger and more open rooms. Posts, beams, and frame members are heavier than other types of framing, and the wood is often left exposed for decorative purposes.

Balloon

In **balloon** framing, long vertical studs run from the foundation to the roof of the house. Horizontal studs (called **ledger boards**) are nailed to these vertical studs to provide support for floor and roof joists. Although this was common in older multi-story brick buildings, it is rarely used today because of its poor fire-resistant design and cost issues.

Roofing

The roof is part of the last step in framing a house. There are several styles of exterior roof design that can be used. (Sample roof styles and roof frame examples appear on the next page.) Roof style can influence the choice of roof frame. Three roof frame types are **truss roofing**, **joist and rafters**, and **sloped joist**.

Truss Roofing

Truss roofing is a type of roof frame that consists of several pieces attached together to a triangular structure that creates a beam of support to hold up the roof covering. Trusses are held together by nails, bolts, or metal plates (called **gusset plates**). A truss must be used when the span or weight of the roof would be too great for a single beam. Trusses are often used because they are less expensive than longer pieces of wood, can be engineered to be stronger than beams, and come to the job site pre-assembled.

Joist and Rafters

Joist and rafters roofing is a type of roof frame where joists are supported by outer load bearing walls and a central load bearing wall (acts as beams do for floor joists). The ceiling joists run horizontally; parallel to the floor. The ceiling rafters begin on the outer load bearing walls, but rise as they come to the center peak of a roof.

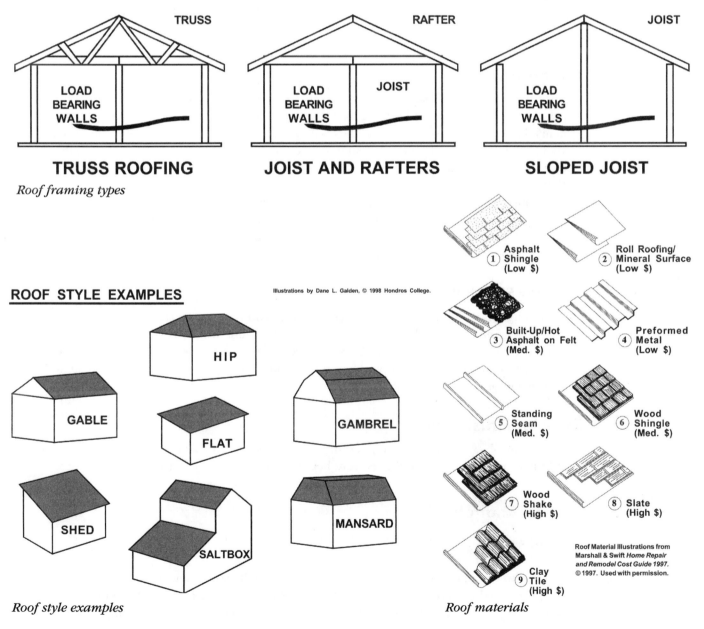

Roof framing types

Roof style examples

Roof materials

This rise is referred to as a roof's *pitch*. **Pitch** is *a roof's vertical rise in inches, divided by the roof's horizontal span in feet*. Where two sets of rafters meet at the peak, there's only a ridge board between them. The rafters are held up by the opposing pressure that each side places on the other.

Sloped Joist

Sloped joist roofing is a type of roof frame where joists go from the outer load bearing walls to a central load bearing wall, which is higher than the outer walls. Instead of having the joists parallel to the floor, the joists actually slope up with the pitch of the roof. There are no rafters because the joists are essentially taking that position.

 This type of roof framing allows for *vaulted ceilings* (also called *cathedral ceilings*). **Vaulted ceilings** are ceilings that rise as they follow the roof line, extending up into the roof peak. They're not flat and don't run parallel to the floor, but create a feeling of openness and are ideal for skylights.

Rough-Ins

After the frame is complete, the next step is to do rough-ins. **Rough-ins** are *any type of interior work to a house or building that is not part of the finish work*. Essentially, these are items that will not be seen because they will be hidden later by the finished walls, but are vital to the operation of a home. Rough-ins include things like electrical wiring, plumbing, heating and air-conditioning, and so on. Usually, **permits** (*official government documents that acknowledge work a person wants to do on a property and allow it to be done*) will need to be obtained and inspections will follow after each type of work has been completed to ensure it complies with building codes and safety rules. **Building codes** are *a means of setting construction standards, requiring builders to use particular methods and materials*. A final inspection is also made after all work is done.

Interior Finish Work

Once rough-in work has been completed and inspections have been made, the next step is for interior finish work to begin. Ceilings and walls of studs will be covered with drywall or other material, and then painted. Floors will be covered with specified flooring materials. Lights and light switches, plumbing fixtures, and kitchen cabinets will be installed, as well as trim and other special finishing touches.

Exterior Finish Work

Exterior finish work may get wrapped up about the same time as the interior, before it, or after it. It depends on when things were begun, and on the choices for exterior finishes.

For Example

Stone and brick exteriors take longer to complete than vinyl siding.

Actually, work on the exterior has been going on for quite some time. Right after framing is completed, and usually before any rough-in work begins, some additional exterior work is done to help keep weather and elements out while the rest of the house is being completed.

Completion

During the completion stage, it is time to finish outside features like patios, driveways, and landscaping. One of the most important completion items is to clean-up the worksite and haul away debris. Perhaps the best gauge of when a house is complete is when final inspections have been performed and the house has been approved for habitation.

Styles of Houses

Now that we've discussed construction steps and issues, let's take a look at some of the styles of houses. There are two ways to define the style:

1. Exterior appearance
2. Functional layout

When discussing the *exterior appearance* of a home, there are basic architectural styles that are popular:

- American Colonial
- Cape Cod
- English Tudor
- Traditional Ranch
- French Provincial
- Modern Contemporary
- Spanish Villa

There are innumerable variations on these basic designs.

In addition to these basic architectural styles, *functional layouts* also serve to describe a home. Some of these are associated so closely with an architectural style, they share a common name:

- One-story, referred to as a "Ranch"
- One-and-a-half story, referred to as a "Cape Cod"
- Split-level—multi-level, short stairs
- Bi-level—2 levels, one sunken, no basement
- Two-story

There are a variety of possible combinations of architectural styles and functional layouts.

ENGLISH TUDOR

AMERICAN COLONIAL

SPANISH VILLA

MODERN CONTEMPORARY

CAPE COD

TRADITIONAL RANCH

Images from Clipart Collection. © 1994, Explore the World of Software Inc.

HOUSE LAYOUT EXAMPLES

Illustrations from Marshall & Swift *Home Repair & Remodel Cost Guide 1997.* © 1997.   Used with permission.

One-Story

One-story residences have one level of living area. The roof structure has a medium slope. The attic space is limited and is not intended for living area.

One-and-One-Half Story

One-and-one-half story residences have two levels of living area. Characterized by a steep roof slope and dormers, the area of the upper level, whether finished or unfinished, usually equals 40% to 60% of the lower level.

Two-Story

Two-story residences have two levels of finished living area. The area of each floor is approximately the same. The roof structure has a medium slope. The attic space is limited and not designed for usable living area.

Two-and-One-Half Story

Two-and-one-half story residences have three levels of living area. Having a steep roof slope with dormers, the area of the third floor, whether finished or unfinished, usually equals 40% to 60% of the second floor.

Two-Story Bi-Level

Two-story bi-level residences have two levels of living area. Unlike a conventional two-story, the lower level, which may be partially below grade, is partially unfinished. A distinguishing characteristic is its split-foyer entry.

Split-Level

Split-level residences have three levels of finished living area—lower level, intermediate level, and upper level. The lower level is immediately below the upper level, as in a two-story. The intermediate level, adjacent to the other levels, is built on a grade approximately four feet higher than that of the lower level.

Calculating Area

Square footage is always calculated by using the outside dimensions of the structure—building costs always should include outside walls. For commercial buildings, the square footage total may be divided by space usage.

For Example

The square footage may be divided between warehouse space and office space, with a different cost manual multiplier used for each type of space.

For residential property, non-living areas (e.g., garage space, screened-in porch) are subtracted from the outer dimension totals when figuring square footage. This is referred to as the gross living area. **Gross living area (GLA)** is *residential space that is finished, livable, and above grade*. Garages, finished basements, and storage areas do not usually count as part of this total area. Finished attics can count as GLA if they have heat, electricity, finished walls, and normal ceiling height.

 A detailed explanation of the math for calculating area can be found in the Appendix.

Home Inspections

Different styles of roofs, foundations, exteriors, and home layouts have been introduced, but there are many more areas covered by a **home inspection**. It's important for real estate agents and appraisers to be familiar with the major parts of a house. Knowing the names, as well as different styles and types that are common, can help agents and appraisers portray an image of professionalism—and help them talk intelligently with the people they'll meet in their real estate career. It's also helpful to know some of the major systems of a house, what their purpose is, and how they function.

 Real estate agents and appraisers must remember not to portray themselves as having expertise in these areas unless they receive additional specialized training or certification.

For further information, refer to the Home Inspection Supplement in the Appendix.

Summary

1. **Steps in building a new home** include site work, foundation, framing, roofing, rough-ins, interior finish, exterior finish, and completion. **Foundation types** include concrete slabs, piers and beams, crawl spaces, or basements. **Framing types** include platform, post and beam, and balloon. **Roofing types** include truss, joist and rafters, and sloped joist. **Roof styles** include gable, hip, gambrel, mansard, saltbox, shed, and flat. **Rough-ins** include things like electrical wiring, plumbing, heating and air-conditioning. **Interior finish** includes things like drywall, floor coverings, light switches, plumbing fixtures, kitchen cabinets, and other finishing touches. **Exterior finish** includes finishing the exterior of the house, whether it be brick, stucco, siding, etc. **Completion** typically includes outside features and landscaping, clean-up of the work site, all final inspections, and when the house is approved for habitation.

2. Usually, **permits** (official government documents that acknowledge work a person wants to do on a property and allow it to be done) will need to be obtained and inspections will follow after each type of work has been completed to ensure that the work complies with all building codes and safety rules. **Building codes** are a means of setting construction standards, requiring builders to use particular methods and materials.

3. **Architectural styles** include American Colonial, English Tudor, French Provincial, Spanish Villa, Cape Cod, Traditional Ranch, and Modern Contemporary.

4. **Functional layouts** include Ranch (1 story), Cape Cod (1 1/2 story), split level (multi-level, short stairs), bi-level (2 levels, one sunken, no basement), and two-story.

Quiz

1. **Which type of roof allows for vaulted ceilings?**
   a. joists and rafters
   b. sloped joists
   c. truss roofing
   d. raised tie trusses

2. **A roof's pitch is the**
   a. rise of the roof.
   b. rise of the roof in feet, divided by the span of the roof in inches.
   c. rise of the roof in inches, divided by the span of the roof in feet.
   d. run of the roof.

3. **The home's plumbing would be installed during the _____ stage.**
   a. completion
   b. interior finish
   c. rough-in
   d. site work

4. **Floor coverings would be installed during the _____ stage.**
   a. completion
   b. foundation
   c. interior finish
   d. rough-in

5. **Landscaping is typically completed during the _____ stage.**
   a. completion
   b. exterior finish
   c. rough-in
   d. site work

6. **A Ranch style home is typically**
   a. one-story.
   b. one–and-a-half-stories.
   c. split-level.
   d. two-stories.

7. **A Cape Cod style home is typically**
   a. one-story.
   b. one-and-a-half-stories.
   c. split-level.
   d. two–stories.

8. **When platform framing is used in construction, each story of the structure**
   a. is built one story at a time.
   b. is constructed simultaneously.
   c. has a crawl space.
   d. has its own footer.

9. **The component of a house on which the foundation rests is known as a**
   a. footer.
   b. lateral.
   c. pier.
   d. sill plate.

10. **Electrical wiring, plumbing, and heating ductwork installed in a house as a step in the construction process, and later connected to their main service points and hidden from view, are known as**
    a. basic essentials.
    b. framing.
    c. rough-ins.
    d. temporary utilities.

11. **The triangular structure that creates a beam of support to hold up the roof of a structure is known as a**
    a. foundation.
    b. gusset plate.
    c. ledger.
    d. truss.

12. **The roofing material installed during the framing process which will serve as a base layer for the final roof covering is known as**
    a. a ledger.
    b. a rafter.
    c. rebar.
    d. sheathing.

Site Valuation

This chapter discusses the theory of site valuation, inclu[de]
the characteristics that give land inherent value, theor[y]
of land value, and increasing land value by assemblage. O[ther]
topics include identifying a site by its legal description and
differences between surveys and location surveys. The collec[tion]
and analysis of site data, including factors that affect value, as
as the five methods of determining site value will be examin[ed].

Key Terms

Assemblage The combining of two or more parcels of land into one larger parcel.

Government Survey System A legal description for land, referencing principal meridians and base lines designated throughout the country. Also called **Governmental Rectangular Survey**.

Location Survey The process of verifying that an improvement properly sits within the boundaries of the property and there are no encroachments from neighboring land onto the subject property.

Lot and Block A legal description used for platted property. The description states only the property's lot and block number in a particular subdivision; to find the exact location of property boundaries, the plat map for that subdivision must be consulted at the county recorder's office.

Metes and Bounds A legal description that starts at an easily identifiable point of beginning (POB), then describes the property's boundaries in terms of courses (compass directions) and distances, ultimately returning to the POB.

Plat A detailed survey map of a subdivision, or other grouped lots of land, recorded in the county where the land is located. Subdivided property is often called platted property. Also called a **Plat Map**.

Plottage Combining two or more parcels into one, with an increase in value over the value of the two parcels individually.

Range Lines In the government survey system, north-south lines that run parallel to principal meridians at six-mile intervals.

Section Part of a township, one mile by one mile square, used for the government survey system; one section equals 640 acres, 36 sections equal one township.

Survey The process of locating and measuring the boundaries of a property, and identifying the improvements, encroachments, and easements associated with that land.

Townships Square divisions of land, six miles by six miles, in the government survey system. One township contains 36 sections.

Theory of Site Valuation

Site valuation is an important process for several reasons. Apart from the fact that sometimes the subject of an appraisal is vacant land or site, site valuation is necessary for developing the cost approach. It is also instrumental in a highest and best use analysis and as a part of other types of analysis.

Inherent Value of Land

While studying the motivation and methods for valuing a site, separate from any structures on it, remember that land itself has some inherent value. The theories discussed regarding the value land has can be summarized as follows:

1. **Scarcity:** Land supply is limited—no more can be created in any location.

2. **Indestructibility:** Land goes on forever—always has potential to make income.

3. **Immobility:** Land can't be moved—regardless of the situation.

Other factors can come into play. Perhaps the most important is a corollary to immobility: Location. **The location of land is the primary determinant of its value**.

For Example

The same amount of land is worth more in downtown Columbus, Ohio than it would be if it were located in downtown Springfield, Ohio. Also, the same amount of land is worth more as waterfront property than if it were not waterfront property.

The previous examples about the different values of land based on location are really a reflection of two larger theorems about land value.

Land Value Theorem #1

Just as location is the primary determinant of land value, **land value is the primary determinant of real property value**. In other words, land and its location are the real factors determining the value of property. That may sound odd if you think about a nice, large house that you've had your eye on and would love to buy. Your first thought is that you're buying a nice, large house. But think again. You're really buying the location first and the house second. Would you be willing to pay the same amount for the house you've always wanted if it were located anywhere else? What about if that same house were located right next to a toxic waste dump? Now how much would you pay for it? People think they're buying a house (and certainly a good part of the value is the cost of the house) but, in reality, they're buying the land and its location.

Land Value Theorem #2

Land derives its value from market demand. This may sound like it contradicts the first land value theorem but, in reality, they go hand in hand. The reason why one location of land is more desirable than another is because of market demand. Remember the example? The same house next to a toxic waste dump has no value because of its location—because nobody would want it if it was located there. There's no market demand for nice, large houses located next to toxic waste dumps, so the value of land (and the house) is much less.

Ways to Increase the Value of Land

Given the "land value theorems" and immobility of land, it may seem like there's nothing that can be done to increase the value of land. Actually, there is—without resorting to improvements. Improvements to raw land to make it into a site can add value, but the inherent value of the land is still the same. If buildings are added, the value of the real estate is increased, but not the inherent value of the land. One way to increase the value of land is to have more of it.

Assemblage

Assemblage is *the combining of two or more parcels of land into one larger parcel*. This is typically done to increase the usefulness (utility) of the land by allowing one larger building to be constructed on the larger parcel than could have been built on the smaller individual parcels. The value of the land will also increase; in fact, this one large parcel is likely worth more than the sum total of the smaller parcels. This is referred to as **plottage**—*combining two or more parcels into one, with an increase in value over the value of the two parcels individually*. The increase in value (over the cost of acquiring the parcels) by successful assemblage is usually due to a change in use. By creating a larger parcel with more utility and higher and better use than the individual sites, the owner has successfully achieved an increase in the inherent value of the land. Actually, individual land owners can benefit as well.

For Example

Mega Co. wants to build a new shopping center. The company picked out an ideal location where ten homes now sit. Each of the ten homes is worth about $100,000. Mega knows, though, that the value of all ten parcels together is $2,000,000. Instead of trying to buy each home for only $100,000, Mega is likely to offer the owners $120,000 as an incentive for them to sell. If every home is purchased for $120,000, Mega's total cost will be $1,200,000—much less than the total value of the larger parcel.

This incentive will likely work at first, but may get more difficult as the last few owners learn what's going on. These last few homes will likely cost Mega more money but home owners have to be careful, too. If they are unrealistic about their homes' worth to Mega's project or its budget, or how high Mega is willing to go, the owners may get nothing. If they hold out too long for too much, Mega may decide to design the project around them.

Value of Frontage

As a corollary to assemblage and plottage, it's important to understand that the addition of some land is more valuable than other land. This is especially true for commercial property, which is compared by the front foot (feet along the road).

 The first number in a lot's size is its frontage. A lot that measures 150' x 200' has 150 frontage feet and a depth of 200 feet.

Adding more front footage to a lot makes land much more valuable than adding more depth—even if the total amount of land added is the same.

For Example

Andy owns a lot that measures 100' by 100'. He buys up an adjacent lot of the same size. Andy's land is worth more if more front footage can be added than if more depth is added. The lot still has the same total area either way, but a 200' x 100' lot is much more valuable than a 100' x 200' lot.

Commercial properties place a higher value on front footage because it is more useful for business purposes. Adding depth increases the value of the lot, but as the depth of a lot increases, the value per front foot increases at a decreasing rate.

For Example

If a lot is 100' wide and 10,000' deep, how much would someone be willing to pay to make the lot 10,005' deep? Not much. The total value increase to the lot would be small.

How much would someone be willing to pay for a few more feet of road frontage? More than that person would for more depth!

Remember, these examples are primarily for commercial properties. Generally, the marketplace does not make the same distinctions for residential properties. An increase in lot size (whether frontage or depth) generally contributes the same amount of extra value to a lot based on the total size of the lot. An exception to this would be residential waterfront property. In this case, extra beachfront or lakefront footage would result in an increase in value.

Highest and Best Use

As mentioned, determining a property's highest and best use is an important element in considering site value. An appraiser will need to gather data and analyze the physical characteristics of the property—whether residential dwelling or commercial property.

However, determination of highest and best use for residential properties, in many cases, is abbreviated by private and public limitations that could single out only one or two potential property uses. It is not uncommon for a non-residential property also to be subject to private and public limitations, but often there is a broad array of potential uses. Thus, the appraiser may need to spend a considerable amount of time performing research and analysis to determine the highest and best use.

Highest and Best Use in Commercial Properties

For our purposes, commercial properties include non-residential land, income-producing properties, multi-family residential properties with more than four units, mixed-use properties, etc.

There are many potential scenarios for determining highest and best use in a non-residential appraisal assignment, depending on whether the site is currently improved or if it is vacant. If the site is improved, the appraiser must first determine if the improvement is bringing the greatest return to the land in terms of market value.

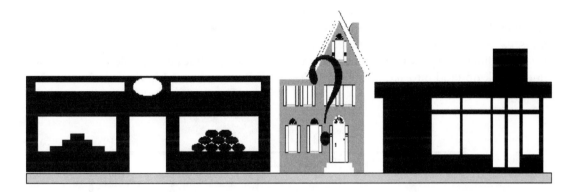

The highest and best use analysis for a residential dwelling on a commercially zoned lot often presents a challenging and complex task for the appraiser.

The appraiser's highest and best use analysis for a non-residential land parcel or site is often more complex and detailed than would be performed for a residential property. The primary reason for this is that non-residential land or site often has multiple uses permitted by zoning. The appraiser's highest and best use analysis would not only include whether the property should be improved with a non-residential improvement or structure, but also extend to the specific type of structure the parcel should be improved with.

Also a challenge in a non-residential highest and best use analysis is the frequency for which a perfectly good structure may not be contributing to the highest and best use of the land. In such case, the appraiser's recommendation may be to tear down the improvement(s).

Identifying the Site

Now that the theory behind site valuation has been discussed, it's time to look at the actual valuation process. Before the appraiser begins to accumulate data for use in the site valuation, he needs to be sure that data is collected on the correct parcel of land. Sometimes, the address is not enough, particularly when dealing with vacant land. Sometimes, the land parcel or site has not been assigned an address at all. Identifying the correct site involves obtaining and verifying the site's legal description. The test of a valid description of property is the ability to identify and distinguish that property from any and all other parcels of land. There are three basic types of legal descriptions used:

1. Government survey system
2. Lot and block system
3. Metes and bounds system

Government Survey System

The **government survey system** is *a legal description for land, referencing principal meridians and base lines designated throughout the country*. It is also called the **government rectangular survey**.

 Some parts of Ohio use the **Virginia Military Survey** (**VMS**), which is a later version of another type of Government Survey System.

With the government survey system, a particular piece of land is identified by directions and coordinates, which count from these lines as reference points. *Additional north-south lines*, called **range lines**, run parallel to principal meridians at six mile intervals. Additional east-west lines, called **township lines**, run parallel to base lines at six mile intervals. These lines break up land into *six mile by six mile squares* called **townships**.

TOWNSHIP IDENTIFICATION: Using principal meridians and base lines
(each principal meridian and base line has a unique name or number.)

The 36 square miles of a township are subdivided into 36 *sections*. A **section** is *one square mile* (640 acres). Each section in a township is numbered sequentially so a person can locate her land by referring to the section number, and subsequent references to half and quarter sections with compass points. Any portion of land that cannot be divided into equal fractional lots is designated as a **government lot**.

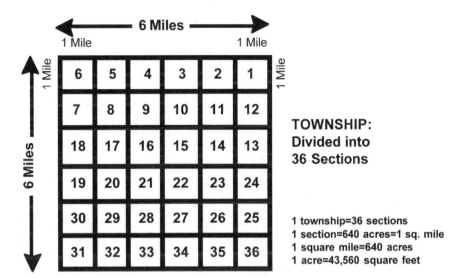

A typical parcel of land is located within a section. A legal description from this method would use directions and quadrants. Look at the following diagram.

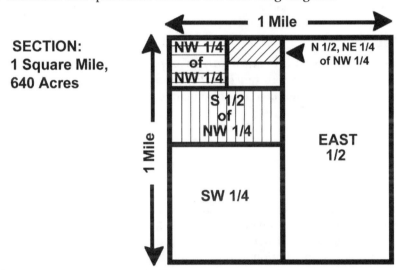

A legal description might read: N 1/2, NE 1/4 of NW 1/4. Always start from the end of the description and work backwards. We are talking about the NW 1/4, so look at the upper left corner of the section, and then read the rest of the description to determine which part of the NW 1/4 is being talked about.

For Example

The above illustration contains different shading:

- The S 1/2 of NW 1/4 is shaded like this:
- The NW 1/4 of NW 1/4 is shaded like this:
- The N 1/2, NE 1/4 of NW 1/4 is shaded like this:

For the real estate prelicensing exam, in addition to being able to locate a parcel of land within a section, students will also need to know how to calculate the land acreage for a given parcel of land. With the government survey system, calculating acreage is rather easy.

Again, start from the end of the legal description and work backwards from right to left. Since an entire section of land in the government survey system always equals 640 acres, take 640 and divide by the denominators (bottom number) for each fractional part.

For Example

- For the S 1/2 of NW 1/4, take 640 ÷ 4 ÷ 2 = 80 acres
- For the NE 1/4 of NW 1/4, take 640 ÷ 4 ÷ 4 = 40 acres
- For the N 1/2, NE 1/4 of NW 1/4, take 640 ÷ 4 ÷ 4 ÷ 2 = 20 acres

Lot and Block System

The **lot and block system** is a *type of legal description used for platted property.* Platted property is any property that has been subdivided from a large tract into smaller lots. These lots are numbered, first with a block number for the area, then individually with each lot receiving its own number. *The lot and block description states only the property's lot and block number in a particular subdivision*; to find the exact location of property boundaries, the *plat* or *plat map* for that subdivision must be consulted at the county recorder's office.

Plat Map

A **plat** (or **plat map**) is *a detailed survey map of a subdivision, or other grouped lots of land, recorded in the county where the land is located.* Different jurisdictions have different rules about when land must be platted and a plat map recorded.

For Example

Dividing land into lots of less than five acres may mean that a person has to file a plat map with local authorities.

Plat maps are generally kept in the county recorder's office in a plat book. The general location of the land indicates which book must be consulted to look at the plat map. The specific map, then, allows a person to look up the exact location of the lot using the lot and block numbers. In addition to the lot and block numbers, the plat map will usually also give details such as streets, public easements, and ownership information. Other information may include zoning, elevations, and flood plains.

For Example

In the following diagram, the legal description of the shaded area is Lot 19, Block 17 of Golden Valley Estate.

SAMPLE SUBDIVISION PLAT MAT: Golden Valley Estate, Block 17, Lots 1-22.

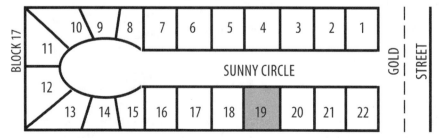

GOLDEN VALLEY ESTATE.

Metes and Bounds System

The metes and bounds system is *a legal description that starts at an easily identifiable point of beginning (POB), then describes the property's boundaries in terms of courses (compass directions) and distances, ultimately returning to the POB.* A legal description may also refer to monuments, which are fixed physical objects used as reference points.

 The point of beginning (POB) may also be called point of origin; monuments may also be called markers.

This type of legal description gets its name from the way land is described. From the point of beginning, a line is extended in a specified direction (metes). The line changes direction at specific points (bounds). The bounds are often permanent physical objects (monuments or markers). Care must be taken when selecting monuments, though, to make sure that they are more or less permanent. A tree that is chosen as a monument may be cut down at a future date. A lake that is chosen as a marker may have the shore recede. Often the safest marker is a pin. A pin is simply a rod that is driven into the ground. This may be done by the original owner, a subsequent owner, or a surveyor.

The final important thing to remember about metes and bounds descriptions is that they must always return to the point of beginning (POB) or the point of origin. Descriptions that do not return to the point of beginning are considered inadequate and inaccurate. They must be corrected if such an error exists, or if any markers or monuments have been moved or destroyed.

For Example

A legal description of the land in the following diagram might read:

Beginning at the pin in the center of Miller Road, go SE 300 feet at an angle till the edge of the road meets another pin, then go due south 250 feet till you hit a pin at the adjoining property's fence, then go due west 350 feet till you hit a pin at the edge of Miller's Pond, go due north 200 feet to another pin, then go due west 100 feet to a pin near the base of an old oak tree, then go due north till you hit the road, then NE at an angle to the point of beginning at the pin in the center of Miller Road.

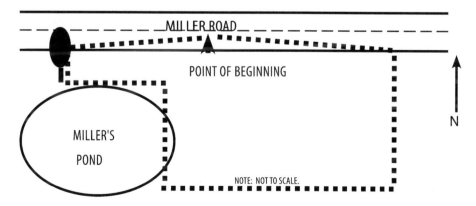

Sample Metes and Bounds Survey.

Other Points about Site Identification

There are a few other things that appraisers and real estate agents should know about locating and identifying a site:

1. Although maps can be used to help locate property that has a government survey system or lot and block legal descriptions, often no precise maps exist for property having a metes and bounds legal description.

2. Locating property by its legal description and verifying that it is the correct lot and more or less in the correct position is not the same as a *survey*. A **survey** is *the process of locating and measuring the boundaries of a property, and identifying the improvements, encroachments, and easements associated with that land*. This process can be very expensive. A location survey is a less expensive alternative often used by lenders. A **location survey** is *the process of verifying that an improvement properly sits within the boundaries of the property and there are no encroachments from neighboring land onto the subject property*. A survey or location survey is not typically part of an appraisal.

3. As an alternative to verifying the legal description of the subject property, an appraiser may simply state as a limiting condition or assumption in the final appraisal report that the legal description was provided to the appraiser by the owner, lender, etc., and was assumed to be correct.

 This does not replace a physical inspection, though, since this is still good practice in order to determine the physical characteristics of the land parcel or site and verify some of the facts and data that will be used in the valuation.

Collecting and Analyzing Site Data

After the site has been identified, the appraiser can begin collecting and analyzing the appropriate data for site valuation. The process that the appraiser uses to arrive at a value for the site is actually similar to the appraisal process discussed in Chapter 4. In addition to looking at general data on economic, governmental, social, and physical forces that are at work on a particular piece of property, the appraiser will focus on the specific data factors that will affect the site analysis.

Specific Data Factors

There are many specific data factors the appraiser will analyze with regard to a specific property. These factors will fall into one of the categories identified previously: Physical, governmental and economic.

 Social factors were not included in the list as they are not as significant a consideration for vacant land or site.

Physical Factors

Some would argue that physical factors are the most important data to be considered when examining the value of a site. In fact, the most important physical factor is size: Width, depth, shape, size of usable area, etc. The appraiser must be very sure that this data is correct. Configuration of the parcel of land is important as well: How the land sits in relation to the road, other parcels of land, etc.

For Example

A large parcel is more valuable than a smaller one and a commercial parcel with more road frontage is more valuable than a land-locked piece (remember the "front footage" discussion earlier in this chapter).

Other physical factors specific to the property include the topography of the land (flat or hilly), drainage, soil type, and view. Also, the presence or absence of utilities or other site improvements should be noted on the appraiser's site data form. The location of the lot within a neighborhood, position of the lot (e.g., corner, cul-de-sac), and access to the lot are other factors that will be taken into consideration. All of this data can be obtained by a personal inspection of the property, and from public records.

Governmental Factors

Governmental factors are also important considerations when examining the value of a site. The most important governmental factor is zoning. As previously discussed, most land would be worth more if used for commercial purposes instead of for residential homes, but the government limits the way a piece of property may be used. Government restrictions on land use also include public easements for roads or sewer, and building codes that restrict building size or placement.

 Some non-government restrictions can also impact value in the same way, namely private easements and deed restrictions.

Other governmental factors that affect site value are taxes and public services. A heavy tax burden can lower the value of a site, whereas tax abatements can make a site more attractive. Public services that are close-by (e.g., police, fire) can make a site more desirable than one where services are perceived as being too far away to provide adequate service and protection. All of this data can be obtained from public records.

Economic Factors

Economic factors also come into play when examining the value of a site. Here, relevant data concerns the specific site, as well as the surrounding lots and the immediate area. The most important economic factor is the specific position or location of the lot with regard to market demand for that type of property.

For Example

Is the property waterfront land? Do people in this area prefer corner lots and are they willing to pay more for them? Would the lot be considered easily accessible by the typical buyer? Other location considerations may come into play as well, depending on the market in the area.

Other site factors include whether or not the current utilities are adequate for the land's ideal use, and what it would cost if it becomes necessary to upgrade them. Surrounding lot considerations include general conformity of lot size and use. Concerns in the immediate area would include positive and negative environmental factors that are present or likely in the near future. This data can be obtained from a number of sources, including personal inspection, public records, and general knowledge of market conditions and future plans for the area.

Using Data to Value the Site

Once data has been gathered, verified, and analyzed, the appraiser must choose a method of valuation that will yield the most accurate results. Once a method is chosen, the appraiser will need to gather additional data to implement the valuation method. Different data are used depending on the method of valuation chosen. This additional data often includes recent comparable sales information on similar properties in the area, as well as economic data for similar types of property.

There are five common methods that the appraiser can use to perform a site valuation:

- Sales comparison method

- Allocation method

- Subdivision analysis method

- Land residual method

- Ground rent capitalization method

The first two methods use an analysis of comparable sales, and can be used for almost any type of property or site. The last three methods use various income analysis methods to arrive at a value. The subdivision analysis is typically used for large tracts of land that will be made into residential lots (although a similar method could be used for subdividing land into an office or industrial park). The last two methods can be used only for commercial properties. Let's look at each of these methods.

Sales Comparison Method

The **sales comparison method** is like the sales comparison approach to appraising property: The value of real estate is estimated by taking a market analysis of recent sales in the area where the subject property is located. While the sales comparison approach is detailed in Chapter 9, an overview is in order here.

The first step for a sales comparison is to obtain data on other similar properties that sold recently in the same market area. The other properties should be as similar to the subject property as possible. Market evidence must be used to adjust the price of the other properties to account for differences between them and the subject.

Adjustments

Any difference a typical buyer might pay more or less for can be considered an adjustment for the other sales.

For Example

If an appraiser analyzes the data and determines that buyers will pay $10,000 more for a waterfront lot than one across the street, this becomes a difference that has to be addressed in the sales comparison approach. On the other hand, if buyers are paying the same price for a cul-de-sac lot as they are for a corner lot of the same size, this difference would not warrant an adjustment.

Typical items considered for adjustments are location of the lot, physical characteristics of the lot, or restrictions on the lot. Other adjustments can be made for financing concessions or other atypical terms of sale.

When adjustments are made, the other sales are adjusted to make them closer to the subject. **The subject is never adjusted**. If a comparable sale has something that is better than the subject property, value must be subtracted from the sale price to make it closer to the subject property. If a comparable sale has something that is inferior to the subject property, value must be added to the sale price to make it closer to the subject property.

For Example

In a subdivision of new homes, 35 vacant lots have been sold and there are five left. Chris wants to buy one of the lots and is having it appraised. In looking at lots that have sold in the last six months, all of the lots are the same in size and shape. The only differences are the location of the lots, and some lots are wooded. Wooded sites and corner lots bring higher prices. From comparing recent sales and market evidence to arrive at adjustment figures, we can conclude the following:

	Subject	Comparable #1		Comparable #2		Comparable #3	
Sale Price	-------	$14,000		$13,500		$14,250	
Wooded	Yes	No	+ $500	No	+ $500	Yes	
Location	Middle	Corner	- $250	Middle		Corner	- $250
Adjusted Sale Price	-------	$14,250		$14,000		$14,000	

Thus, the appraiser would likely conclude, based on the comparable sales data, that a middle wooded lot is worth about $14,000.

Remember that the previous example is a simplified scenario. Although the appraiser tries to find comparable sales that are as similar to the subject as possible, there are usually more adjustments than this—especially for houses or other improved properties. Also, the appraiser correctly identifies what an adjustment should be from gathered market data for each feature that is different from the subject. This will be discussed in detail in Chapter 9, which covers the sales comparison approach.

Allocation Method

The **allocation method** is a method of site valuation whereby the value of the land is determined by establishing a typical ratio of site value to total property value in an area, then applying that same ratio to the subject property.

For Example

In a subdivision, houses with lots are selling for $100,000 and vacant lots are selling for $20,000. Thus, using the allocation method for valuing the site, we can see a ratio of one to five, or 1:5. So if an appraiser is trying to determine the value of a site for another home that is worth $150,000, he should apply the 1:5 ratio to determine that the $150,000 home has a site worth of $30,000.

Actually, the appraiser would look at several comparable sales before arriving at a ratio. The allocation method can also be used to derive the value of the building or improvement as well. In the previous example, since the site has a value ratio of 1:5, the building value could be derived using a ratio of 4:5 of the total value. Going back to our example above, using the allocation method, the $150,000 home's actual building worth is $120,000 out of the total value.

The major drawback to the allocation method is that it does not have a mechanism to consider differences between the properties or sites. As mentioned before, location, size, and many other factors can influence the value of property. Still, the allocation method can be useful if there are few other comparable sales available in the immediate area. A ratio for the allocation method can even be derived from tax records and assessed values, if necessary, due to lack of comparable sales or other useful data recent enough to be considered accurate and reliable.

Subdivision Analysis Method

The **subdivision analysis method** is a method of valuing raw land that will become residential land for subdivision development, by taking the total projected sale value of all finished lots and subtracting out all costs of development. The resulting figure is the calculated value of the raw land.

 This method of analysis can also be done for industrial land, commercial land, or other investment projects where a large tract of land will be divided and sold in lots.

The calculations for this can actually become quite involved. All costs of development must include many things: Construction of access roads, excavation, providing utilities to each lot, sales people to sell the lots, developer's profit, the interest the developer must pay to borrow the money, and the list goes on. Any cost the developer will incur before all lots are sold is counted as a development cost.

For Example

A developer is looking at a 100-acre tract of land, and deciding how much it's worth in its raw state. The developer calculates that the 100-acre tract could be divided into 250 lots, which could be sold for $10,000 each:

250 lots x $10,000 = $2,500,000

The developer's total costs (including profit and interest) would be $1,500,000:

$2,500,000 - $1,500,000 = $1,000,000

So, the raw land is worth about $1,000,000 to the developer. The developer can choose to pay this much, or get the land at a lower price to make extra profit. Either way, this figure represents a probable ceiling value.

Actually, the calculations are a lot more complex, but the previous simplified example illustrates the theory. First, the developer needs to determine how many lots can physically be created from the raw land—from a practical standpoint as well as within zoning laws. The developer may even have to spend some money here to do an analysis or perform a feasibility study.

When the developer is doing the actual calculations on the total costs, the developer must also take into account how long the project will take, what cash flow will be during those months or years, and the time value of money. All of these calculations take into account not only interest paid on borrowed money, but also the opportunity cost of having the money invested in this project instead of elsewhere. The developer expects a return on investment and a profit.

An analysis must also be made of the developer's ongoing expenses in getting the lots developed and sold, as well as analyzing the cash flow resulting from the eventual sale of the individual lots. Projecting income and expenses into the future is a difficult task. And again, time is a critical element—time to complete the first phase of the project, time to get the first lots sold, time to finish the project, and time to get all of the lots sold.

 This method can also be called the **subdivision development method**, **anticipated use method**, **cost of development method**, or **development method**.

Land Residual Method

The **land residual method** is an income method of site valuation that attributes a certain part of the income produced by a property to the building or other improvement, and then attributes the remaining income to the land. By using a **capitalization rate** (essentially a rate of return on investment that is typical for that type of investment), the value of the land is then calculated. This method is useful when the value of the building or improvement is known and the value of the land is unknown.

For Example

An appraiser is determining a value opinion for a warehouse facility. The appraiser is using the land residual method to verify another income approach. The building is valued at $600,000. Net income is $45,000 per year, with 65% being attributable to the building. The market derived capitalization rate is 8.75%.

$45,000 x 65% = $29,250

$45,000 - $29,250 = $15,750

$15,750 ÷ 8.75% (0.0875) = $180,000

The indicated land value is $180,000. The total value of the property is $780,000 ($600,000 + $180,000).

The complexity of the land residual technique is found in determining how much income is contributed by and, thus, attributed to the land compared to the total property, as well a determining a market-level rate of capitalization.

This method is used mainly as a check or verification of other income or appraisal methods. It's used as a primary appraisal tool when there are few comparable sales in the area.

Ground Rent Capitalization Method

The **ground rent capitalization method** is another income method of valuing land based on the annual income it could potentially generate, divided by an appropriate **capitalization rate**. The appropriate capitalization rate is determined by examining other comparable sales, and using their sale price and the net income they generate in a year. Research must be done to obtain comparable sales of leased sites that are similar to the subject site.

 This method is primarily used for commercial properties but can be also used (especially in waterfront or resort type areas) where residential homes, condos, apartments, etc., are built on leased land.

The calculations for this method are relatively simple. Take the annual net income of similar properties and divide that number by the site's sale price. That number produces a capitalization rate. Then, take the net income from ground rent of the subject site divided by that capitalization rate to derive a value for the subject site.

For Example

The subject property generated $5,400 in net income. What's the value? A comparable property, with $4,500 in net income, sold for $50,000.

$4,500 (Net Income of Comparable) ÷ $50,000 (Comparable Sale Price) = 0.09 (Capitalization Rate)

$5,400 (Net Income of Subject) ÷ 0.09 (Capitalization Rate) = $60,000 (Value of Subject)

Thus, the value of the subject property is $60,000 based on a 9% capitalization rate.

The capitalization rate is actually derived after examining several comparable sales properties. Also, if net income is not given, certain expenses must be subtracted from gross income to derive net income. These concepts will be examined in detail in Chapter 11, which details the income approach to appraisal.

Summary

1. Site valuation is important when the subject of the appraisal is a vacant land parcel or site. Also, site valuation is important as a component of a highest and best use analysis and for other applications and techniques. Land has inherent value due to scarcity, indestructibility, and immobility. Location is the primary determinant of land value. **Land value theorem #1**: Land value is primary determinant of real property value. **Land value theorem #2**: Land derives its value from market demand.

2. Land value can be increased beyond merely adding improvements. Inherent land value can be increased by **assemblage** (combining two or more parcels of land into one larger parcel). **Plottage** is an increase in value (over cost) by successful assemblage, usually due to change in use.

3. Three methods are used to identify site by legal description. 1. The **government survey system** references principal meridians and base lines, divides land into 6-mile square townships, one **township** has 36 sections (1 mile square), a **section** has 640 acres, one acre = 43,560 sq. ft., the description has directions and fractional quadrants. 2. The **lot and block system** uses platted property, a **plat map** shows lot and block numbers. 3. The **metes and bounds system** starts at point of beginning (POB), uses compass directions and distances, may reference markers, and returns POB.

4. A **survey** is the process of locating and measuring the boundaries of a property, and identifying improvements, encroachments, and easements. Surveys can be expensive so lenders often use a location survey. A **location survey** is the process of verifying that an improvement properly sits within the boundaries of a property, and that there are no encroachments from neighboring improvements onto the subject property. As an alternative to verifying legal description, an appraiser can state as limiting condition or assumption in appraisal: "Legal description was given, assumed to be correct."

5. Collecting and analyzing site data involves general data factors and property-specific factors. Property-specific factors are **physical** (size, configuration, topography, drainage, soil type, view, utilities, location, and access), **governmental** (zoning, public easements, taxes, and public services), and **economic** (location, utilities, conformity, and environmental factors).

6. There are five common methods to value a site: 1. **Sales comparison method**—value of site is estimated by taking market analysis of recent sales in area; adjustments are made to comparable sales, making them as similar as possible to subject site; 2. **Allocation method**—value of site is determined by finding a typical ratio of site value to total property value in an area; ratio can change over time; 3. **Subdivision analysis method**—value of raw land is determined by taking total projected sale value of all finished lots and subtracting all development costs; costs must include developer profit and time value of money, as well as projected cash flow of expenses and income from sale of lots as they're completed; 4. **Land residual method**—site value is calculated by attributing part of the income a property produces to the building and part to the land; a cap rate is then used to calculate value; and 5. **Ground rent capitalization method**—value is calculated as net yearly rent income divided by cap rate to get value; capitalization rate is derived from comparable sales.

Quiz

1. **Which does NOT contribute to land's inherent value?**
   a. immobility
   b. improvements
   c. indestructibility
   d. scarcity

2. **The combining of two or more parcels of land into one larger parcel is known as**
   a. annexation.
   b. assemblage.
   c. platted.
   d. plottage.

3. **"S 1/2 of NW 1/4" represents which type of legal description?**
   a. government survey system
   b. lot and block system
   c. metes and bounds system
   d. plottage system

4. **How many acres are in a section?**
   a. 406
   b. 460
   c. 640
   d. 6,400

5. **A detailed survey map of a subdivision is called a(n)**
   a. county recorded map.
   b. plat map.
   c. plot map.
   d. elevation map.

6. **Which may NOT be found in a metes and bounds legal description?**
   a. compass directions
   b. monuments
   c. point of beginning
   d. township markers

7. **The process of verifying that an improvement properly sits within the boundaries of the property, and that there are no encroachments from neighboring land onto the subject property is called a**
   a. encroachment survey.
   b. location analysis.
   c. location survey.
   d. survey.

8. **The most important physical factor in determining site value is**
   a. demographics.
   b. improvements.
   c. size.
   d. taxes.

9. **The most important governmental factor in determining site value is**
   a. census data.
   b. private deed restrictions.
   c. public utility easements.
   d. zoning.

10. **The most important economic factor in determining site value is**
    a. land is more valuable with improvements than vacant.
    b. land is valuable no matter where it is.
    c. location of the lot with regard to market demand.
    d. the size of any existing improvements.

11. **Which site valuation method uses adjustments to make other properties closer to the subject property?**
    a. allocation method
    b. ground rent capitalization method
    c. sales comparison method
    d. subdivision analysis method

12. **Which site valuation method uses a ratio of land value to total property value?**
    a. allocation method
    b. land residual method
    c. sales comparison method
    d. subdivision analysis method

13. **Which site valuation method takes the total projected sales value of all lots and subtracts development costs to arrive at a land value?**
    a. allocation method
    b. ground rent capitalization method
    c. sales comparison method
    d. subdivision analysis method

Sales Comparison Approach

This chapter will thoroughly overview the sales comparison approach: First defining the concept and key terms, then going into the exact procedure. Comparable sales will be discussed, as well as the techniques for identifying and applying adjustments to comparable properties. A sample sales comparison approach will be illustrated, followed by a discussion of the pros and cons of sales comparisons and differences between the sales comparison approach and a competitive market analysis (CMA).

Key Terms

Amenity A tangible or intangible feature that enhances and adds value to real estate.

Comparable Properties Sold properties that ideally represent the most similar market conditions, physical design and features, and market appeal as the subject property.

Competitive Market Analysis (CMA) A method of determining a recommended listing price and anticipated sale price of a property by comparing the subject property to other properties that have sold, are presently for sale, or did not sell in a given area. Also called **Comparative Market Analysis**.

Gross Adjustments The overall total of all adjustments applied regardless of whether the adjustment is applied as positive or negative.

Matched Pair Analysis Process of developing the contributory value of specific property characteristics or features by comparing pairs of similar properties. Also called **Paired Data Analysis**.

Net Adjustments The sum of the adjustments taking into account whether the adjustment was positive or negative.

Sales Comparison Approach An appraisal method that develops an indication of the value of real property by comparing the property being appraised with other recently sold properties. Data are collected and adjustments made for differences. Also called **Market Approach**.

Subject Property Property for which a value opinion is sought.

Defining the Sales Comparison Approach

The **sales comparison approach** is *an appraisal method that develops an indication of the value of real property by comparing the property being appraised with other recently sold properties. Data are collected and adjustments made for differences.* This method is also called the **market approach.** The **subject property** is *the property being appraised or for which a value opinion is sought.* With the sales comparison approach, the value of the subject property is determined by comparing it to *other similar properties that are ideally from the same market area,* called **comparable properties.** When a sales comparison approach is applicable, most lenders require that an appraiser analyze as many comparable sales as are necessary, but no less than three, to reach a conclusion of value.

The sales comparison approach is considered the most useful and accurate of the three appraisal methods because it's rooted in actual market activity. Provided, of course, that sufficient sales data is available for the analysis to be meaningful.

 Remember: An appraisal is an opinion of value. The marketplace establishes the value of a property. An appraisal reflects the appraiser's opinion of what the marketplace's reaction will be, in terms of dollars.

Since the sales comparison approach relies on historic market actions, this method is considered to be the most dependable in the majority of situations. The reliability of the approach, however, depends on the quantity and quality of the data available to the appraiser from which he forms and supports his conclusions.

Sometimes, appraisers may give consideration to similar currently listed properties since they tend to represent the upper limit of value as of the appraisal's effective date. Currently listed properties evidence competition a subject property would be up against if it were available to the market on the effective date.

Market Value and the Sales Comparison Approach

When an appraisal is being done for the purpose of a real estate purchase or for a mortgage refinance transaction, the type of value being sought is almost always market value. In this scenario, the appraiser must evaluate the value of a home based on what he feels a typical buyer would pay. Just because one person really wants a property and is willing to pay a particular price does not necessarily mean a typical buyer would pay that much. When the appraiser is performing his analysis, he is forming an opinion of value based on the typical buyer because lenders (or other parties requesting the appraisal) want to limit their risk in making the loan.

 In Other Words: They want to know that the buyer isn't paying more for the property than a typical buyer would pay.

Lenders must consider the possibility of **foreclosure** as a contingency that could occur at any time. If a property must be foreclosed on, lenders want to know what price they can reasonably expect to get out of the property, and that typical buyers would pay that price.

Substitution and the Typical Buyer

It's important to understand that market value appraisals are based on the actions of a "typical buyer." A **typical buyer** is one who is acting in her own best interest, without undue pressure, influence, or emotional attachment, and would rationally and readily accept a less expensive substitute if one were available in the marketplace. This goes back to the theory of **substitution** discussed in Chapter 3.

Comparable Data

The sales comparison approach analyzes comparable sales to arrive at a value conclusion, where the comparable properties must be part of an arm's length transaction. Properties where parties were related, the property was sold as part of a liquidation sale (e.g., foreclosure), or the sale had other unusual terms or concessions are eliminated. A minimum of three comparables is required by most lenders to ensure a reliable appraisal from sufficient data. Although not a USPAP requirement, it's best if these comparables are as recent as possible (usually sold no more than six months or a year prior to the date of the current appraisal being performed) and as similar as possible to the subject property in terms of physical characteristics and locational attributes.

For Example

A two-story house would not usually be compared to a single-story Ranch.

If there aren't enough recently sold properties in the subject's immediate neighborhood, the appraiser may look in another similar area, or use older sales, making price adjustments up or down depending on market conditions at the time of the sale. The preferable route is to find another similar area. In either case, the appraiser must make note in the appraisal report of the fact that a different area or older comparable sales were used, and explain why this needed to be done.

Of course, it's often difficult to find properties that are exactly the same as the subject property in all respects. Therefore, the sales comparison approach provides a method of adjusting properties so that meaningful comparisons can be performed between the comparables and the subject property.

Adjusting Properties

Adjusting properties is *the process of making chosen comparables come as close as possible in features to the subject so that meaningful price comparisons can be made.* The process for adjusting comparable data is simple:

1. The subject property is the starting point and *never changes*.

2. If the comparable is missing a feature that the subject has, the appraiser *adds* (+) to the comparable to make the properties equal.

3. If the comparable has a feature that subject property does not, the appraiser *subtracts* (-) from the comparable to make the properties equal.

For Example

An appraiser needs to develop adjusted values for three comparable sales he is analyzing. The comparables are similar to the subject in all respects, except for the garage. (From a separate analysis, it was determined that $5,000 is the contributory value in this neighborhood for a garage.) The comparison would look as follows:

	Subject Property	Comparable 1	Comparable 2	Comparable 3
Feature	1-car garage	No garage	1-car garage	2-car garage
Pre-adjustment Value	--	$91,000	$100,000	$110,000
Adjustment Needed	Never adjust!	(Missing feature; add to make equal to subject property) + $5,000	(Equal to subject property; no need to adjust) $0	(Additional feature; subtract to make equal to subject property) - $5,000
Final Value	$100,000	$96,000	$100,000	$105,000

Based on this analysis (and other features not listed here), the appraiser would reach a conclusion of estimated value for the subject property.

The adjustment scenario in the previous example is repeated for each significant feature that's different between the subject property and comparables. There are three important things to know about adjusting properties:

1. Adjustments are applied only for features present or absent the day the comparables sold.
2. Adjustments are made only for significant features.
3. Adjustment totals are *sometimes* limited by lenders and others.

Adjustments Only as of the Day the Comparables Sold

Adjustments are made to comparable properties for differences between them and the subject property, as of the day the comparables sold. Changes to comparables after they were sold are not considered because this would not be reflected in their sale prices. If an appraiser is considering a comparable, but learns it needed extensive repair after it sold to bring it to the condition level of the subject on the effective date, a condition adjustment would be made to the comparable for its inferior condition on the effective date of the appraisal.

Adjustments Only for Significant Features and Conditions

Adjustments are made to comparables only for significant features and conditions. A significant feature generally refers to physical features of the properties. The term "conditions" implies conditions of the transaction (e.g., when a sale occurred with special financing terms offered), or for market condition differences between the date the comparable property sold and the effective date of the subject appraisal.

 In Other Words: Significant features or conditions warranting an adjustment would be features or conditions that would factor into a typical buyer's decision, in dollars, regarding what they would pay for the subject property.

Significant features or conditions could vary from property to property and from market to market.

For Example

A view of the golf course may be a significant feature in a golf course community, while access to a waterway would be a significant feature for riverfront property.

Here's a partial list of features usually considered for most homes:

1. **Date the sale took place**—An older sale could have appreciated, or a supply and demand situation could have changed since the comparable was sold

2. **Property location**—Position of lot (e.g., corner lot vs. middle lot, cul-de-sac vs. main road)

3. **Size of lot**—Overall size/area of lot is usually most important for residential; for commercial, lot frontage is usually worth more than lot depth

4. **Condition**—Upkeep and overall quality (e.g., does the home need to be painted or the yard landscaped to meet the level of the average home in the neighborhood?)

5. **Age**—A newer home *may* be worth a little more

6. **Style and construction of home**—Adjustments should be made if homes are different styles or made from different materials (e.g., wood vs. stone) that would be noticed by the market

7. **Size of home/square footage**—Usually counts only livable space, not basements, and finished basements are often a separate point to compare

8. **Total number of rooms**—Note dining rooms or breakfast nooks

9. **Number of bedrooms**—Include master bedroom, or lack of, and any rooms that may double as bedrooms, offices, or dens

10. **Number of full/half bathrooms**—Half baths usually refer to a toilet and sink; also note special features like all-tile walls

11. **Basement**—Note kind of basement (e.g., full, half, or walk-out) and whether or not any finishing has been done and quality of the work

12. **Garage**—Note not only size, but also attached, detached, or built-in

13. **Heating/cooling/water**—Note type of cooling or heating system (e.g., heat pump), and well water or septic tank vs. city utilities

14. **Other**—Note unique features (e.g., patio, deck, porch, breezeway, fireplace, built-in shelves, walk-in closets, hot tubs, swimming pools)

15. **Terms of sale**—Note special financing arrangements, points being paid by the seller, or other conditions

If differences in features between the comparable sales and the subject property did not result in differences in sale prices, only those features which appeared to contribute to any price differences should be noted.

For Example

Two similar comparables sold for almost exactly the same price, even though one had central air-conditioning and one had a heat pump, so the conclusion is that the presence of central air or a heat pump didn't have a significant affect on the sale price. Therefore, this would not warrant an adjustment.

Adjustment Totals are Sometimes Limited

Total adjustments that may be made to comparables are considered by underwriters. The reason for this is to provide a benchmark as to how closely the comparable sales compare to the subject property. If the comparable sales are too dissimilar, they will result in an excessive amount of adjustments. Most lenders observe two basic guidelines:

1. The total net value of all adjustments *should* not exceed 15% of comparable's sale price.

2. The total gross (absolute) value of all adjustments *should* not exceed 25% of the comparable's sale price.

Observing the adjustment total also helps the appraiser to recognize the relevance of the data analyzed in the sales comparison approach, given that all differences have been addressed and resulted with a corresponding adjustment. In general, the rationale demonstrated here is that the less a comparable must be adjusted, the more relevant and comparable the data is.

Gross adjustments are *the overall total of all adjustments applied regardless of whether the adjustment is applied as a positive or negative.* In comparison, **net adjustments** are *the sum of the adjustments, taking into account whether the adjustment was a positive or negative.* Net adjustments reflect the percent of absolute adjustments when compared to the sale price of the comparable.

For Example

If a comparable that sold for $100,000 requires a +$15,000 adjustment and a -$5,000 adjustment, the total **net adjustment** would be +$10,000, or +10%.

Gross adjustments address the sum of all adjustments as a running total. So, that same comparable that sold for $100,000 and required a +$15,000 adjustment and a -$5,000 adjustment would have $20,000 in gross adjustments, or 20%.

Deriving and Applying Adjustments

Once the necessity of an adjustment to a comparable property is determined by an appraiser, he must know how much of an adjustment to make before it can be made. An adjustment can be applied for any **amenity** or **condition** which, in the marketplace, results in a difference in price between two properties. An **amenity** is *any tangible or intangible feature that enhances and adds value to real estate.* In an earlier example, a garage was the amenity in question. How did we know a garage was worth $5,000? The value of the garage likely would have been determined by performing a **matched pair analysis**.

Matched Pair Analysis

Matched pair analysis is *the process of developing the contributory value of specific property characteristics or features by comparing pairs of similar properties.* (This is also called **paired data analysis**.) Ideally, there should be only one different characteristic between the pairs of properties being analyzed so the difference in sale price can be attributed directly to that feature. Of course, in reality, the analysis may be more involved, with multiple adjustments derived in some instances.

For Example

An appraiser is trying to find the contributory value of a fireplace for a given subject property. In researching recent sales in the area, the appraiser finds Ranch homes that have nearly identical features—same number of bedrooms and baths, both with basements, both on a cul-de-sac, and both sold within the past six months and were on the market for about the same amount of time. One sold for $110,000, the other sold for $112,500. The only difference is one had a fireplace and one did not, so from this the appraiser may conclude that the fireplace is worth $2,500 for this property type, in this area.

Of course, an appraiser will rarely rely on only one set of comparables to arrive at a conclusion of value for a feature when using a matched pair analysis. In fact, the more comparables or sets of comparables that can be used to derive a contributory value, the more meaningful the results will be.

Very often, adjustments may be derived from comparable sales data other than from the actual comparable properties being used as in the sales comparison approach. Appraisers may not perform a matched pair analysis for each appraisal. Instead, like general market data, the appraiser will gather matched pair data and information on a regular basis and store that information for use in the regular course of his appraisal business. Typical updating may call for new information to be gathered and analyzed periodically. Of course, in each assignment, an appraiser must ensure the adjustments being applied using stored data are relevant and represent market reaction to the feature or condition.

Next, let's take a look at an example grid used for matched pair analysis.

For Example

The following market data was gathered on recent sales in an area.

Note: These values are for example purposes only and may vary greatly in your area.

Comparable	Bedrooms	Baths	Square Feet	Garage	Basement	Sale Price
#1	3	1.5	1,250	Yes	Yes	$77,000
#2	3	1.5	1,100	Yes	Yes	$74,000
#3	2	1.0	850	Yes	No	$63,500
#4	4	1.5	1,250	Yes	Yes	$79,000
#5	3	1.5	1,175	No	Yes	$69,500
#6	3	1.0	1,000	No	No	$65,000
#7	2	1.0	950	Yes	No	$65,500
#8	3	1.5	1,175	Yes	Yes	$72,500
#9	3	1.0	1,000	No	Yes	$67,500
#10	3	1.0	1,100	Yes	Yes	$72,500

(continued on next page)

For Example (cont.)

In picking the pairs, look for comparables where features are the same, except for one. The following matched pair sets were deduced from the given information. By finding the difference in price, the feature's contributory value can be determined.

Matched Pairs:

Feature	Matched Pairs	Value
Bedrooms	#1 and #4	$2,000
Baths (Half)	#2 and #10	$1,500
Square Feet	#3 and #7	$20/square foot
Garage	#5 and #8	$3,000
Basement	#6 and #9	$2,500

You will also note that the square footage between comparables #1 and #2 can be compared, and a $20 per square foot adjustment is derived from this pairing as well. This lends additional support for the appraiser's conclusions.

Percentage Adjustments

With matched pair analysis, dollar amounts for physical feature adjustments were derived. So if it is determined that a half bath had a contributory value of $1,500, $1,500 was added to or subtracted from the comparables in the sales comparison analysis to "make" the comparables more similar to the subject property. Sometimes, a dollar figure is not appropriate. Often, adjustments for conditions other than physical features are more appropriate when derived and applied as a percentage of the sale price, rather than a dollar amount derived from paired data. These include things like financing concessions, terms of sale, and date of sale.

Financing Concessions

Financing concessions include such things as seller-paid points, interest rate buy downs, assumptions, and owner/seller financing. Any or all of these should be addressed by the appraiser if they affected the sale price. The appraiser must study the transaction to ascertain whether financing concessions influenced the transaction and perhaps allowed the seller to get a higher price for the property than she would have gotten with a conventional financing transaction.

Here, though, a straight dollar amount derived from comparable data would not yield an accurate adjustment when applied to other comparable data.

For Example

In a comparable transaction, if the seller carried a small second mortgage which resulted in a $10,000 increase in sale price on a $100,000 home, this would not indicate that a $10,000 adjustment should be applied for any price home where the seller carried a second mortgage. It would be unacceptable to apply this same dollar figure of appreciation to a $150,000 home. Instead, a 10% adjustment would be reasonable for the $150,000 home (since $10,000 is 10% of the $100,000 home price), provided the appraiser determines that this reflects typical market reaction. This percentage is still derived using matched pair analysis, but the dollar figure has been converted to, and will be applied as, a percentage.

Terms of Sale

Terms of sale covers most other types of concessions a seller may have made in selling a home. This could include the seller paying for any fees or inspections, personal property included in the sale, or any other special terms (e.g., decorating allowance). The appraiser must analyze the marketplace to ascertain whether these concessions are typical, and if the payment of these items by the seller influenced the transaction. Again, the percentage is derived from a matched pair analysis, converted to and applied as a percent to the comparable sales used in the sales comparison approach.

Date of Sale

It is not always the case, but usually the older a comparable transaction is, the less likely it is to reflect current market conditions. Property values in an area may have gone up or down since the comparable was sold, or supply and demand may be different. Using comparable properties less than six months old is usually preferred. However, this purely depends on what has been going on in a particular market. Property values, though, whether increasing or decreasing, go up or down in percentages—not whole dollar amounts (e.g., previous example).

The best way to derive this percentage is still using the matched pair analysis technique, with the dollar figure converted to a percentage of the home's value. One favorable method used for observing market condition change would be the sale of the same home (in the same condition) twice over a given period of time. The advantage would be that no other adjustments would likely be necessary, but the disadvantage is that homes do not usually sell again very quickly except under duress or in distressed situations. Again, an appraiser must be very careful that market condition adjustments are properly derived and applied, and adequately supported.

How to Apply Percentage Adjustments

Percentage adjustments are used slightly differently than straight dollar adjustments. With percentage adjustments, the appraiser must translate a dollar figure from the matched pair analysis into a percentage, and then convert that percentage back to a dollar figure when applying the adjustment.

For Example

An appraiser is determining how much of an adjustment should be made for the seller taking back a second mortgage. The appraiser uses a matched pair analysis. Two houses are identical, except for the financing in the transaction. The first sold for $100,000 with no seller financing, but the second, with seller financing, sold for $110,000. Thus, the appraiser concludes the buyer paid $10,000 more for the property where seller financing was included. The appraiser converts the dollar amount from the matched pair analysis ($10,000) into a percentage (10%), which is stored in his files for future use.

Later on, the appraiser is developing the sales comparison approach in another appraisal assignment. One comparable used in his analysis sold for $55,000, but the seller carried a second mortgage. Since the subject in this appraisal is not being appraised subject to any favorable financing, the appraiser needs to adjust the comparable for the seller carrying the second mortgage. The percentage derived from his prior analysis and contained in his file indicates that seller financing increases the sale price by 10%. When this is applied to the comparable he is analyzing in the current appraisal, it is converted back into a dollar figure of $5,000, and subtracted from the sale price of the comparable property.

Priority of Adjustments

The priority of adjustments becomes particularly important when percentage adjustments are being applied. Appraisers use a systematic order in which they apply adjustments. The **priority of adjustments** is:

1. Financing concessions

2. Terms of sale

3. Date of sale (market conditions)

4. Location

5. Physical features or differences

Sales Comparison Approach Sample

Let's apply what we've learned so far by looking at a sample sales comparison approach that has been transferred to the URAR form.

 The complete appraisal appears at the end of Chapter 12.

By analyzing the sample on the next page, you can gain a perspective of how the sales comparison approach appears in its final reported form. Note that the appraiser's indicated value conclusion was $178,000—equal to the contract sale price. While it would be unethical for the appraiser to conclude at a target price, the action of offer and acceptance between the buyer and seller in this transaction (provided the transaction was determined to be arm's length) is a good indication of typical market action for the property. Also note the final conclusion of $178,000 is well supported by two of the three comparable sales (#2 and #3). This may not be the case in all transactions. Per USPAP, the appraiser must analyze the purchase agreement between the buyer and the seller. This can be important if there are special terms or conditions that may affect the transaction.

Competitive Market Analysis

A **competitive market analysis (CMA)**, also referred to as a **comparative market analysis**, is a method of determining the recommended listing price and/or anticipated sale price of a property by comparing the subject property to other properties that have sold, are presently for sale, or did not sell in a given area. This is **not** the equivalent of an appraisal. A similarity exists between the sales comparison approach and a CMA: Both follow a similar presentation format, comparing features of the subject property to a series of comparables. However, a CMA includes active and expired listings.

A CMA is performed by a real estate agent to assist clients in determining a suggested price at which they could buy or sell a home. A typical CMA does not involve the mass collection of data the other three appraisal approaches use. Furthermore, a CMA tends to be more subjective because it depends on visual impressions of the properties and does not involve the same amount of detail as an appraisal. Finally, a CMA gives different weight to properties depending on how quickly they sold or how long they've been on the market. Properties currently for sale or that did not sell could yield additional insight into market conditions that may affect the marketability and resulting sale price of the subject property.

Uniform Residential Appraisal Report   File # 18988

| There are | 7 | comparable properties currently offered for sale in the subject neighborhood ranging in price from $ 174,900 to $ 192,500 . |
| There are | 12 | comparable sales in the subject neighborhood within the past twelve months ranging in sale price from $ 168,500 to $ 191,000 . |

FEATURE	SUBJECT	COMPARABLE SALE # 1		COMPARABLE SALE # 2		COMPARABLE SALE # 3	
Address	22 OAKWOOD DRIVE WESTERVILLE, OH 43081	21 VALLEYVIEW COURT WESTERVILLE, OHIO		337 CHRIS COURT WESTERVILLE, OHIO		321 PEARSON DRIVE WESTERVILLE, OHIO	
Proximity to Subject		0.37 MILE		0.33 MILE		0.62 MILE	
Sale Price	$ 178,000		$ 180,000		$ 185,000		$ 172,000
Sale Price/Gross Liv. Area	$ sq.ft.	$ 89.82 sq.ft.		$ 97.16 sq.ft.		$ 99.48 sq.ft.	
Data Source(s)		FRANKLIN CO. AUDITOR		FRANKLIN CO. AUDITOR		FRANKLIN CO. AUDITOR	
Verification Source(s)		COLS. MLS, BROKER		COLS. MLS, BROKER		COLS. MLS, BROKER	
VALUE ADJUSTMENTS	DESCRIPTION	DESCRIPTION	+(-) $ Adjustment	DESCRIPTION	+(-) $ Adjustment	DESCRIPTION	+(-) $ Adjustment
Sales or Financing		CONV		CONV		CONV	
Concessions		NONE		SELLER PAID	-5,000	NONE	
Date of Sale/Time		4/30/2005		3/5/2005		5/14/2005	
Location	AVERAGE	AVERAGE		AVERAGE		AVERAGE	
Leasehold/Fee Simple	FEE SIMPLE	FEE SIMPLE		FEE SIMPLE		FEE SIMPLE	
Site	16,500 SQ.FT.	17,200 SQ. FT.		15,740 SQ. FT		13,650 SQ. FT.	
View	RES/AVG	RES/AVG		PARK/GOOD	-2,500	RES/AVG	
Design (Style)	2 STORY	2 STORY		2 STORY		2 STORY	
Quality of Construction	AVERAGE	AVERAGE		AVERAGE		AVERAGE	
Actual Age	6 YEARS	5 YEARS		6 YEARS		8 YEARS	
Condition	GOOD	GOOD		GOOD		AVERAGE	+2,500
Above Grade	Total/Bdrms/Baths	Total/Bdrms/Baths		Total/Bdrms/Baths		Total/Bdrms/Baths	
Room Count	7 / 3 / 2.1	6 / 3 / 2.1		8 / 3 / 2.1		7 / 3 / 2	+500
Gross Living Area	1,952 sq.ft.	2,004 sq.ft.	-500	1,904 sq.ft.	+500	1,729 sq.ft.	+2,200
Basement & Finished	642 Sq.Ft.	1,002 SQ. FT.	-2,000	700 SQ. FT.		600 SQ. FT.	
Rooms Below Grade	2 RMS, F BA	UNFINISHED	+3,000	1 RM. FIN	+2,000	2 RMS, F BA	
Functional Utility	AVERAGE	AVERAGE		AVERAGE		AVERAGE	
Heating/Cooling	GFA/CENTRAL	GFA/CENTRAL		GFA/CENTRAL		GFA/CENTRAL	
Energy Efficient Items	TYPICAL	TYPICAL		STANDARD		STANDARD	
Garage/Carport	2-C ATT GAR	2-C ATT GAR		2-C ATT GAR		2-C ATT GAR	
Porch/Patio/Deck	PORCH, PATIO	PORCH, DECK		PORCH, PATIO		PORCH, DECK	
	B-I SPA	NONE	+500	IN-GRD POOL	-500	B-I SPA	
	WD PRIV FNC	WD PRIV FNC		WD PRIV FNC		NONE	+500
	FIREPLACE	FIREPLACE		2 FIREPLACES	-1,000	FIREPLACE	
Net Adjustment (Total)		☒ + ☐ -	$ 1,000	☐ + ☒ -	$ 6,500	☒ + ☐ -	$ 5,700
Adjusted Sale Price of Comparables		Net 0.6 % Gross 3.3 %	$ 181,000	Net 3.5 % Gross 6.2 %	$ 178,500	Net 3.3 % Gross 3.3 %	$ 177,700

I ☒ did ☐ did not research the sale or transfer history of the subject property and comparable sales. If not, explain

My research ☐ did ☒ did not reveal any prior sales or transfers of the subject property for the three years prior to the effective date of this appraisal.
Data Source(s)   FRANKLIN COUNTY AUDITOR
My research ☒ did ☐ did not reveal any prior sales or transfers of the comparable sales for the year prior to the date of sale of the comparable sale.
Data Source(s)   FRANKLIN COUNTY AUDITOR
Report the results of the research and analysis of the prior sale or transfer history of the subject property and comparable sales (report additional prior sales on page 3).

ITEM	SUBJECT	COMPARABLE SALE #1	COMPARABLE SALE #2	COMPARABLE SALE #3
Date of Prior Sale/Transfer	NONE IN 36 MONTHS	9/23/2004	NONE IN 12 MONTHS	NONE IN 12 MONTHS
Price of Prior Sale/Transfer		$155,000		
Data Source(s)		FRANKLIN CO AUDITOR		
Effective Date of Data Source(s)		6/3/2005		

Analysis of prior sale or transfer history of the subject property and comparable sales   RESEARCH REVEALED THAT SALE #1 TRANSFERRED ON 9/23/2004 FOR $155,000. FURTHER INQUIRY WITH THE SELLER IN THE MOST RECENT TRANSACTION REVEALED THAT THE PURCHASE WAS VIA SHERRIFF'S AUCTION. COSMETIC RENOVATIONS WERE PERFORMED PRIOR TO THE PROPERTY BEING RE-MARKETED.

Summary of Sales Comparison Approach   THE SALES REFLECT A REASONABLE VALUE RANGE. ALL SALES ARE FROM THE IMMEDIATE MARKET AREA. CORRELATION IS TOWARD THE UPPER PART OF THE VALUE RANGE, WITH TWO OF THE THREE SALES INDICATING THAT DIRECTION. THESE SALES ARE THE MOST RECENT AND REQUIRE THE FEWEST NET ADJUSTMENTS.

Indicated Value by Sales Comparison Approach $ 178,000

Sample Sales Comparison Analysis section from the URAR

A CMA does not attempt to derive and apply adjustments for differences between the subject property and the data being compared. Rather, a CMA primarily examines observable differences between properties that would attract a buyer to one property over another. If the subject property is lacking a significant feature that's present in the comparables, the agent may suggest a lower price to attract buyers to the property. But if a feature is present in the subject property that is not in any comparables, a higher price may be suggested.

 For more detail on CMAs, refer to the Appendix.

CMA CASE STUDY

Competitive Market Analysis — CMA Project

The following project is a simulation of a Competitive Market Analysis (CMA) that might be done for a buyer or seller. We begin with the picture and description of the subject property below. Then, using the CMA sheet on the next page, analyze the subject by comparing it to the competing properties, sold properties, and the offered not sold properties (expired, withdrawn, etc.) which appear on the following pages.

Although there is not a single "right" answer, certainly some analyses will be more reliable than others. Above all, you need to be able to substantiate your recommendation for the subject property. This is not like an appraisal, though. Instead, a CMA assists with pricing:

- As the listing agent, you want to help the seller get the best price possible for the home, while minimizing the chance that the property is overpriced and hence more difficult to sell.

- As a buyer's agent, you want to help the buyert make a good offer on the home so that it is more likely to be accepted, but without the buyer paying more than he would pay for a comparable property.

SUBJECT PROPERTY:

1259 WINTER COVE

RANCH STYLE; 3 BEDROOMS; 2 BATHS; FULL BASEMENT, FINISHED, WITH A FAMILY ROOM, BEDROOM, AND FULL BATH. IT HAS A COVERED FRONT PORCH, REAR PATIO, FENCED REAR YARD, AND ATTACHED 2-CAR GARAGE.

COMPETITIVE MARKET ANALYSIS

SUBJECT

ADDRESS	STYLE	BDRMS	BATHS	BSMT/FIN	FEATURES	AGE	CONDITION

COMPETING PROPERTIES

ADDRESS	STYLE	BDRMS	BATHS	BSMT/FIN	FEATURES	AGE	CONDITION	DOM	PRICE

SOLD PROPERTIES

ADDRESS	STYLE	BDRMS	BATHS	BSMT/FIN	FEATURES	AGE	CNDTN	DOM	SALE DATE	LISTED PRICE	SALE PRICE	FNNC

OFFERED, BUT DID NOT SELL

ADDRESS	STYLE	BDRMS	BATHS	BSMT/FIN	FEATURES	AGE	CNDTN	DOM	FINAL LIST PRICE

VALUE RANGE INDICATED _____ TO _____

ASKING PRICE RANGE _____ TO _____

COMPETING PROPERTIES

630 SPRING HILL DRIVE
(1 STREET FROM SUBJECT)

RANCH STYLE; 3 BEDROOMS; 2 BATHS; BUILT ON A CRAWL SPACE. IT HAS A COVERED FRONT PORCH, REAR DECK, AND ATTACHED 2-CAR GARAGE. HOUSE IS 4 YEARS OLD AND IN GOOD CONDITION.
LISTING PRICE: $124,900
DAYS ON MARKET: 60

2420 HARDING HILL COURT
(4 BLOCKS FROM SUBJECT)

RANCH STYLE; 3 BEDROOMS; 1.5 BATHS; PARTIAL BASEMENT. IT HAS A REAR DECK, AND ATTACHED 2-CAR GARAGE. HOUSE IS 12 YEARS OLD AND IN ABOVE AVERAGE CONDITION.
LISTING PRICE: $117,900
DAYS ON MARKET: 180

1247 WINTER COVE
(SAME STREET AS SUBJECT)

RANCH STYLE; 3 BEDROOMS; 2 BATHS; FULL BASEMENT, UNFINISHED. IT HAS A FRONT PORCH, REAR DECK, AND ATTACHED 2-CAR GARAGE. HOUSE IS NEW AND RECENTLY FINISHED.
LISTING PRICE: $133,500
DAYS ON MARKET: 1

1257 WINTER COVE
(NEXT DOOR TO SUBJECT)

BI-LEVEL; 3 BEDROOMS; 2 BATHS; PARTIAL BASEMENT WITH FAMILY ROOM. IT HAS A REAR DECK, FIREPLACE, AND ATTACHED 2-CAR GARAGE. HOUSE IS 5 YEARS OLD AND IN ABOVE AVERAGE CONDITION.
LISTING PRICE: $122,900
DAYS ON MARKET: 45

<u>SOLD PROPERTIES</u>

465 LOCUST WOODS DRIVE
(2 BLOCKS FROM SUBJECT)

RANCH STYLE; 3 BEDROOMS; 2 BATHS; BUILT ON A CRAWL SPACE. IT
HAS A COVERED FRONT PORCH, REAR DECK, AND ATTACHED 2-CAR
GARAGE. HOUSE IS 2 YEARS OLD AND IN GOOD CONDITION.
LIST PRICE: $124,900
SALE PRICE: $119,900
SOLD 4 MONTHS AGO
DAYS ON MARKET: 47
FINANCED BY FHA; SELLER PAID $3,000 IN POINTS AND CLOSING COSTS

6432 HILL VIEW COURT
(3 BLOCKS FROM SUBJECT)

2 STORY; 4 BEDROOMS; 2.5 BATHS; CRAWL SPACE. IT HAS A REAR DECK,
AND ATTACHED 2-CAR GARAGE. HOUSE IS 8 YEARS OLD AND IN ABOVE
AVERAGE CONDITION.
LIST PRICE: $129,900
SALE PRICE: $123,900
SOLD 3 MONTHS AGO
DAYS ON MARKET: 120
CONVENTIONAL FINANCING; SELLER PAID A $1,500 DECORATING
ALLOWANCE

1049 WINTER COVE
(SAME STREET AS SUBJECT)

1½ STORY; 3 BEDROOMS; 2 BATHS; FULL BASEMENT FINISHED WITH
FAMILY ROOM AND FULL BATH. IT HAS A FRONT PORCH, REAR DECK,
AND ATTACHED 2-CAR GARAGE. HOUSE IS 1 YEAR OLD AND IN GOOD
CONDITION.
LIST PRICE: $126,900
SALE PRICE $125,000
SOLD 5 MONTHS AGO
DAYS ON MARKET: 30
SOLD FOR CASH

958 WINTER COVE
(SAME STREET AS SUBJECT)

RANCH STYLE; 3 BEDROOMS; 1.5 BATHS; CRAWL SPACE. IT HAS A
PORCH, REAR DECK, AND ATTACHED 1-CAR GARAGE. HOUSE IS 5 YEARS
OLD AND IN GOOD CONDITION.
LIST PRICE: $122,900
SALE PRICE: $118,000
SOLD 10 MONTHS AGO
DAYS ON MARKET: 30
CONVENTIONAL FINANCING; NO CONCESSIONS

OFFERED NOT SOLD

313 MAPLE POINT
(3 BLOCKS FROM SUBJECT)

RANCH STYLE, 3 BEDROOMS, 2 BATHS, FULL BASEMENT, UNFINISHED.
IT HAS A SMALL FRONT DECK, REAR DECK, AND AN ATTACHED 2-CAR
GARAGE. HOUSE IS 2 YEARS OLD AND IN GOOD CONDITION.
LIST PRICE: $134,900
DAYS ON THE MARKET: 180

641 PINEHURST CROSSING
(1 BLOCK FROM SUBJECT)

2 STORY, 4 BEDROOMS, 2.5 BATHS, CRAWL SPACE. IT HAS A REAR DECK,
AND ATTACHED 2-CAR GARAGE. HOUSE IS 8 YEARS OLD AND IN ABOVE
AVERAGE CONDITION.
LIST PRICE: $129,900
DAYS ON THE MARKET: 90

1539 WINTER COVE
(SAME STREET AS SUBJECT)

RANCH STYLE, 3 BEDROOMS, 2 BATHS, FULL BASEMENT FINISHED WITH
FAMILY ROOM AND FULL BATH. IT HAS A FRONT PORCH, REAR DECK,
AND AN ATTACHED 2-CAR GARAGE. THE HOUSE IS NEW AND IN GOOD
CONDITION.
LIST PRICE: $131,900
DAYS ON THE MARKET: 180

958 AUTUMN WOODS
(1 BLOCK FROM SUBJECT)

RANCH STYLE, 3 BEDROOMS, 2.5 BATHS, CRAWL SPACE. IT HAS A FRONT
PORCH, REAR DECK, AND ATTACHED 3-CAR GARAGE. HOUSE IS 1 YEAR
OLD AND IN GOOD CONDITION.
LIST PRICE: $142,900
DAYS ON THE MARKET: 120

NOTES

Summary

1. The **sales comparison approach** is an appraisal method in which an appraiser develops an opinion of value by using market data and analyzing comparable sold properties. It can be a very reliable method for developing an opinion of value given there is sufficient reliable data which may be analyzed.

2. For most appraisals for mortgage finance transactions, at least three comparable sales are analyzed. **Comparables**, ideally, should be recent sales, physically similar to the subject, and in a similar market. **Adjustments** are made to comparables for differences. The comparable is always adjusted and **never** the subject. If the comparable lacks something the subject has, an adjustment is added to the comparable to "make" it like the subject; if the comparable has something the subject does not, an adjustment is subtracted. Adjustments are made only for features or conditions as of the day the comparable sold; adjustments are made only for significant features; and adjustment totals are sometimes limited.

3. Dollar amount of adjustments is determined by **matched pair analysis**. Ideally, one difference between a pair of properties indicates contributory value of a particular feature. Physical features are **dollar adjustments**, but dates of sale, terms of sale, and time on market are most often applied as **percentage adjustments**.

4. **Priority of adjustments**: Financing concessions, terms of sale, date of sale, location, and physical features or differences.

5. A **competitive market analysis (CMA)** is used to determine a recommended listing price and anticipated sale price by comparing the subject to comparables sold, for sale, or no longer on the market. A CMA depends on visual impressions and observable differences. A CMA weighs properties by how quickly they sold.

Quiz

1. **Which of the following is NOT necessary to perform the sales comparison approach?**
   a. comparable sales
   b. matched pair analysis data for significant features
   c. subject property
   d. cost manuals

2. **Matched pair analysis**
   a. is a means of determining the contributory value of specific property characteristics or features by comparing pairs of similar properties.
   b. is a means of using comparable sales to determine the value of a subject property.
   c. is unimportant as appraisers attempt to find comparables which are as similar to the base as possible.
   d. is a means of considering the total of all adjustments, whether positive or negative.

3. **What is the priority of adjustments (beginning with the most important)?**
   a. financing concessions, location, terms of sale, physical features, and date of sale
   b. financing concessions, terms of sale, date of sale, location, and physical features
   c. physical features, location, date of sale, terms of sale, financing concessions
   d. physical features, terms of sale, date of sale, financing concessions, and location

4. **An amenity is**
   a. always adjusted for in an appraisal.
   b. always a physical, tangible feature.
   c. any feature for which there is a ready substitute in the marketplace.
   d. any tangible or intangible feature that enhances and adds value to real estate.

5. **A competitive market analysis is _____ equal to an appraisal.**
   a. always
   b. more or less
   c. never
   d. sometimes

6. **Analyzing properties currently listed as part of the appraiser's analysis assists with**
   a. determining contributory value of a particular feature.
   b. establishing replacement cost.
   c. estimating land value.
   d. evidencing competition and the upper limit of value.

7. **When a dollar amount of difference attributable to a particular property feature cannot be observed by comparing the sale prices of a matched pair,**
   a. an adjustment must be applied to address the difference.
   b. the appraiser is using an unacceptable technique.
   c. the need for an adjustment is not supported.
   d. the properties in the matched pair should be discarded.

8. **A comparable property which sold for $150,000 required $10,000 in upward adjustments and $5,000 in downward adjustments. What was the percent of total gross adjustments applied?**
   a. 5%
   b. 10%
   c. 17%
   d. 20%

9. **If in a comparable sale which sold for $80,000, the seller contributed $4,000 to buy-down the buyer's interest rate, what would be the percent of adjustment observed from this transaction?**
   a. 2%
   b. 5%
   c. 7.5%
   d. 10%

10. **The date for which the appraiser's value opinion is valid is known as the**
    a. appraised date.
    b. date of the report.
    c. effective date.
    d. inspection date.

Cost
Approach

This chapter will overview the cost approach: First defining the concept and key terms, then concentrating on the exact procedure. Replacement and reproduction costs of a building will be discussed, as will the use of cost manuals and other cost approach methods. Finally, different types of depreciation, as well as methods for calculating, will be examined before taking a look at a sample cost approach.

Key Terms

Cost Approach An appraisal method that develops an indication of the value of real property by figuring the cost of building the house or other improvement on the land, minus (-) depreciation, plus (+) the value of the vacant land.

Cost Manuals Books, electronic media, and online sources that provide estimated construction costs for various types of buildings in different areas of the country.

Depreciation A loss in value to property for any reason.

Economic Life The time during which a building can be used for its intended purpose, or generate more income than is paid out for operating expenses.

Effective Age The age of a structure based on physical deterioration, functional obsolescence, or external obsolescence.

External Obsolescence When something outside of a property's boundaries makes a property less desirable.

Functional Obsolescence When an improvement is less desirable because of something inherent in its design.

Remaining Economic Life The period of usefulness (physically, functionally, and externally) that an improvement has remaining as of the day of the appraisal.

Replacement Building the functional equivalent (substitute) of the original building using modern materials, methods, and design.

Reproduction Building as exact duplicate (replica) of the original building.

Defining the Cost Approach

The **cost approach** is *an appraisal method that develops an indication of the value of real property by figuring the cost of building the house or other improvement on the land, minus (-) depreciation, plus (+) the value of the vacant land.* USPAP states that when a cost approach is applicable, an appraiser must:

- Develop an opinion of site value by an appropriate appraisal method (discussed in Chapter 8).

- Analyze such comparable cost data as are available to estimate the cost new of the improvements.

- Analyze such comparable cost data as are available to estimate the difference between cost new and the present worth of the improvements (accrued depreciation).

We'll look at building costs and depreciation here.

The cost approach is typically a more reliable method of indicating a value opinion for most newer structures as typically there is less (if any) physical depreciation to consider. However, the method is also useful when a replacement cost for a building is required, or for buildings that are unusual, with few comparable sales. The cost approach is also useful as a secondary check of other appraisal approaches developed by the appraiser, or to support the value indications reached through other methods. But, an informed buyer will rarely look at cost when making a purchase decision. The buyer may look at the cost of other new buildings as a benchmark of value, or as an alternative, but not in deciding what price to offer. That is dictated more by market conditions, comparable sales, or anticipated income.

Of course, it's important to remember that cost does not always equal value. If a house is overbuilt (too many features) or a building has other forms of obsolescence, market value would likely be less than the cost of building. An informed buyer's primary concern is what similar properties are selling for in the area, rather than the cost to build the house.

Substitution and the Typical Buyer

Just as the actions of a "typical buyer" are important in sales comparison, they are considered here as well. Remember, a **typical buyer** is one who is acting in his own best interest, and would rationally and readily accept a less expensive substitute. Assuming no delay, the typical buyer would pick the less expensive substitute. Keep in mind that implicit in the definition of the word "substitute" is that the structures are more or less comparable in features and quality.

Cost of Building and Improvement

The cost of building a house or improvement on land can be determined several ways. Before a specific cost method is chosen, the appraiser must know whether the estimate is for replacing or reproducing the building. There's a significant difference:

- **Replacement** of a structure is building the functional equivalent (substitute) of the original building using modern materials, methods, and design.

- **Reproduction** of a structure is building an exact duplicate (replica) of the original building.

Usually, cost estimates are performed for *replacing* a building with one that's of similar size and utility. Most of the time, a similar building is an acceptable, less expensive alternative. Cost estimates for *reproducing* a building are typically done for historical buildings where it's important for the new structure to have the exact same appearance and materials as the original structure. This is more common for Insurance Valuations than Market Valuations.

The particular costing methods are determined by the appraiser based on the scope of work determined early in the assignment. Common cost approach methods are **square foot method**, **comparative unit method**, **quantity survey method**, **unit-in-place method**, and **index method**. We will briefly overview those methods here.

Square Foot Method

The typical method for determining the cost of replacing a building is the **square foot method**. This method relies on cost manuals. **Cost manuals** are *books, electronic media, and online sources that give estimated construction costs for various types of buildings in different areas of the country*. Appraisers subscribe to these cost services, which are frequently updated.

Cost manuals detail the "per square foot" cost new of specific building types and can, if necessary, be broken down by individual components.

For Example

An appraiser is figuring the cost of a 1,250 square foot, one-story home in the Midwest. The cost service indicates a total cost per square foot of $48.65 (assuming replacement cost is being used), so 1,250 x $48.65 = $60,812.50 cost estimate.

Comparative Unit Method

The **comparative unit method** uses the cost of recently built comparable structures, using recently constructed buildings as a basis for estimating the cost of replacing the subject property.

This method is favored by many appraisers as it more closely reflects costs observed in the subject market. Often, appraisers use data from other new construction projects they have appraised as a basis. Interviews with local builders and contractors are another way to gather this cost data.

Quantity Survey Method

The **quantity survey method** is the most detailed of the cost approaches because it requires a thorough itemization of every building component used. This method duplicates the process a contractor goes through when determining a bid for a contract. The process is painstaking and not often practiced. However, because of the detail involved, the method is often considered to be the most accurate.

Unit-in-Place Method

The **unit-in-place method** estimates the cost of reproducing a building by looking at the unit cost of each of the structure's component parts, and adding all of these unit costs together based on actual need and usage.

For Example

Rather than counting up the cost of each part and the labor involved as in the quantity survey method, the unit-in-place method would break down the total cost of each building component (e.g., electrical, plumbing, framing, roofing) and use this to estimate the cost of the building.

Index Method

The **index method** estimates the cost of a building by taking its original cost and multiplying that number by an index factor, based on when the building was originally constructed.

For Example

A building cost $500,000 in 1990. A current index factor for that type of building might be 1.60. By multiplying $500,000 x 1.60, you get a present day estimated cost of $800,000 to build the same building.

This method is not very common. It is considered less accurate than the other methods because it takes minimal factors into account. It may also prove difficult to determine because the original building cost must be known.

Calculating Depreciation

Depreciation is *a loss in value to property for any reason*. That loss in value could be attributable to physical deterioration, functional obsolescence, or external (or economic) obsolescence. The common mindset is that depreciation relates exclusively to physical deterioration. While it is true in many appraisal assignments that the estimation of physical depreciation is the only form that must be addressed, depreciation could also extend to components that would not be well accepted by the market for some reason, or conditions (physical or economic) outside the boundaries of the property.

 Keep in mind that depreciation is **never** applied to land. Only improvements depreciate. This becomes an important point when developing the cost approach.

There are three types of depreciation:

- Straight-line depreciation
- Age life method
- Breakdown method

Straight-Line Depreciation

Straight-line depreciation takes the total amount of depreciation divided by the number of years, or age of the structure.

For Example

If a 10-year-old structure has depreciated $20,000 since it was built, the depreciation is $2,000 per year.

Straight-line depreciation is not typically used by appraisers. More commonly, appraisers use the **age-life method** or the **breakdown method**.

Age Life Method

The **age life method** is a depreciation technique that considers the ratio of the effective age to the total economic life. This is also called the **economic age-life method**. **Economic life** is *the time during which a building can be used for its intended purpose, or generate more income than is paid out for operating expenses*. **Remaining economic life** is *the period of usefulness that a building has remaining as of the day of the appraisal*.

The **effective age** could be thought of as *what has been used up of the life of a structure*. The remaining economic life could be thought of as what life is left in the structure:

Effective Age + Remaining Economic Life = Economic Life

The **effective age** of a structure is based on both physical and economic concepts. Deterioration is a physical concept while obsolescence is an economic concept. The **effective age** *addresses all forms of depreciation by considering the presence of physical deterioration, functional obsolescence, and external obsolescence*. The determination of a structure's effective age is heavily reliant on an appraiser's judgment and experience. Keep in mind that a building's effective age is not necessarily equal to its actual age:

- **Physically**—Maintenance and upkeep can lengthen a building's useful life; neglect can shorten it. When a property is renovated or repaired, the effective age becomes less and remaining economic life is lengthened.

- **Functionally**—When design and functional elements of the improvements do not meet current market standards (such as an odd floor plan), the obsolescence will be reflected in the effective age.

- **Externally**—If an undesirable element is present outside the subject property boundaries and is negatively affecting the subject property, the condition will be considered in the subject's effective age,

To calculate age-life depreciation, a simple formula is used:

Effective Age ÷ Total Economic Life = Depreciation Percentage

Current Cost of Building x Depreciation Percentage = Estimated Amount of Depreciation

For Example

The current cost of a building is $500,000. An appraiser has determined that the building has an effective age of 10 years and a total economic life of 50 years. Using the age-life depreciation formula, the calculation is as follows:

10 ÷ 50 = 0.20   (20%)

So, $500,000 (cost new) x 20% (depreciation estimate) =
   $100,000 – estimated amount of depreciation

Regarding physical deterioration, a building:

- In good condition has more useful economic life.
- In well-kept condition could remain at the same effective age for many years.
- With significant deferred maintenance may have an effective age that's greater than its actual age.

When a building is renovated, remodeled, or updated, the effective age decreases, but the clock for effective age begins moving forward once the modifications have been completed.

Breakdown Method

The **breakdown method** (sometimes called the **observed depreciation method**) breaks the total depreciation into three categories:

- Physical deterioration
- Functional obsolescence
- External obsolescence

This is accomplished by the appraiser's inspection of the structure, study of demographics, and analysis of the market or other external conditions.

Here, we will need to better define the three causes of depreciation. As well, an appraiser must also consider whether the condition is **curable** or **incurable**.

Physical Deterioration

Physical deterioration is *actual wear and tear on something due to age, the elements, or other forces*. This type of depreciation is often observable during the appraiser's personal inspection of the subject property. Regular maintenance can slow the process, and many types of physical deterioration are **curable**.

A depreciation figure for physical deterioration is calculated by taking the new price of the item and subtracting a percentage for the wear and tear. The depreciation percentage is somewhat subjective, and depends on the appraiser's experience. This calculation is easier for physical items (e.g., shingles, a furnace) than for less-tangible items (e.g., stucco, paint).

Price x Depreciation Percentage = Dollar Depreciation

For Example

The furnace in a house cost $5,000 new. Based on an inspection, current wear and tear appears to have diminished the furnace's life by about 20%. So, to figure the amount of depreciation attributed to that item:

$5,000 x 20% = $1,000

If an item *cannot be replaced or reasonably repaired*, the physical deterioration is said to be **incurable**.

The test for deciding if physical deterioration is curable or incurable is quite simple. The cost to repair the item must not exceed the value the repair would contribute to the sale value. Return on investment for money spent on repairs may also be taken into consideration:

- If the cost to repair is less than the value the repair would contribute to the sale value, then physical deterioration is **curable**.

- If the cost to repair is more than the value the repair would contribute to the sale value, then physical deterioration is **incurable**.

That does not necessarily mean that the item should not be fixed, but it does provide a basis for deciding whether or not it is worth the time, effort, and money to repair a property's shortcomings. For extensive repairs, the time needed to complete the repairs and the time value of money are additional considerations that can complicate the calculations and decision.

Long-Lived and Short-Lived Items

Long-lived items are *items in a property expected to last for the life of the structure*. Severe damage to long-lived items that result in incurable physical deterioration include:

- Basements
- Foundations
- Load bearing walls/Framing
- Insulation
- Roof trusses
- Floor joists

Usually, these are not expected to need major repair or replacement during the building's useful life, and repairing or replacing them is very expensive. For this type of depreciation, the appraiser will typically use a percentage of the building's total value to determine a depreciation value attributed to the incurable item.

For Example

A basement wall with severe water damage has buckled. Although this can actually be fixed, it's classified as incurable due to the tremendous expense involved: The house is worth $150,000, but repairing this damage will run about $25,000, or 16.67% depreciation attributable to the condition of the basement wall.

$25,000 ÷ $150,000 = 16.67%

Knowing the cost of the repair helps the appraiser determine what depreciation percentage to attribute to a particular type of physical deterioration.

Short-lived items are *items in a property expected to be replaced during the lifetime of the structure*:

• Carpet

• HVAC system

• Paint

Functional Obsolescence

Functional obsolescence occurs *when a building is less desirable because of something inherent in the design of the structure*. This type of depreciation is observable during an inspection, but may sometimes need to be confirmed with a demographics study or market analysis.

For Example

Some older homes have two bedrooms in tandem—you must go through the first bedroom to get to the second one. While this feature can be observed, additional data are often needed to determine if this feature constitutes functional obsolescence. A demographics study may show that this feature is not a setback as long as the home has enough separate bedrooms to accommodate a typical family. A market analysis may show that this feature is a drawback when many newer homes are in the area, but not when the subject is in an area of older homes with the same feature.

Other examples of functional obsolescence are outdated home styles, out-of-date fixtures, or homes with only one bathroom. Unusual floor plans can also fall under the category of functional obsolescence. These undesirable features may be **curable**, like outdated fixtures; or **incurable**, based on whether a return could be realized by curing the feature.

Sometimes, major costs or renovations may be classified as curable if the major cost would make a significant contribution to the home's value (e.g., adding a room or a garage). The test for classification as curable or incurable is whether the cost of the renovation can be recovered when the property is sold.

A depreciation figure for functional obsolescence is based upon whether the undesirable feature is curable or incurable. If the obsolescence is curable, depreciation may be equal to the cost of curing the undesirable feature. If the undesirable feature is incurable, depreciation is figured using a matched pair analysis: Comparing sale prices of properties with and without the feature to determine an adjustment figure for the undesirable feature.

External Obsolesence

External obsolescence occurs *when something outside the boundaries of a property makes it less desirable.* The causes of the obsolescence may be economic, environmental, or location. This type of depreciation may be observable, but often requires additional research. This additional research typically looks at the cause of the problem and the likelihood it will continue; as well as research into the effect the external obsolescence has on the market value of the property.

For Example

External obsolescence may be caused by the closing of a plant that was important to the economic base of an area. Appraisers will gather as much information as possible: Is the plant shut-down permanent or temporary? Are there any parties interested in buying the facility? Answers to these questions may or may not influence the value of the subject property or the depreciation factor cited as external obsolescence, but they would likely be included in a final appraisal report.

Other examples of external obsolescence are a declining neighborhood, a nearby landfill, or a new highway that creates noise or re-routes traffic. These conditions and their external causes are **incurable**—property owners can typically do little to stop or change these conditions. Even when action can be taken (e.g., trying to close a landfill), the outcome is uncertain and often far into the future. Such actions do not make something **curable** until the circumstance has actually changed.

A depreciation figure for external obsolescence is determined by a market analysis or matched pair analysis; comparing the difference in sale prices from a property with the external obsolescence and a similar property without it.

Cost Approach Example

Let's look at a cost approach example using the square foot method and depreciation using the age-life method.

 This is a continuation of the appraisal from Chapters 5 and 9. The complete appraisal can be found at end of Chapter 12.

COST APPROACH TO VALUE (not required by Fannie Mae)							
Provide adequate information for the lender/client to replicate the below cost figures and calculations.							
Support for the opinion of site value (summary of comparable land sales or other methods for estimating site value) ESTIMATED SITE VALUE IS DERIVED FROM A SALES COMPARISON ANALYSIS OF LOT SALES WITHIN THE SUBJECT'S SUBDIVISION. THIS ANALYSIS IS CONTAINED IN THE APPRAISER'S WORKFILE.							
ESTIMATED ☐ REPRODUCTION OR ☒ REPLACEMENT COST NEW	OPINION OF SITE VALUE					=$	35,000
Source of cost data MARSHALL SWIFT COSTING SERVICE	DWELLING	1,952 Sq.Ft. @ $	67.40			=$	131,565
Quality rating from cost service AVG Effective date of cost data 3/1/2005	FOUNDATION	642 Sq.Ft. @ $	12.00			=$	7,704
Comments on Cost Approach (gross living area calculations, depreciation, etc.)						=$	
GROSS LIVING AREA HAS BEEN DETERMINED FROM EXTERIOR	Garage/Carport	528 Sq.Ft. @ $	18.00			=$	9,504
DIMENSIONS. LOCAL COST DATA CONTAINED IN THE	Total Estimate of Cost-New					=$	148,773
APPRAISER'S FILES HAS ALSO BEEN RESEARCHED.	Less	Physical	Functional	External			
DEPRECIATION HAS BEEN CALCULATED USING THE AGE/LIFE	Depreciation	5,951				=$(	5,951)
METHOD.	Depreciated Cost of Improvements					=$	142,822
	"As-is" Value of Site Improvements					=$	5,000
Estimated Remaining Economic Life (HUD and VA only) 72 Years	INDICATED VALUE BY COST APPROACH					=$	182,822

Sample Cost Approach section from URAR

Summary

1. The **cost approach** is an appraisal method that estimates the value of real estate by figuring the cost of the improvements, minus (-) depreciation, plus (+) the value of the site (vacant land and site improvements). A typical buyer won't pay more for a property than they would for a comparable substitute.

2. **Replacement** is building the functional equivalent of the original building; **reproduction** is building an exact replica of the original building. Except for historical buildings, replacement is usually used. The cost approach methods are: **Square foot method** (cost manuals), **comparative unit method** (local cost data), **quantity survey** (total of parts/ materials and labor), **unit-in-place method** (total unit cost for each component), and **index method** (original cost multiplied by an index factor).

3. **Depreciation** is loss in value of real estate, for any reason. Land does not depreciate. **Economic life** is the amount of time a building can be used for its intended purpose, or generate more income than cost. **Age life depreciation** is the effective age of the building divided by economic life. This determines depreciation percentage.

4. Loss of property value occurs from physical deterioration, functional obsolescence, and external obsolescence. **Physical deterioration** is the actual wear and tear due to age, elements, and other forces. Items become **incurable** when the cost to repair them exceeds the contribution to sale value. **Functional obsolescence** occurs when a property is less desirable due to the design of building (this is **curable** if cost adds value to property). **External obsolescence** occurs when things outside the property boundaries make it less desirable—**incurable** because it is outside the control of the property owner.

5. **Cost approach** uses data gathered from cost manuals or other sources that track information on cost of building materials and labor. Site value is usually derived from comparable sales. Depreciation is often seen through observation. The cost approach is often used as support for the sales comparison approach. The cost approach is more often reliable for unique buildings, new buildings, and insurance purposes.

Quiz

1. **Which is NOT necessary to perform the cost approach?**
   a. depreciation
   b. replacement or reproduction cost data
   c. site value
   d. matched pair data

2. **Depreciation is**
   a. always the result of external obsolescence.
   b. always the result of functional obsolescence.
   c. always the result of physical deterioration.
   d. a loss in value for any reason.

3. **The cost approach is NOT the most applicable method for**
   a. determining an insurance replacement value.
   b. a recently constructed building.
   c. a residential condo in a complex with 50% occupancy and many recent sales.
   d. an unusual building for which there are no comparable sales available.

4. **_____ cost is more commonly used because _____.**
   a. Replacement / most of the time, a similar building is an acceptable, less expensive alternative.
   b. Replacement / people are always interested in replacing a damaged home with one that is exactly like their old one.
   c. Reproduction / most of the time, a similar building is an acceptable, less expensive alternative.
   d. Reproduction / people are always interested in replacing a damaged home with one that is exactly like their old one.

5. **Which is the most important consideration in developing the cost approach?**
   a. a building's actual age
   b. a building's effective age
   c. both a and b
   d. neither a nor b

6. **Age life depreciation takes the _____ of a building and divides by the _____ of a building to arrive at a depreciation percentage.**
   a. economic life / effective age
   b. economic life / actual age
   c. effective age / economic life
   d. actual age / economic life

7. **Severe structural damage to a basement and foundation would likely be considered**
   a. curable functional obsolescence.
   b. curable physical deterioration.
   c. incurable external obsolescence.
   d. incurable physical deterioration.

8. **External obsolescence is**
   a. related to things outside the property boundaries.
   b. always curable.
   c. always the same as functional obsolescence.
   d. related to something on the exterior of the home.

9. **A house with a poor floor plan that would be very difficult and costly to change would likely suffer from**
   a. curable external obsolescence.
   b. curable functional obsolescence.
   c. incurable external obsolescence.
   d. incurable functional obsolescence.

10. **How does the appraiser determine the appropriate weight to be given to the cost approach?**
    a. The appraiser always uses the cost approach as supporting evidence for the other appraisal methods.
    b. The appraiser considers what the purpose of the appraisal is before deciding how much weight to give the cost approach.
    c. If the figure for the cost approach is very different from the other figures, the appraiser uses a weighted average to bring it in line.
    d. If the figures for the cost approach and the sales comparison approach come out very different, the appraiser knows not to give the cost approach much weight.

Income Approach

This chapter will review the income approach: First defining the concept and key terms, then discussing the procedure. Income capitalization methods using a gross monthly rent multiplier and a direct capitalization rate will be illustrated.

Key Terms

Anticipation An economic principle that says value is created by the expectation of future benefits, such as profit on resale, pleasure, tax shelter, production, income, etc. Anticipation is the foundation of the income approach.

Capitalization An income approach technique that converts the income of a property into a value opinion through the application of either a direct capitalization rate or a factor, such as a multiplier.

Contract Rent What tenants are actually paying for in rent, as stated in the terms of the lease.

Direct Capitalization An income capitalization method that takes a property's single-year net operating income (or NOI) divided by a direct capitalization rate: NOI ÷ Rate = Value.

Direct Capitalization Rate A rate of return, stated as a percent, used to derive a value opinion from the anticipated net operating income a property could generate. It is used for direct capitalization in the income approach. Also called **Cap Rate** or **Rate**.

Effective Gross Income Potential gross income, less (-) vacancy and collection losses.

Fixed Expenses Ongoing operating expenses that do not vary based on occupancy levels of the property (e.g., taxes, insurance).

Gross Income The estimated income a property has the potential to generate, before vacancy and collection losses and expenses.

Gross Monthly Rent Multiplier (GMRM) A rate of return, stated as a factor or multiplier, used to derive a value opinion from the anticipated monthly rent a property could generate. The technique takes a single month's gross rent and multiplies it by the GMRM to indicate a value conclusion: Monthly gross rent x GMRM = Value.

Market Rent What the property could rent for in the open market if unencumbered by any lease and available.

Net Operating Income (NOI) Net income after all operating expenses have been deducted.

Potential Gross Income The income that could be produced by a property in an ideal situation, with no vacancy or collection losses.

Reserves for replacement An amount of money, considered as an operating expense, set aside for future replacement of major items, such as the roof or heating system.

Variable Expenses Operating expenses necessary to the property, but typically dependent on the property's occupancy level.

Defining the Income Approach

The **income approach** is *an appraisal method that develops an indication of the value of real property by analyzing the amount of rent or income the property could generate using market data.* **Capitalization** is *an income approach technique that converts the income of a property into a value opinion through either the application of a direct capitalization rate or a factor, such as a multiplier.* USPAP states that when an income approach is applicable, an appraiser must, as appropriate:

• Analyze such comparable rental data as are available to estimate the market rental of the property.

• Analyze such comparable operating expense data as are available to estimate the operating expenses of the property.

• Analyze such comparable data as are available to estimate rates of capitalization.

• Base projections of future rent on reasonably clear and appropriate evidence.

The appraiser must weigh historical information and trends, current supply and demand, factors affecting such trends, and anticipated events; such as competition from other developments under construction.

There are two ways to derive value using the income approach:

1. Employing a **gross monthly rent multiplier** to analyze the market rent of a property

2. Direct capitalization using a **direct capitalization rate** to analyze the net income stream produced by the property

The income approach is very useful for appraising income-producing, or potentially income-producing, properties because it analyzes the rent or income and produces a direct correlation with the value of the property. This also makes it easy to make comparisons between properties. Investors are typically not emotional about their buying decisions and like to have objective means to compare properties. The income approach parallels the thought process typical investors go through when making a buying decision.

Substitution, Anticipation, and the Typical Investor

A **typical investor** is *one who is acting in his own best interest.* In fact, a typical investor and typical buyer share similar characteristics. The distinction is made only to emphasize that investors are typically more rational than other buyers, and even less likely to make a decision based on emotional attachment.

For Example

Either the numbers work or they don't. Either Property A has a higher value because of its income stream or Property B does.

There is some room for independent evaluation of future worth—the investor might feel that he can increase rents or decrease expenses—but overall, the indications produced through the analysis form a basis for direct comparison. This involves the theory of **substitution**, as well as the theory of **anticipation**.

Theory of Substitution

Substitution says that an informed buyer—or, in this case, a prudent investor—will not pay more for a property than for a comparable substitute. This is even truer for an investor interested in a future income stream than a buyer interested in a nice place to live. Theoretically, for an investor, income from one property may be as good as another.

Theory of Anticipation

Anticipation is *an economic theory that says value is created by the expectation of future benefits; such as profit on resale, pleasure, tax shelter, production, income, etc.* Here, the investor looks at the future expected income stream, as well as the expected future resale value. The projection of future anticipated benefits limits what a property is worth in the market place.

Gross Monthly Rent Multiplier (GMRM)

An income approach using a **gross monthly rent multiplier** or GMRM is the simplest technique of the income capitalization approach. In most cases, the GMRM is used for small residential income properties.

 A GMRM factor may also be expressed as a GRM. They are the same—both use gross monthly market rent in their analysis.

Let's look at this method.

About the GMRM

The **gross monthly rent multiplier (GMRM)** is *a rate of return, stated as a factor or multiplier, used to derive a value opinion from the anticipated monthly rent a property could generate.* Once this factor or multiplier is determined, it can be used to estimate the value of another rental property. The GMRM is most commonly used for one- to four-unit residential properties and is based on the total gross monthly rent of a property.

 With this method, *no consideration is given to expenses, vacancies, collection losses, debt service, or depreciation.*

The GMRM is most applicable and reliable for forming a value opinion of residential income properties when relevant income and sales data exists. Since the technique does not consider any operating expenses, the comparable properties being used must be similar in respect to lease terms and physical characteristics. The GMRM identifies the subject property's ranking within the market of similar properties by giving a means of comparing gross monthly rent and sale prices or value. This method can also be used as support for value indications derived from other appraisal methods. The GMRM is a benchmark to gauge the property's potential profitability by analyzing the potential gross income against the investment dollars needed to buy that future income stream.

Deriving the GMRM

The GMRM is derived with a very simple formula. Data are collected on a number of rental properties that have recently sold in a certain area. The selling price for each is divided by the gross monthly rent the property commanded in the marketplace, thus arriving at a GMRM figure:

Rental Home Sale Price ÷ Gross Monthly Rent = GMRM

GMRMs are calculated for a number of comparable properties which are similar to the subject property. The GMRMs are then analyzed and weighted, giving the most consideration to properties most like the subject. From these comparables, a GMRM figure is selected to apply to the subject property to estimate a value.

For Example

An appraiser has determined that market rent for the subject property is $550 per month. He researches and analyzes transaction data from the market and identifies an indicated GMRM. The following is revealed:

	Sale Price	Monthly Rent	Formula	GMRM
1	$66,200	$530	66,200 ÷ 530	124.91
2	$73,000	$590	73,000 ÷ 590	**123.73**
3	$75,000	$610	75,000 ÷ 610	**122.95**
4	$65,000	$525	65,000 ÷ 525	**123.81**
5	$65,500	$500	65,500 ÷ 500	131.00
6	$70,000	$575	70,000 ÷ 575	121.74
7	$72,800	$650	72,800 ÷ 650	112.00
8	$68,000	$520	68,000 ÷ 520	130.77

In the appraiser's final analysis of the developed range of GMRMs, he notes that the most common result is around 123.00, with those results ranging from just slightly less than 123.00 to the upper 123.00 range (illustrated in bold type).

In reconciling a GMRM conclusion, the appraiser could choose to use 123.00 as a GMRM, or probably better, place most weight on #2 (123.73) and #4 (123.81), since the GMRM from those transactions most closely brackets the subject's estimated market rent of $550 (as highlighted). For this reason, the appraiser chooses a GMRM of 123.75 to apply to the subject.

Using the GMRM

The subject property's determined GMRM is then put into another simple formula to arrive at an estimate of value. The gross monthly market rent from the subject property is then multiplied by the GMRM derived in the first step:

Gross Monthly Market Rent x GMRM = Estimated Value

Let's illustrate this application by continuing with our previous example.

For Example

The appraiser has chosen $550 per month as a reasonable opinion of market rent for the subject property and a GMRM of 123.75 to apply to the rent. Thus, the results of the appraiser's conclusions are as follows:

123.75 x $550 = $68,062.50, or rounded to the nearest thousand, $68,000

Income Approach Analysis of the URAR Form

The URAR form is used only for single-family properties. The income approach is developed and reported for single-family properties in fewer cases primarily due to the prominence of owner-occupied properties as well as lack of sufficient data from which reliable value indications can be produced. The URAR accommodates only one line for the reporting of the income approach.

When the income approach is not applicable or sufficient data does not exist from which to develop conclusions using an income technique, the appraiser's reconciliation notes must contain an explanation, as seen in the sample below.

The technique specified by the form uses a multiplier. Also, this complete appraisal—with the reconciliation section notes—appears at the end of Chapter 12.

INCOME APPROACH TO VALUE (not required by Fannie Mae)						
Estimated Monthly Market Rent $	N/A	X Gross Rent Multiplier	N/A	= $	N/A	Indicated Value by Income Approach
Summary of Income Approach (including support for market rent and GRM)			THE INCOME APPROACH HAS NOT BEEN PROCESSED DUE TO A LACK			
OF COMPARABLE MARKET DATA. THE MARKET IS PRIMARILY OWNER-OCCUPIED.						

Sample income approach section from URAR form

Direct Capitalization Method

Investment property analysis can become quite involved. There are many ways to derive value, and different ways to attribute that value to the building, land, and property as a whole. A property's value can also be estimated by examining income, expenses, and other items. This discussion will focus on a simplified income capitalization method that relies on a property's past income performance. **Direct capitalization** is *an income capitalization method that takes a property's single-year net operating income (or NOI) divided by a direct capitalization rate.*

Determining the Net Operating Income of the Subject Property

The **net operating income (NOI)** of the subject property is *the estimated amount the property owner or investor should realize after accounting for certain losses and operating expenses (including replacement reserves) for the property.*

The steps in estimating NOI require a systematic and careful analysis. These steps are:

1. Determine PGI (potential gross income)
2. Estimate rates of vacancy and collection losses
3. Determine EGI (effective gross income)
4. Estimate operating expenses
5. Determine NOI

While these five steps may seem outwardly simple, the appraiser may spend a significant amount of time in analyzing the various components leading to an estimated NOI. For direct capitalization, the method considers all of these components on an *annual* basis.

The mathematical formula for NOI is as follows:

> **PGI**
> **- Vacancy and Collection Losses**
> **= EGI**
> **- Operating Expenses**
> **= NOI**

Potential Gross Income (PGI)

Potential gross income (PGI) is *the income that could be produced by a property in an ideal situation, with no vacancy or collection losses* (e.g., rent that could not be collected due to a tenant who failed to pay). The key here is that PGI is the income a property *could* generate if the property is fully rented and occupied during the particular period being analyzed. In most cases, PGI is based on an *annual* amount.

Effective Gross Income (EGI)

Effective gross income (**EGI**) is *the potential gross income, less vacancy and collection losses*. EGI is the income that could be (or is) realized from an income property after deducting an amount for vacancy and collection losses, but before any operating expenses are considered. If PGI is what the property owner *could* have taken in, EGI can be thought of as what that property owner *did* take in. The formula for EGI is:

PGI - Vacancy and Collection Losses = EGI

Estimating Vacancy and Collection Losses

In most cases, both losses (vacancy and collection) are based on a percentage of the PGI. The percentage applied in the development of NOI is determined by analysis of market data.

Net Operating Income (NOI)

As previously mentioned, NOI is *the income after expenses.*

 In Other Words: Net operating income is the effective gross income minus (-) operating expenses.

Do not confuse NOI with cash flow. Cash flow considers other obligations, such as payments toward loan debt and income tax obligations not considered in the NOI. The formula for NOI is:

PGI - Vacancy and Collection Losses = EGI – Operating Expenses = NOI

Operating Expenses

Operating expenses are *day-to-day costs of running of a property, like repairs and maintenance, but not including debt service or depreciation*. These are expenses that must be incurred by the property owner in order to adequately maintain a property at a level that allows it to continue producing revenue. Since income is analyzed at an annual level, the operating expenses are also considered on an *annual* basis.

Operating expenses are divided into three types:

1. Fixed expenses
2. Variable expenses
3. Reserves for replacement

Let's discuss each expense type a little further.

Fixed Expenses

Fixed expenses are *ongoing expenses that do not vary based on occupancy levels of the property*. Real estate taxes and insurance on the property are items that are most always considered fixed expenses. Even though the cost of these items might vary from year to year, the change is not usually great, and these expenses are not based upon occupancy.

Other examples of fixed expenses might be services that are contracted at a level rate for, perhaps, a year at a time. A good example might be refuse collection, where the lessor pays for a certain number of collections per week or month, regardless of how much refuse he has. Another fixed expense might be the cost of a security light for a parking area where the expense is a reoccurring flat fee. Again, think of costs not associated with occupancy.

Variable Expenses

Variable expenses are *operating expenses necessary to the property, but dependent on the property's occupancy level.* Maintenance and repairs are typically considered a variable expense, as are any utilities to the living units furnished by the lessor. Another common variable expense is management fees (often expressed as a percent). Since it is not logical that property managers, or a management company, are rewarded for vacant units or property, the percentage is typically based upon EGI rather than PGI. Thus, management fees are considered a variable expense since the expense varies based on occupancy. Other examples of variable expenses *might* be legal or accounting fees charged on a non-consistent basis.

Reserves for Replacement

There are certain components or items of any structure that will need to be replaced from time to time throughout the life of the building. For an income-producing property, the anticipated cost of replacing these components or items is addressed by reserves for replacement. **Reserves for replacement** (sometimes just called **reserves**) *refers to an amount of money set aside for future replacement of major items.* When used in an income analysis, the replacement reserve is most often applied as an annual dollar (sometimes as a percentage) amount.

Although there could certainly be others, common components or items for residential income properties for which a replacement reserve is typically considered include roof, heating and/or air-conditioning systems, carpeting, and lessor furnished appliances.

Deriving a Direct Capitalization Rate

The **direct capitalization rate** (also called a **cap rate** or **rate**) is *a rate of return, stated as a percent, used to derive a value opinion from the anticipated net operating income a property could generate. It is used for direct capitalization in the income approach.* Here, we will discuss how a direct capitalization rate is derived from market data using this formula.

(Net Operating) Income ÷ Value = (Direct Capitalization) Rate

(Easily remembered as IVR)

For Example

In the course of analyzing an investment property, the appraiser collected the following sales and income data:

	Sale Price	NOI	I ÷ V = R	Rate (%)
Sale #1	$425,000	$39,600	39,600 ÷ 425,000 = 0.0932	9.32%
Sale #2	$470,000	$42,300	42,300 ÷ 470,000 = 0.0900	**9.00%**
Sale #3	$395,000	$39,100	39,100 ÷ 395,000 = 0.0990	9.90%
Sale #4	$452,000	$40,900	40,900 ÷ 452,000 = 0.0905	**9.05%**
Sale #5	$405,000	$36,500	36,500 ÷ 405,000 = 0.0901	**9.01%**

In forming conclusions from this example, it can be noted that three of the five resulting indications are most closely related at 9.00% - 9.05%. Thus, the appraiser has the best support for concluding somewhere within this range, and probably at the lower end, since two of those conclusions are suggesting 9.00% as being a reasonable indication for an overall capitalization rate.

Applying a Direct Capitalization Rate

When a direct capitalization rate is applied to the subject's net operating income, a value conclusion is revealed. The formula used is as follows:

(Net Operating) Income ÷ (Direct Capitalization) Rate = Value

For Example

An appraiser has determined that a reasonable market level net operating income of a subject property is $39,200.

In the previous example, the appraiser derived a direct capitalization rate of 9.00% to apply to the subject's net operating income. By dividing the NOI by the direct capitalization rate (using the IRV formula), the appraiser can determine a value conclusion:

$39,200 ÷ 9.00% = $435,556

Before concluding our discussion of the direct capitalization approach, we should probably point out that, most generally, the income capitalization approach is used for larger residential properties with more than four units, or for non-residential commercial properties.

Summary

1. The **income approach** is an appraisal method that develops an opinion of value for real estate by analyzing the amount of rent or income the property could generate. A factor such as a **gross monthly rent multiplier (GMRM)** or a **direct capitalization rate** is derived from market data and then applied to the subject property's market rent or income.

2. A **typical investor** is one acting in his own best interests. **Substitution** says an informed buyer (prudent investor) won't pay more for a property than for a comparable substitute. **Anticipation** says value is created by expectation of future benefits.

3. **Direct capitalization** is an income capitalization method that takes a property's single-year net operating income (NOI) divided by a direct capitalization rate. A **direct capitalization rate** is a rate of return, stated as a percent, used to derive a value opinion from the anticipated net operating income a property could generate. **Potential gross income (PGI)** is income before vacancy and/or collection losses, and expenses (100% occupancy, no vacancy/collection losses). **Effective gross income (EGI)** is potential gross income, minus (-) vacancy and collection losses. **Net operating income (NOI)** is the income after expenses have been subtracted from EGI.

4. **Market rent** is what the property could rent for on the open market. **Fixed expenses** are ongoing and do not vary based on occupancy (e.g., taxes, insurance). **Variable expenses** depend on occupancy (e.g., maintenance, management, utilities). **Reserves for replacement** are monies, considered as an operating expense, set aside for future replacement of major items. Operating expenses do **not** include debt service or depreciation.

5. **A direct capitalization rate** is a rate of return, stated as a percent, used to derive a value opinion from the anticipated net operating income a property could generate. It is used to for direct capitalization in the income approach and is also called a **cap rate** or **rate**. Most small residential properties use the **gross monthly rent multiplier (GMRM)**. A GMRM is derived from comparable rental properties. To derive a GMRM, sale price is divided by gross monthly rent. To apply a GMRM, the gross monthly market rent of the subject is multiplied by the GMRM to arrive at a value indication.

Quiz

1. **Which is NOT necessary to develop the direct capitalization technique?**

   a. expenses

   b. income

   c. rate

   d. debt service

2. **The theory of anticipation says**

   a. a buyer won't pay more for the subject than for a comparable property.

   b. a property is worth more if an investor is excited about acquiring the property.

   c. real estate will always appreciate in value.

   d. value is created by the expectation of future benefits.

3. **Which would NOT be considered an operating expense?**

   a. debt service

   b. fixed expenses

   c. reserves

   d. variable expenses

4. **Vacancy and collection losses**

   a. are always 10%.

   b. are considered when using a GMRM.

   c. are not considered when doing a direct capitalization method appraisal.

   d. determined by analysis of market data.

5. **Which element is used to determine the gross monthly rent multiplier?**

   a. collection losses

   b. expenses

   c. vacancy losses

   d. sale price

6. **A main disadvantage of the gross monthly rent multiplier is**

   a. the capitalization rate is not accurate enough.

   b. it can be used only to support the cost approach, not the sales comparison approach.

   c. the lack of very similar comparable data.

   d. using the GMRM is more complicated than the capitalization rate.

7. **Potential gross income, less vacancy and collection losses is the**

   a. capitalization rate.

   b. effective gross income (EGI).

   c. gross rent multiplier (GRM).

   d. net operating income (NOI).

8. **Using IRV, what would be the indicated value (rounded to the nearest one hundred dollars) of a property that has NOI of $8,000 if the overall capitalization rate is indicated at 9.25%?**

   a. $65,300

   b. $74,000

   c. $86,500

   d. $92,400

9. **If a subject property has a market rent of $625 per month and a GMRM of 183.75 is deemed applicable, what is the appraiser's indicated value conclusion (rounded to the nearest one thousand dollars)?**

   a. $103,000

   b. $115,000

   c. $132,000

   d. $184,000

10. **A six-unit apartment building with a net operating income of $24,000 recently sold for $390,000. What is the indicated overall capitalization rate (carried to two places) derived from this data?**

    a. 6.15%

    b. 6.95%

    c. 7.10%

    d. 7.25%

11. **An unfurnished house rents for $8,100 per year, which is determined to represent market level. The property recently sold for $147,000 in an arm's length transaction. What is the GMRM indicated (rounded to two places)?**

    a. 5.51

    b. 18.15

    c. 181.48

    d. 217.78

12. *A GMRM is applied to _____ to produce a value indication.*

   a. contract rent

   b. effective gross income

   c. market rent

   d. net operating income

Reconciling Estimates of Value and Reporting Conclusions

This chapter is the culmination of everything discussed in this text. It will examine how the value indications produced from the various approaches to value are reconciled and how they are reported. Next, the steps in the reconciliation process will be examined, including a few points on when each of the appraisal approaches would be given the most weight. This chapter will also look at reporting conclusions and some of the USPAP obligations that must be followed. Finally, it will illustrate a completed URAR appraisal report (including addenda).

Key Terms

Addenda Additional parts of an appraisal report. Addenda usually consist of photos of the subject and comparables, a sketch of the subject's floor plan, a table for calculating the area of the subject, a location map, or additional necessary comments that do not fit in the space on the appraisal form.

Reconciliation Analyzing the values derived from the different appraisal approaches to arrive at a final opinion of value.

Reconciling Estimates of Value

As touched on briefly in Chapter 4, **reconciliation** is the appraisal process of *analyzing the values derived from the different appraisal approaches to arrive at a final opinion of value.* This is the appraiser's opportunity to bring together all data collected, verified, and analyzed during the appraisal process. As part of the reconciliation, the appraiser must determine the strengths and weaknesses of each appraisal approach used—reflecting on the quality and quantity of data analyzed and the relevance of a particular approach. Skill and experience are important as the appraiser goes through the appraisal reconciliation process.

Steps in the Reconciliation Process

There are several steps the appraiser must take when reconciling the appraisal values. The appraiser:

1. Looks at the strengths and weaknesses of each appraisal method and technique used.

2. Considers the quality and quantity of the data that were gathered and used.

3. Decides which of the approaches to value is the most applicable to solving the valuation problem at hand for the subject property.

4. Reviews each step in the approaches developed and considers their relevance and reliability.

If the appraiser determines in the scope of work *not* to include one or more of the valuation approaches in his analysis, USPAP requires the appraiser to explain his reasoning for the exclusion in the appraisal report.

When reconciling the value indications produced and deciding the weight to give each approach, the appraiser takes several points into consideration. Each approach has different considerations.

Sales Comparison Approach

When considering the sales comparison approach, the appraiser primarily considers *what type of property the subject is.* If the appraisal is for a property for which there is sufficient meaningful data to perform the analysis, the sales comparison approach would be a reliable method of indicating value. For most residential assignments of owner-occupied residential properties, this would likely be the best indicator of value.

Cost Approach

When considering the cost approach, the appraiser considers *the type and age of the subject property.* If the appraisal is for a special purpose or single-use type property for which there is not sufficient comparable data, the cost approach may be the most relevant. Also, the newer the structure, the more applicable the cost approach would be.

Income Approach

When considering the income approach, the appraiser considers *whether or not the property currently has, or has the potential to generate, an income stream which can be analyzed,* or if there are other similar properties with an income stream which could form a basis of comparison. The appraiser would also consider the *amount and sufficiency of income, expense, and other data available* on the subject property and comparable properties to allow for meaningful value conclusions.

Giving Each Approach Appropriate Weight

The appraiser must give final consideration to each estimate of value from each appraisal approach. The appraiser uses some of the criteria mentioned previously to decide which approach will be given the most weight in the final value opinion in the appraisal. This is an important step because it would be rare for the values to be equal. The appraiser must decide which of the appraisal approaches is the most relevant and reliable given the available data, and which best reflects the market value of the subject property. The appraiser will then use this as the basis for his final opinion of value.

The value conclusions from the other approaches to value could, in some cases, be used to support the value indication derived by the approach being primarily relied upon. Or, in other circumstances, multiple approaches could be used together to determine the final value opinion. However, the results are **not** simply mathematically averaged; although, the appraiser could determine that each approach is a valid indication and therefore, arrive at a final value conclusion somewhere within the range of indications. The report should provide details of the appraiser's reasoning and logic used in forming his final opinion of value and must be clear, understandable, and not misleading.

Finally, the appraisal report states the final value opinion. For the purpose of most appraisal reports, including the URAR form report, this will be a single number. However, USPAP allows for a value opinion to also be stated as a range of numbers or a relationship to a benchmark (e.g., more than, less than).

Reconciliation Sample

This reconciliation is a continuation of the sample appraisal discussed throughout this textbook, beginning in Chapter 5. The completed URAR appraisal report form follows.

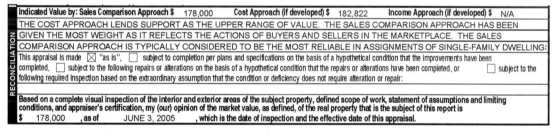

Sample Reconciliation section of URAR

Completed URAR Appraisal Report

The final section of this chapter includes a complete residential appraisal using a **Uniform Residential Appraisal Report (URAR)** form. The complete appraisal also includes additional sections and addenda, which are typical parts of a standard appraisal report.

Appraisal Addenda

The additional parts of an appraisal report—collectively referred to as the **addenda**—are an important part of the supporting evidence used by the appraiser in defense of the appraiser's estimate or opinion of value. Pages of a typical addenda contain such things as:

- Photographs of the subject
- A sketch of the floor plan of the improvements, as well as a chart/table used to calculate the area of the house
- Photographs and information on the comparable sales used in the appraisal
- A location map that pinpoints the location of the subject and comparables

Addenda may also include other exhibits or illustrations an appraiser determines relevant, which would assist the client and other intended users with understanding the report.

Uniform Residential Appraisal Report
File # 18988

The purpose of this summary appraisal report is to provide the lender/client with an accurate, and adequately supported, opinion of the market value of the subject property.

Property Address 22 OAKWOOD DRIVE	City WESTERVILLE	State OH	Zip Code 43081
Borrower CHRISTOPHER S. JONES	Owner of Public Record JAMES R. & MARIA S. HOLDER	County FRANKLIN	

Legal Description LOT #27, PHASE II, LAKE RIDGE SUBDIVISION

Assessor's Parcel # 62-42316000	Tax Year 2004	R.E. Taxes $ 4,397.00
Neighborhood Name LAKE RIDGE SUBDIVISION	Map Reference 45 P40	Census Tract 0071.93

Occupant ☒ Owner ☐ Tenant ☐ Vacant   Special Assessments $ ☐ PUD HOA $ N/A ☐ per year ☐ per month

Property Rights Appraised ☒ Fee Simple ☐ Leasehold ☐ Other (describe)

Assignment Type ☒ Purchase Transaction ☐ Refinance Transaction ☐ Other (describe)

Lender/Client SECOND FEDERAL MORTGAGE   Address 2723 NORTH MAIN STREET, HILLIARD, OHIO

Is the subject property currently offered for sale or has it been offered for sale in the twelve months prior to the effective date of this appraisal? ☒ Yes ☐ No

Report data source(s) used, offering price(s), and date(s). THE SUBJECT HAS BEEN LISTED THROUGH THE COLUMBUS MULTIPLE LISTING SERVICE FOR $179,900. THE PROPERTY HAS BEEN LISTED APPROXIMATELY 35 +/- DAYS.

I ☒ did ☐ did not analyze the contract for sale for the subject purchase transaction. Explain the results of the analysis of the contract for sale or why the analysis was not performed. THE CURRENT AGREEMENT TO PURCHASE INCLUDES THE FOLLOWING PERSONALTIES: RANGE, REFRIGERATOR AND MISCELLANEOUS WINDOW COVERINGS. NONE ARE CONSIDERED TO CONTRIBUTE SIGNIFICANT VALUE TO THE TRANSACTION.

Contract Price $ $178,000   Date of Contract 6/1/2005   Is the property seller the owner of public record? ☒ Yes ☐ No Data Source(s) FRANKLIN CO. REC.

Is there any financial assistance (loan charges, sale concessions, gift or downpayment assistance, etc.) to be paid by any party on behalf of the borrower? ☒ Yes ☐ No

If Yes, report the total dollar amount and describe the items to be paid. $3,000.00   THE SELLER IS PAYING UP TO $3,000 TOWARD THE PURCHASER'S POINTS AND/OR CLOSING COSTS.

Note: Race and the racial composition of the neighborhood are not appraisal factors.

Neighborhood Characteristics			One-Unit Housing Trends				One-Unit Housing		Present Land Use %	
Location ☐ Urban	☒ Suburban	☐ Rural	Property Values ☒ Increasing	☐ Stable	☐ Declining	PRICE	AGE	One-Unit	90 %
Built-Up ☐ Over 75%	☒ 25-75%	☐ Under 25%	Demand/Supply ☐ Shortage	☒ In Balance	☐ Over Supply	$ (000)	(yrs)	2-4 Unit	%
Growth ☒ Rapid	☐ Stable	☐ Slow	Marketing Time ☒ Under 3 mths	☐ 3-6 mths	☐ Over 6 mths	155 Low	2	Multi-Family	%
Neighborhood Boundaries SPRINGHILL DRIVE TO THE NORTH, STONERIDGE DRIVE TO THE EAST,						279 High	9	Commercial	%
FLOWER AVENUE TO THE SOUTH, CUSTER DRIVE TO THE WEST.						180 Pred.	5	Other	10 %

Neighborhood Description THE IMMEDIATE MARKET AREA IS PREDOMINATELY SINGLE-FAMILY HOUSING OF VARIOUS STYLES WITH SCATTERED UPPER-MID RANGE CUSTOM CONSTRUCTION. PROXIMITY TO SERVICES, EMPLOYMENT, AND RECREATION IS CONSIDERED AVERAGE. OTHER LAND USE IS THE INFLUENCE OF A PUBLIC PARK WITHIN THE DEFINED NEIGHBORHOOD.

Market Conditions (including support for the above conclusions) INTEREST RATES APPEAR TO BE STABLE AND REMAIN FAVORABLE, WITH MANY FINANCING AVENUES AVAILABLE. ONGOING NEW CONSTRUCTION SUPPORTS STEADY TO RAPID GROWTH PATTERN OF THE OVERALL MARKET. EXISTING HOUSING RESALES COUPLED WITH NEW CONSTRUCTION MAINTAIN SUPPLY/DEMAND IN BALANCE.

Dimensions 110' X 150'	Area 16,500 SQ.FT.	Shape RECTANGULAR	View RESID. HOUSING

Specific Zoning Classification R-4   Zoning Description LOW DENSITY RESIDENTIAL DISTRICT

Zoning Compliance ☒ Legal ☐ Legal Nonconforming (Grandfathered Use) ☐ No Zoning ☐ Illegal (describe)

Is the highest and best use of subject property as improved (or as proposed per plans and specifications) the present use? ☒ Yes ☐ No If No, describe

Utilities	Public	Other (describe)		Public	Other (describe)	Off-site improvements – Type	Public	Private
Electricity	☒		Water	☒		Street ASPHALT	☒	
Gas	☒		Sanitary Sewer	☒		Alley NONE		

FEMA Special Flood Hazard Area ☐ Yes ☒ No   FEMA Flood Zone X   FEMA Map # 39049C0069H   FEMA Map Date 4/21/1999

Are the utilities and off-site improvements typical for the market area? ☒ Yes ☐ No If No, describe

Are there any adverse site conditions or external factors (easements, encroachments, environmental conditions, land uses, etc.)? ☐ Yes ☒ No If Yes, describe

NO ADVERSE SITE CONDITIONS OR ENCROACHMENTS HAVE BEEN NOTED. FLOOD INFORMATION IS PER FLOODSOURCE FLOOD MAPPING SERVICE, AND IS NOT TO BE RELIED UPON FOR FLOOD INSURANCE DETERMINATION. THE CLIENT SHOULD RELY UPON THEIR FLOOD CERTIFICATION SOURCE FOR FINAL DETERMINATION.

General Description	Foundation	Exterior Description materials/condition	Interior materials/condition
Units ☒ One ☐ One with Accessory Unit	☐ Concrete Slab ☒ Crawl Space	Foundation Walls POURED CONC.	Floors WOOD/CRPT/CER
# of Stories 2	☐ Full Basement ☒ Partial Basement	Exterior Walls VINYL/BRICK	Walls DRYWALL
Type ☒ Det. ☐ Att. ☐ S-Det./End Unit	Basement Area 642 sq.ft.	Roof Surface DIM. SHINGLE	Trim/Finish STND. OAK
☒ Existing ☐ Proposed ☐ Under Const.	Basement Finish 75 %	Gutters & Downspouts ALUMINUM	Bath Floor CERAMIC
Design (Style) 2 STORY	☐ Outside Entry/Exit ☒ Sump Pump	Window Type DOUBLE HUNG	Bath Wainscot CERAMIC
Year Built 1999	Evidence of ☐ Infestation	Storm Sash/Insulated INSULATED	Car Storage ☐ None
Effective Age (Yrs) 3 YEARS	☐ Dampness ☐ Settlement	Screens YES	☒ Driveway # of Cars 2
Attic ☐ None	Heating ☒ FWA ☐ HWBB ☐ Radiant	Amenities ☐ Woodstove(s) #	Driveway Surface CONCRETE
☐ Drop Stair ☐ Stairs	☐ Other Fuel NAT. GAS	☒ Fireplace(s) # 1 ☒ Fence WD. PRIV.	☒ Garage # of Cars 2
☐ Floor ☒ Scuttle	Cooling ☒ Central Air Conditioning	☒ Patio/Deck REAR ☒ Porch FRONT	☐ Carport # of Cars
☐ Finished ☐ Heated	☐ Individual ☐ Other	☐ Pool ☒ Other B-I SPA	☒ Att. ☐ Det. ☐ Built-In

Appliances ☐ Refrigerator ☐ Range/Oven ☒ Dishwasher ☒ Disposal ☒ Microwave ☐ Washer/Dryer ☒ Other (describe) TRASH COMPACTOR

Finished area above grade contains: 7 Rooms 3 Bedrooms 2.1 Bath(s) 1,952 Square Feet of Gross Living Area Above Grade

Additional features (special energy efficient items, etc.). MONITORED SECURITY AND FIRE ALARM SYSTEM. GARAGE HAS FINISHED INTERIOR, 2 ELECTRIC DOOR OPENERS AND BUILT-IN STORAGE AREA.

Describe the condition of the property (including needed repairs, deterioration, renovations, remodeling, etc.). THE SUBJECT WAS FOUND TO BE IN OVERALL ABOVE AVERAGE CONDITION AND REASONABLY MAINTAINED. THE EFFECTIVE AGE IS SLIGHTLY LESS THAN ACTUAL DUE TO OVERALL CONDITION.

Are there any physical deficiencies or adverse conditions that affect the livability, soundness, or structural integrity of the property? ☐ Yes ☒ No If Yes, describe

Does the property generally conform to the neighborhood (functional utility, style, condition, use, construction, etc.)? ☒ Yes ☐ No If No, describe

Uniform Residential Appraisal Report

File # 18988

| There are | 7 | comparable properties currently offered for sale in the subject neighborhood ranging in price from $ | 174,900 | to $ | 192,500 |

| There are | 12 | comparable sales in the subject neighborhood within the past twelve months ranging in sale price from $ | 168,500 | to $ | 191,000 |

FEATURE	SUBJECT	COMPARABLE SALE # 1		COMPARABLE SALE # 2		COMPARABLE SALE # 3	
Address	22 OAKWOOD DRIVE	21 VALLEYVIEW COURT		337 CHRIS COURT		321 PEARSON DRIVE	
	WESTERVILLE, OH 43081	WESTERVILLE, OHIO		WESTERVILLE, OHIO		WESTERVILLE, OHIO	
Proximity to Subject		0.37 MILE		0.33 MILE		0.62 MILE	
Sale Price	$ $178,000	$ 180,000		$ 185,000		$ 172,000	
Sale Price/Gross Liv. Area	$ sq.ft.	$ 89.82 sq.ft.		$ 97.16 sq.ft.		$ 99.48 sq.ft.	
Data Source(s)		FRANKLIN CO. AUDITOR		FRANKLIN CO. AUDITOR		FRANKLIN CO. AUDITOR	
Verification Source(s)		COLS. MLS, BROKER		COLS. MLS, BROKER		COLS. MLS, BROKER	
VALUE ADJUSTMENTS	DESCRIPTION	DESCRIPTION	+(-) $ Adjustment	DESCRIPTION	+(-) $ Adjustment	DESCRIPTION	+(-) $ Adjustment
Sales or Financing		CONV		CONV		CONV	
Concessions		NONE		SELLER PAID	-5,000	NONE	
Date of Sale/Time		4/30/2005		3/5/2005		5/14/2005	
Location	AVERAGE	AVERAGE		AVERAGE		AVERAGE	
Leasehold/Fee Simple	FEE SIMPLE	FEE SIMPLE		FEE SIMPLE		FEE SIMPLE	
Site	16,500 SQ.FT.	17,200 SQ. FT.		15,740 SQ. FT		13,650 SQ. FT.	
View	RES/AVG	RES/AVG		PARK/GOOD	-2,500	RES/AVG	
Design (Style)	2 STORY	2 STORY		2 STORY		2 STORY	
Quality of Construction	AVERAGE	AVERAGE		AVERAGE		AVERAGE	
Actual Age	6 YEARS	5 YEARS		6 YEARS		8 YEARS	
Condition	GOOD	GOOD		GOOD		AVERAGE	+2,500
Above Grade	Total Bdrms. Baths	Total Bdrms. Baths		Total Bdrms. Baths		Total Bdrms. Baths	
Room Count	7 3 2.1	6 3 2.1		8 3 2.1		7 3 2	+500
Gross Living Area	1,952 sq.ft.	2,004 sq.ft.	-500	1,904 sq.ft.	+500	1,729 sq.ft.	+2,200
Basement & Finished	642 Sq.Ft.	1,002 SQ. FT.	-2,000	700 SQ. FT.		600 SQ. FT.	
Rooms Below Grade	2 RMS, F BA	UNFINISHED	+3,000	1 RM. FIN	+2,000	2 RMS, F BA	
Functional Utility	AVERAGE	AVERAGE		AVERAGE		AVERAGE	
Heating/Cooling	GFA/CENTRAL	GFA/CENTRAL		GFA/CENTRAL		GFA/CENTRAL	
Energy Efficient Items	TYPICAL	TYPICAL		STANDARD		STANDARD	
Garage/Carport	2-C ATT GAR	2-C ATT GAR		2-C ATT GAR		2-C ATT GAR	
Porch/Patio/Deck	PORCH, PATIO	PORCH, DECK		PORCH, PATIO		PORCH, DECK	
	B-I SPA	NONE	+500	IN-GRD POOL	-500	B-I SPA	
	WD PRIV FNC	WD PRIV FNC		WD PRIV FNC		NONE	+500
	FIREPLACE	FIREPLACE		2 FIREPLACES	-1,000	FIREPLACE	
Net Adjustment (Total)		☒ + ☐ -	$ 1,000	☐ + ☒ -	$ 6,500	☒ + ☐ -	$ 5,700
Adjusted Sale Price of Comparables		Net 0.6 % Gross 3.3 %	$ 181,000	Net 3.5 % Gross 6.2 %	$ 178,500	Net 3.3 % Gross 3.3 %	$ 177,700

I ☒ did ☐ did not research the sale or transfer history of the subject property and comparable sales. If not, explain

My research ☐ did ☒ did not reveal any prior sales or transfers of the subject property for the three years prior to the effective date of this appraisal.
Data Source(s) FRANKLIN COUNTY AUDITOR

My research ☒ did ☐ did not reveal any prior sales or transfers of the comparable sales for the year prior to the date of sale of the comparable sale.
Data Source(s) FRANKLIN COUNTY AUDITOR

Report the results of the research and analysis of the prior sale or transfer history of the subject property and comparable sales (report additional prior sales on page 3).

ITEM	SUBJECT	COMPARABLE SALE #1	COMPARABLE SALE #2	COMPARABLE SALE #3
Date of Prior Sale/Transfer	NONE IN 36 MONTHS	9/23/2004	NONE IN 12 MONTHS	NONE IN 12 MONTHS
Price of Prior Sale/Transfer		$155,000		
Data Source(s)		FRANKLIN CO AUDITOR		
Effective Date of Data Source(s)		6/3/2005		

Analysis of prior sale or transfer history of the subject property and comparable sales RESEARCH REVEALED THAT SALE #1 TRANSFERRED ON 9/23/2004 FOR $155,000. FURTHER INQUIRY WITH THE SELLER IN THE MOST RECENT TRANSACTION REVEALED THAT THE PURCHASE WAS VIA SHERRIFF'S AUCTION. COSMETIC RENOVATIONS WERE PERFORMED PRIOR TO THE PROPERTY BEING RE-MARKETED.

Summary of Sales Comparison Approach THE SALES REFLECT A REASONABLE VALUE RANGE. ALL SALES ARE FROM THE IMMEDIATE MARKET AREA. CORRELATION IS TOWARD THE UPPER PART OF THE VALUE RANGE, WITH TWO OF THE THREE SALES INDICATING THAT DIRECTION. THESE SALES ARE THE MOST RECENT AND REQUIRE THE FEWEST NET ADJUSTMENTS.

Indicated Value by Sales Comparison Approach $ 178,000

Indicated Value by: Sales Comparison Approach $ 178,000   Cost Approach (if developed) $ 182,822   Income Approach (if developed) $ N/A

THE COST APPROACH LENDS SUPPORT AS THE UPPER RANGE OF VALUE. THE SALES COMPARISON APPROACH HAS BEEN GIVEN THE MOST WEIGHT AS IT REFLECTS THE ACTIONS OF BUYERS AND SELLERS IN THE MARKETPLACE. THE SALES COMPARISON APPROACH IS TYPICALLY CONSIDERED TO BE THE MOST RELIABLE IN ASSIGNMENTS OF SINGLE-FAMILY DWELLINGS

This appraisal is made ☒ "as is", ☐ subject to completion per plans and specifications on the basis of a hypothetical condition that the improvements have been completed, ☐ subject to the following repairs or alterations on the basis of a hypothetical condition that the repairs or alterations have been completed, or ☐ subject to the following required inspection based on the extraordinary assumption that the condition or deficiency does not require alteration or repair:

Based on a complete visual inspection of the interior and exterior areas of the subject property, defined scope of work, statement of assumptions and limiting conditions, and appraiser's certification, my (our) opinion of the market value, as defined, of the real property that is the subject of this report is
$ 178,000 , as of JUNE 3, 2005 , which is the date of inspection and the effective date of this appraisal.

Uniform Residential Appraisal Report   File # 18988

ADDITIONAL COMMENTS

COST APPROACH TO VALUE (not required by Fannie Mae)

Provide adequate information for the lender/client to replicate the below cost figures and calculations.

Support for the opinion of site value (summary of comparable land sales or other methods for estimating site value)   ESTIMATED SITE VALUE IS DERIVED FROM A SALES COMPARISON ANALYSIS OF LOT SALES WITHIN THE SUBJECT'S SUBDIVISION. THIS ANALYSIS IS CONTAINED IN THE APPRAISER'S WORKFILE.

ESTIMATED ☐ REPRODUCTION OR ☒ REPLACEMENT COST NEW	OPINION OF SITE VALUE		=$	35,000
Source of cost data MARSHALL SWIFT COSTING SERVICE	DWELLING 1,952 Sq.Ft. @ $ 67.40		=$	131,565
Quality rating from cost service AVG Effective date of cost data 3/1/2005	FOUNDATION 642 Sq.Ft. @ $ 12.00		=$	7,704
Comments on Cost Approach (gross living area calculations, depreciation, etc.)			=$	
GROSS LIVING AREA HAS BEEN DETERMINED FROM EXTERIOR	Garage/Carport 528 Sq.Ft. @ $ 18.00		=$	9,504
DIMENSIONS. LOCAL COST DATA CONTAINED IN THE	Total Estimate of Cost-New		=$	148,773
APPRAISER'S FILES HAS ALSO BEEN RESEARCHED.	Less Physical Functional External			
DEPRECIATION HAS BEEN CALCULATED USING THE AGE/LIFE	Depreciation 5,951		=$(	5,951)
METHOD.	Depreciated Cost of Improvements		=$	142,822
	"As-is" Value of Site Improvements		=$	5,000
Estimated Remaining Economic Life (HUD and VA only) 72 Years	INDICATED VALUE BY COST APPROACH		=$	182,822

INCOME APPROACH TO VALUE (not required by Fannie Mae)

Estimated Monthly Market Rent $ N/A X Gross Rent Multiplier N/A = $ N/A					Indicated Value by Income Approach

Summary of Income Approach (including support for market rent and GRM)   THE INCOME APPROACH HAS NOT BEEN PROCESSED DUE TO A LACK OF COMPARABLE MARKET DATA. THE MARKET IS PRIMARILY OWNER-OCCUPIED.

PROJECT INFORMATION FOR PUDs (if applicable)

Is the developer/builder in control of the Homeowners' Association (HOA)? ☐ Yes ☐ No   Unit type(s) ☐ Detached ☐ Attached

Provide the following information for PUDs ONLY if the developer/builder is in control of the HOA and the subject property is an attached dwelling unit.

Legal Name of Project

Total number of phases	Total number of units	Total number of units sold
Total number of units rented	Total number of units for sale	Data source(s)

Was the project created by the conversion of existing building(s) into a PUD? ☐ Yes ☐ No If Yes, date of conversion.

Does the project contain any multi-dwelling units? ☐ Yes ☐ No Data Source

Are the units, common elements, and recreation facilities complete? ☐ Yes ☐ No If No, describe the status of completion.

Are the common elements leased to or by the Homeowners' Association? ☐ Yes ☐ No If Yes, describe the rental terms and options.

Describe common elements and recreational facilities.

Freddie Mac Form 70 March 2005   Page 3 of 6   Fannie Mae Form 1004 March 2005

Uniform Residential Appraisal Report   File # 18988

This report form is designed to report an appraisal of a one-unit property or a one-unit property with an accessory unit; including a unit in a planned unit development (PUD). This report form is not designed to report an appraisal of a manufactured home or a unit in a condominium or cooperative project.

This appraisal report is subject to the following scope of work, intended use, intended user, definition of market value, statement of assumptions and limiting conditions, and certifications. Modifications, additions, or deletions to the intended use, intended user, definition of market value, or assumptions and limiting conditions are not permitted. The appraiser may expand the scope of work to include any additional research or analysis necessary based on the complexity of this appraisal assignment. Modifications or deletions to the certifications are also not permitted. However, additional certifications that do not constitute material alterations to this appraisal report, such as those required by law or those related to the appraiser's continuing education or membership in an appraisal organization, are permitted.

SCOPE OF WORK: The scope of work for this appraisal is defined by the complexity of this appraisal assignment and the reporting requirements of this appraisal report form, including the following definition of market value, statement of assumptions and limiting conditions, and certifications. The appraiser must, at a minimum: (1) perform a complete visual inspection of the interior and exterior areas of the subject property, (2) inspect the neighborhood, (3) inspect each of the comparable sales from at least the street, (4) research, verify, and analyze data from reliable public and/or private sources, and (5) report his or her analysis, opinions, and conclusions in this appraisal report.

INTENDED USE: The intended use of this appraisal report is for the lender/client to evaluate the property that is the subject of this appraisal for a mortgage finance transaction.

INTENDED USER: The intended user of this appraisal report is the lender/client.

DEFINITION OF MARKET VALUE: The most probable price which a property should bring in a competitive and open market under all conditions requisite to a fair sale, the buyer and seller, each acting prudently, knowledgeably and assuming the price is not affected by undue stimulus. Implicit in this definition is the consummation of a sale as of a specified date and the passing of title from seller to buyer under conditions whereby: (1) buyer and seller are typically motivated; (2) both parties are well informed or well advised, and each acting in what he or she considers his or her own best interest; (3) a reasonable time is allowed for exposure in the open market; (4) payment is made in terms of cash in U. S. dollars or in terms of financial arrangements comparable thereto; and (5) the price represents the normal consideration for the property sold unaffected by special or creative financing or sales concessions* granted by anyone associated with the sale.

*Adjustments to the comparables must be made for special or creative financing or sales concessions. No adjustments are necessary for those costs which are normally paid by sellers as a result of tradition or law in a market area; these costs are readily identifiable since the seller pays these costs in virtually all sales transactions. Special or creative financing adjustments can be made to the comparable property by comparisons to financing terms offered by a third party institutional lender that is not already involved in the property or transaction. Any adjustment should not be calculated on a mechanical dollar for dollar cost of the financing or concession but the dollar amount of any adjustment should approximate the market's reaction to the financing or concessions based on the appraiser's judgment.

STATEMENT OF ASSUMPTIONS AND LIMITING CONDITIONS: The appraiser's certification in this report is subject to the following assumptions and limiting conditions:

1. The appraiser will not be responsible for matters of a legal nature that affect either the property being appraised or the title to it, except for information that he or she became aware of during the research involved in performing this appraisal. The appraiser assumes that the title is good and marketable and will not render any opinions about the title.

2. The appraiser has provided a sketch in this appraisal report to show the approximate dimensions of the improvements. The sketch is included only to assist the reader in visualizing the property and understanding the appraiser's determination of its size.

3. The appraiser has examined the available flood maps that are provided by the Federal Emergency Management Agency (or other data sources) and has noted in this appraisal report whether any portion of the subject site is located in an identified Special Flood Hazard Area. Because the appraiser is not a surveyor, he or she makes no guarantees, express or implied, regarding this determination.

4. The appraiser will not give testimony or appear in court because he or she made an appraisal of the property in question, unless specific arrangements to do so have been made beforehand, or as otherwise required by law.

5. The appraiser has noted in this appraisal report any adverse conditions (such as needed repairs, depreciation, the presence of hazardous wastes, toxic substances, etc.) observed during the inspection of the subject property or that he or she became aware of during the research involved in performing the appraisal. Unless otherwise stated in this appraisal report, the appraiser has no knowledge of any hidden or unapparent physical deficiencies or adverse conditions of the property (such as, but not limited to, needed repairs, deterioration, the presence of hazardous wastes, toxic substances, adverse environmental conditions, etc.) that would make the property less valuable, and has assumed that there are no such conditions and makes no guarantees or warranties, express or implied. The appraiser will not be responsible for any such conditions that do exist or for any engineering or testing that might be required to discover whether such conditions exist. Because the appraiser is not an expert in the field of environmental hazards, this appraisal report must not be considered as an environmental assessment of the property.

6. The appraiser has based his or her appraisal report and valuation conclusion for an appraisal that is subject to satisfactory completion, repairs, or alterations on the assumption that the completion, repairs, or alterations of the subject property will be performed in a professional manner.

164

Uniform Residential Appraisal Report
File # 18988

APPRAISER'S CERTIFICATION: The Appraiser certifies and agrees that:

1. I have, at a minimum, developed and reported this appraisal in accordance with the scope of work requirements stated in this appraisal report.

2. I performed a complete visual inspection of the interior and exterior areas of the subject property. I reported the condition of the improvements in factual, specific terms. I identified and reported the physical deficiencies that could affect the livability, soundness, or structural integrity of the property.

3. I performed this appraisal in accordance with the requirements of the Uniform Standards of Professional Appraisal Practice that were adopted and promulgated by the Appraisal Standards Board of The Appraisal Foundation and that were in place at the time this appraisal report was prepared.

4. I developed my opinion of the market value of the real property that is the subject of this report based on the sales comparison approach to value. I have adequate comparable market data to develop a reliable sales comparison approach for this appraisal assignment. I further certify that I considered the cost and income approaches to value but did not develop them, unless otherwise indicated in this report.

5. I researched, verified, analyzed, and reported on any current agreement for sale for the subject property, any offering for sale of the subject property in the twelve months prior to the effective date of this appraisal, and the prior sales of the subject property for a minimum of three years prior to the effective date of this appraisal, unless otherwise indicated in this report.

6. I researched, verified, analyzed, and reported on the prior sales of the comparable sales for a minimum of one year prior to the date of sale of the comparable sale, unless otherwise indicated in this report.

7. I selected and used comparable sales that are locationally, physically, and functionally the most similar to the subject property.

8. I have not used comparable sales that were the result of combining a land sale with the contract purchase price of a home that has been built or will be built on the land.

9. I have reported adjustments to the comparable sales that reflect the market's reaction to the differences between the subject property and the comparable sales.

10. I verified, from a disinterested source, all information in this report that was provided by parties who have a financial interest in the sale or financing of the subject property.

11. I have knowledge and experience in appraising this type of property in this market area.

12. I am aware of, and have access to, the necessary and appropriate public and private data sources, such as multiple listing services, tax assessment records, public land records and other such data sources for the area in which the property is located.

13. I obtained the information, estimates, and opinions furnished by other parties and expressed in this appraisal report from reliable sources that I believe to be true and correct.

14. I have taken into consideration the factors that have an impact on value with respect to the subject neighborhood, subject property, and the proximity of the subject property to adverse influences in the development of my opinion of market value. I have noted in this appraisal report any adverse conditions (such as, but not limited to, needed repairs, deterioration, the presence of hazardous wastes, toxic substances, adverse environmental conditions, etc.) observed during the inspection of the subject property or that I became aware of during the research involved in performing this appraisal. I have considered these adverse conditions in my analysis of the property value, and have reported on the effect of the conditions on the value and marketability of the subject property.

15. I have not knowingly withheld any significant information from this appraisal report and, to the best of my knowledge, all statements and information in this appraisal report are true and correct.

16. I stated in this appraisal report my own personal, unbiased, and professional analysis, opinions, and conclusions, which are subject only to the assumptions and limiting conditions in this appraisal report.

17. I have no present or prospective interest in the property that is the subject of this report, and I have no present or prospective personal interest or bias with respect to the participants in the transaction. I did not base, either partially or completely, my analysis and/or opinion of market value in this appraisal report on the race, color, religion, sex, age, marital status, handicap, familial status, or national origin of either the prospective owners or occupants of the subject property or of the present owners or occupants of the properties in the vicinity of the subject property or on any other basis prohibited by law.

18. My employment and/or compensation for performing this appraisal or any future or anticipated appraisals was not conditioned on any agreement or understanding, written or otherwise, that I would report (or present analysis supporting) a predetermined specific value, a predetermined minimum value, a range or direction in value, a value that favors the cause of any party, or the attainment of a specific result or occurrence of a specific subsequent event (such as approval of a pending mortgage loan application).

19. I personally prepared all conclusions and opinions about the real estate that were set forth in this appraisal report. If I relied on significant real property appraisal assistance from any individual or individuals in the performance of this appraisal or the preparation of this appraisal report, I have named such individual(s) and disclosed the specific tasks performed in this appraisal report. I certify that any individual so named is qualified to perform the tasks. I have not authorized anyone to make a change to any item in this appraisal report; therefore, any change made to this appraisal is unauthorized and I will take no responsibility for it.

20. I identified the lender/client in this appraisal report who is the individual, organization, or agent for the organization that ordered and will receive this appraisal report.

Freddie Mac Form 70 March 2005   Page 5 of 6   Fannie Mae Form 1004 March 2005

Uniform Residential Appraisal Report

File # 18988

21. The lender/client may disclose or distribute this appraisal report to: the borrower; another lender at the request of the borrower; the mortgagee or its successors and assigns; mortgage insurers; government sponsored enterprises; other secondary market participants; data collection or reporting services; professional appraisal organizations; any department, agency, or instrumentality of the United States; and any state, the District of Columbia, or other jurisdictions; without having to obtain the appraiser's or supervisory appraiser's (if applicable) consent. Such consent must be obtained before this appraisal report may be disclosed or distributed to any other party (including, but not limited to, the public through advertising, public relations, news, sales, or other media).

22. I am aware that any disclosure or distribution of this appraisal report by me or the lender/client may be subject to certain laws and regulations. Further, I am also subject to the provisions of the Uniform Standards of Professional Appraisal Practice that pertain to disclosure or distribution by me.

23. The borrower, another lender at the request of the borrower, the mortgagee or its successors and assigns, mortgage insurers, government sponsored enterprises, and other secondary market participants may rely on this appraisal report as part of any mortgage finance transaction that involves any one or more of these parties.

24. If this appraisal report was transmitted as an "electronic record" containing my "electronic signature," as those terms are defined in applicable federal and/or state laws (excluding audio and video recordings), or a facsimile transmission of this appraisal report containing a copy or representation of my signature, the appraisal report shall be as effective, enforceable and valid as if a paper version of this appraisal report were delivered containing my original hand written signature.

25. Any intentional or negligent misrepresentation(s) contained in this appraisal report may result in civil liability and/or criminal penalties including, but not limited to, fine or imprisonment or both under the provisions of Title 18, United States Code, Section 1001, et seq., or similar state laws.

SUPERVISORY APPRAISER'S CERTIFICATION: The Supervisory Appraiser certifies and agrees that:

1. I directly supervised the appraiser for this appraisal assignment, have read the appraisal report, and agree with the appraiser's analysis, opinions, statements, conclusions, and the appraiser's certification.

2. I accept full responsibility for the contents of this appraisal report including, but not limited to, the appraiser's analysis, opinions, statements, conclusions, and the appraiser's certification.

3. The appraiser identified in this appraisal report is either a sub-contractor or an employee of the supervisory appraiser (or the appraisal firm), is qualified to perform this appraisal, and is acceptable to perform this appraisal under the applicable state law.

4. This appraisal report complies with the Uniform Standards of Professional Appraisal Practice that were adopted and promulgated by the Appraisal Standards Board of The Appraisal Foundation and that were in place at the time this appraisal report was prepared.

5. If this appraisal report was transmitted as an "electronic record" containing my "electronic signature," as those terms are defined in applicable federal and/or state laws (excluding audio and video recordings), or a facsimile transmission of this appraisal report containing a copy or representation of my signature, the appraisal report shall be as effective, enforceable and valid as if a paper version of this appraisal report were delivered containing my original hand written signature.

APPRAISER RICHARD P. JACKSON	SUPERVISORY APPRAISER (ONLY IF REQUIRED)
Signature _____	Signature _____
Name RICHARD P. JACKSON	Name _____
Company Name THE JACKSON GROUP	Company Name _____
Company Address 44224 BRISTOL SQUARE	Company Address _____
WESTERVILLE, OHIO 43081	
Telephone Number 614-333-3333	Telephone Number _____
Email Address rpj@jckgrp.com	Email Address _____
Date of Signature and Report JUNE 5, 2005	Date of Signature _____
Effective Date of Appraisal JUNE 3, 2005	State Certification # _____
State Certification # _____	or State License # _____
or State License # 20026111111	State _____
or Other (describe) _____ State # _____	Expiration Date of Certification or License _____
State OHIO	
Expiration Date of Certification or License 3/3/2006	**SUBJECT PROPERTY**
	☐ Did not inspect subject property
ADDRESS OF PROPERTY APPRAISED	☐ Did inspect exterior of subject property from street
22 OAKWOOD DRIVE	Date of Inspection _____
WESTERVILLE, OH 43081	☐ Did inspect interior and exterior of subject property
APPRAISED VALUE OF SUBJECT PROPERTY $ 178,000	Date of Inspection _____
LENDER/CLIENT	
Name ROBERTA GLASS	**COMPARABLE SALES**
Company Name SECOND FEDERAL MORTGAGE	
Company Address 2723 NORTH MAIN STREET	☐ Did not inspect exterior of comparable sales from street
	☐ Did inspect exterior of comparable sales from street
Email Address rg@secondfederal.com	Date of Inspection _____

Location Map

Borrower/Client	CHRISTOPHER S. JONES			
Property Address	22 OAKWOOD DRIVE			
City WESTERVILLE	County FRANKLIN	State OH	Zip Code 43081	
Lender SECOND FEDERAL MORTGAGE				

Location Map

Building Sketch (Page - 1)

Borrower/Client CHRISTOPHER S. JONES				
Property Address 22 OAKWOOD DRIVE				
City WESTERVILLE	County FRANKLIN	State OH	Zip Code 43081	
Lender SECOND FEDERAL MORTGAGE				

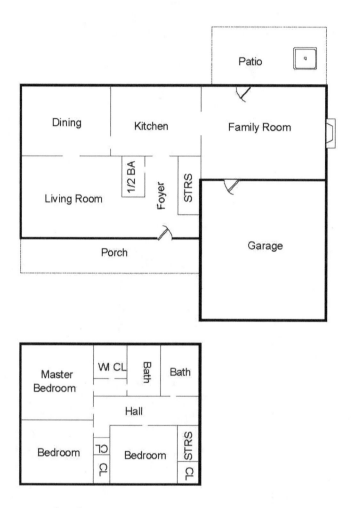

Improvement Sketch

Building Sketch (Page - 2)

Borrower/Client CHRISTOPHER S. JONES	
Property Address 22 OAKWOOD DRIVE	
City WESTERVILLE County FRANKLIN State OH Zip Code 43081	
Lender SECOND FEDERAL MORTGAGE	

AREA CALCULATIONS SUMMARY

Code	Description	Size	Net Totals
GLA1	First Floor	1184.0000	1184.0000
GLA2	Second Floor	768.0000	768.0000
P/P	Porch	192.0000	
	Patio	200.0000	392.0000
GAR	Garage	528.0000	528.0000

TOTAL LIVABLE   (rounded)   1952

LIVING AREA BREAKDOWN

Breakdown			Subtotals
First Floor			
4.00	x	54.00	216.0000
10.00	x	32.00	320.0000
12.00	x	54.00	648.0000
Second Floor			
24.00	x	32.00	768.0000

4 Calculations Total (rounded)   1952

First Floor   GLA1

4.00	x	54.00	=	216.0000
10.00	x	32.00	=	320.0000
12.00	x	54.00	=	648.0000

Area total (rounded)   =   1184

Garage   GAR

22.00	x	24.00	=	528.0000

Area total (rounded)   =   528

Porch   P/P

6.00	x	32.00	=	192.0000

Area total (rounded)   =   192

Patio   P/P

10.00	x	20.00	=	200.0000

Area total (rounded)   =   200

Second Floor   GLA2

24.00	x	32.00	=	768.0000

Area total (rounded)   =   768

Improvement Calculations

Subject Photo Page

Borrower/Client	CHRISTOPHER S. JONES			
Property Address	22 OAKWOOD DRIVE			
City WESTERVILLE	County FRANKLIN	State OH		Zip Code 43081
Lender SECOND FEDERAL MORTGAGE				

Subject Front

22 OAKWOOD DRIVE
Sales Price $178,000
Gross Living Area 1,952
Total Rooms 7
Total Bedrooms 3
Total Bathrooms 2.1
Location AVERAGE
View RES/AVG
Site 16,500 SQ FT.
Quality AVERAGE
Age 6 YEARS

Subject Rear

Subject Street

Subject Photos

Comparable Photo Page

Borrower/Client	CHRISTOPHER S. JONES				
Property Address	22 OAKWOOD DRIVE				
City WESTERVILLE		County FRANKLIN		State OH	Zip Code 43081
Lender SECOND FEDERAL MORTGAGE					

Comparable 1

21 VALLEYVIEW COURT

Prox. to Subject	0.37 MILE
Sale Price	180,000
Gross Living Area	2,004
Total Rooms	6
Total Bedrooms	3
Total Bathrooms	2.1
Location	AVERAGE
View	RES/AVG
Site	17,200 SQ. FT.
Quality	AVERAGE
Age	5 YEARS

Comparable 2

337 CHRIS COURT

Prox. to Subject	0.33 MILE
Sale Price	185,000
Gross Living Area	1,904
Total Rooms	8
Total Bedrooms	3
Total Bathrooms	2.1
Location	AVERAGE
View	PARK/GOOD
Site	15,740 SQ. FT
Quality	AVERAGE
Age	6 YEARS

Comparable 3

321 PEARSON DRIVE

Prox. to Subject	0.62 MILE
Sale Price	172,000
Gross Living Area	1,729
Total Rooms	7
Total Bedrooms	3
Total Bathrooms	2
Location	AVERAGE
View	RES/AVG
Site	13,650 SQ. FT.
Quality	AVERAGE
Age	8 YEARS

Comparable Photos

Summary

1. **Reconciliation** is the process of analyzing the quality and relevance of the approaches to value used to arrive at a final value opinion. The appraiser must consider all data to determine the relevance and reliability of the data analyzed and the developed approaches to value. The appraiser must consider the quality and quantity of data.

2. The **sales comparison approach** may be given the most weight if the subject is residential and there is sufficient data to analyze. The **cost approach** may be given the most weight if the subject is new or unique and sales data is scarce or non-existent. The **income approach** may be given the most weight for income-producing properties for which income data is available.

3. **Reconciliation** includes the appraiser's reasoning for his conclusions and value opinion.

4. The **report** states the appraiser's final value opinion and is a means of communicating with the client and other intended users. The appraisal report details the appraiser's thought process and should be clear, concise, logical, supported, and not misleading.

Quiz

1. *During the reconciliation process,*

   a. the appraiser decides which approach to give the most weight, then throws out the other approaches.

   b. the appraiser decides which approach or approaches to give the most weight.

   c. the appraiser must always determine an exact dollar amount to present as his final opinion of value.

   d. value approaches are mathematically averaged.

2. *In the final appraisal report, the appraiser will NOT*

   a. detail the reasoning he used in arriving at the final opinion of value.

   b. explain why one or more of the appraisal methods may not have been used.

   c. note any specific conditions, unusual circumstances, or assumptions.

   d. reference the listing or sales contract price of the subject property as a factor in developing the value opinion.

3. *When using the URAR form, which income approach technique does the form accommodate?*

   a. comparative unit

   b. direct capitalization

   c. gross income multiplier

   d. gross rent multiplier

4. *During reconciliation, the value indication produced by the sales comparison approach for a residential property*

   a. cannot be the only appraisal approach used to develop a final value opinion.

   b. is never used as the final opinion of value; it is used as support for either the income or cost approach.

   c. may be given the most weight if the data is reliable and the approach is applicable.

   d. must be used in every assignment to develop a final value opinion

5. *When an appraiser decides to use one particular approach as a primary indicator of value in an appraisal,*

   a. any other approaches developed are not reported in the appraisal report.

   b. he has violated USPAP as it prohibits correlating with only one approach.

   c. he must not discuss in the report the other approaches developed.

   d. other approaches may be used to support that opinion.

Final Exams

Real Estate Appraisal Final Exam #1

1. **The opinion of value in an appraisal report is valid**
   a. as of the effective date of the appraisal only.
   b. for three months after the appraisal date.
   c. for six months after the appraisal date.
   d. for one year after the appraisal date.

2. **An appraisal report is NOT required to include**
   a. the address of the subject property.
   b. a final estimate of value.
   c. the signature of the appraiser.
   d. the contract price of the property.

3. **Which value approach would most likely be emphasized for an apartment building in an established neighborhood?**
   a. cost approach
   b. income approach
   c. sales comparison approach
   d. all three approaches would be averaged

4. **A vacant land parcel described as the NE ¼ of Section 17 is selling for $1,200 per acre. What is the sale price of the parcel?**
   a. $48,000
   b. $96,000
   c. $192,000
   d. $768,000

5. **Market value is**
   a. equal to the cost of production.
   b. the most probable selling price to a typical buyer.
   c. what a property sold for.
   d. what one buyer is willing to pay.

6. **Market price is the**
   a. amount, in dollars, actually paid for the property.
   b. amount, in dollars, asked for by the seller.
   c. amount, in dollars, a property should bring on the open market.
   d. the most probable selling price to a typical buyer.

7. **The cost approach does NOT require an estimate of**
   a. depreciation.
   b. site improvements and building costs.
   c. site value.
   d. net operating income.

8. **When using the income approach, appraisers do NOT assume that**
   a. buyers estimate the duration of income when buying income property.
   b. future income is always less valuable than present income.
   c. value is directly related to income.
   d. future income is always more valuable than present income.

9. **Using the information in the following table, calculate depreciation using the age-life method.**

Replacement Cost	$173,000
Effective Age	15 years
Remaining Economic Life	60 years

   a. $6,920
   b. $8,650
   c. $34,600
   d. $43,250

10. **The single most important value factor is**
    a. age.
    b. condition.
    c. location.
    d. size.

11. **Which characteristics create value in real estate?**
    a. durability and transferability
    b. immobility and durability
    c. scarcity and utility
    d. utility and immobility

12. **The four broad forces which affect value are**
    a. cost, income, market, and correlation.
    b. demand, scarcity, utility, and transferability.
    c. density, variety, human scale, and architecture.
    d. economic, governmental, social, and physical.

13. **A neighborhood's life cycle is an example of**
    a. anticipation.
    b. change.
    c. highest and best use.
    d. substitution.

14. **In analyzing a vacant site to estimate its value, the first step is to determine**
    a. its highest and best use.
    b. its list price.
    c. the price of comparable vacant sites.
    d. the price the owner paid for it.

15. **If a developer purchased a lot measuring 348' x 1,000' and the sale price was $5,000 per acre, how much did the developer pay?**
    a. $34,800
    b. $37,395
    c. $38,360
    d. $39,945

16. **The data required for a site analysis includes**
    a. economic characteristics of the neighborhood and community.
    b. physical characteristics of the site.
    c. zoning information.
    d. all of the above

17. **Prior to inspecting the site, an appraiser should obtain information on the**
    a. size and shape of the parcel.
    b. utilities and soil type.
    c. zoning and easements.
    d. all of the above

18. **As the depth of the lot increases, the value per front footage**
    a. decreases.
    b. decreases, and then begins to increase.
    c. increases at a decreasing rate.
    d. increases in direct proportion to the depth.

19. **If a property's effective gross income is $14,351.40 and vacancy is calculated at 6.2%, what is the potential gross income?**
    a. $15,200.00
    b. $15,241.19
    c. $15,267.45
    d. $15,300.00

20. **The utility of property is most affected by**
    a. building codes, restrictions, and zoning.
    b. credit controls and the Federal Reserve.
    c. interest rates and time value of money.
    d. property taxes and escheat.

21. **When reflected to the subject, the comparable property had a fireplace with a contributory value of $1,500, but lacked a half bath with a contributory value of $2,500. What was the net adjustment to the comparable?**
    a. - $1,000
    b. + 1,000
    c. - $4,000
    d. + $4,000

22. **What type of obsolesence is represented by severe structural damage to a basement foundation?**
    a. economic
    b. external
    c. functional
    d. physical

23. **The effective age of a house does NOT consider**
    a. external market area factors.
    b. the floor plan and design.
    c. the physical condition and marketability.
    d. the actual age of the house.

24. **The gross living area of an improved residential property is determined by measuring the**
    a. exterior dimensions of the dwelling, including the garage.
    b. exterior dimensions of the dwelling, not including the garage.
    c. interior dimensions of each room, added together.
    d. interior dimensions of each room and the garage, added together.

25. *When building a new home, what is the order of the first four construction steps?*

    a. foundation, framing, drywall, and rough-ins

    b. framing, rough-ins, site work, and foundation

    c. rough-ins, framing, foundation, and site work

    d. site work, foundation, framing, and rough-ins

26. *Of the following architectural styles, which is typically a one-floor plan design?*

    a. bi-level

    b. Cape Cod

    c. Ranch

    d. split-level

27. *The maximum a typical buyer will pay for a property feature is related to the theory of*

    a. change.

    b. conformity.

    c. progression.

    d. substitution.

28. *In analyzing comparable sales, an appraiser should*

    a. adjust the comparable sales to the subject property.

    b. adjust the subject property to the comparable sales.

    c. average all of the comparable sales and adjust the subject accordingly.

    d. adjust the comparable sales relative to each other.

29. *Which circumstance might cause a transaction NOT to be arm's length?*

    a. Market conditions are known by seller.

    b. Property has been adequately exposed.

    c. Seller was not influenced by haste or duress.

    d. Seller was not knowledgeable of value.

30. *You would expect market price to equal market value if the*

    a. parties to the sale were related.

    b. sale was a foreclosure.

    c. sale was made with an anticipation of change in use (zoning change).

    d. transaction was arm's length.

31. *An appraiser is performing an appraisal of an older apartment building in an established neighborhood for which he has data on several similar apartment buildings. However, none have sold in the past five years. Which approach will be concluded as the most credible?*

    a. comparative unit

    b. cost

    c. income

    d. sales comparison

32. *What sales data does NOT need to be confirmed for the sales comparison approach?*

    a. gross living area

    b. property condition at the time of the sale

    c. terms and circumstances of the sale

    d. names of the previous owners

33. *Adjustments to the sale price of comparable sale properties are measured by the*

    a. amount a typical buyer will pay for an item.

    b. cost per square foot.

    c. principle of conformity.

    d. quantity survey method.

34. *For the appraisal of an older single-family residential dwelling, where should the appraiser put his reliance?*

    a. cost conclusions

    b. market rents

    c. recent listings

    d. recent sales

35. *The increase or decrease in value that helps estimate market value of a property by comparing its features to those of comparable sales is referred to as an*

    a. adjustable comparison.

    b. adjusted basis.

    c. adjustment.

    d. amended value.

36. *A document also referred to as a tax or assessors map is a(n)*

    a. assemblage plan.

    b. plat map.

    c. plottage map.

    d. topographical map.

37. **Which is an example of general data on a subject property?**
    a. school district
    b. site topography
    c. utility source
    d. view

38. **If a property is functionally and physically sound and acceptable to the market, but located next to a noisy and dirty industrial site, the effective age will be**
    a. at its peak.
    b. higher.
    c. lower.
    d. unaffected.

39. **The sales comparison approach for valuing a site is difficult in older, built-up neighborhoods because**
    a. adjustments to sale prices are not required.
    b. the method is too indirect.
    c. the ratio of land to building is not constant.
    d. vacant site sales are often scarce.

40. **In valuing acreage suitable for residential development, a commonly applied method is the _____ method.**
    a. abstraction
    b. land residual
    c. plottage
    d. subdivision analysis

41. **The subject of an appraisal is a two-story dwelling with an exterior dimension of 22' x 66' and a full basement. Half of the basement is finished. What is the gross living area?**
    a. 1,452 square feet
    b. 2,904 square feet
    c. 3,630 square feet
    d. 4,356 square feet

42. **Which is NOT a recognized method of site valuation?**
    a. land residual
    b. plottage comparison
    c. sales comparison
    d. subdivision analysis

43. **In the income approach, residential properties are usually analyzed using**
    a. a capitalization rate.
    b. comparable listings.
    c. contract rent for apartment buildings in the same area as the subject.
    d. a gross rent multiplier.

44. **An appraiser is asked to appraise a vacant residential site. The neighborhood is about 75% built up. Most lots in the area are 55' to 65' wide. The vacant lot is 60' wide. Comparable sales indicate lots are selling from $180 to $225 per front foot. What is the estimate for the subject lot?**
    a. $7,100 - $10,125
    b. $9,900 - $11,400
    c. $10,800 - $13,500
    d. $13,500 - $16,500

45. **Physical differences and their affect on the value of land or site can be determined only by the**
    a. adjustments shown for the date of sale.
    b. land development method.
    c. market's reaction in terms of dollars.
    d. rules of excess depth.

46. **Which approach would be most appropriate in the appraisal of a uniquely designed and recently constructed public library building?**
    a. building residual approach
    b. cost approach
    c. income approach
    d. sales comparison approach

47. **The use of the reproduction cost new of a building when cost estimating for a subject building eliminates all**
    a. external obsolescence.
    b. functional obsolescence.
    c. physical deterioration.
    d. physical deterioration and functional obsolescence.

48. ***Replacement cost refers to estimating the cost of a***

    a. building of the same age.
    b. replica building.
    c. rural appurtenance.
    d. similar building using modern materials.

49. ***In the cost approach, an opinion of value is developed by adding the***

    a. depreciated cost new of improvements to depreciated site value.
    b. depreciated cost new of improvements to estimated site value.
    c. new cost of the improvements to the depreciated site value.
    d. new cost of the improvements to the estimated site value.

50. ***Which is a functional obsolescence?***

    a. broken A/C unit
    b. clogged drain
    c. inoperable faucet
    d. no heating source

Real Estate Appraisal Final Exam #2

1. *Which is NOT an item for which the appraiser would normally be responsible?*
   a. accurately describing the subject
   b. completing a survey of the site
   c. estimating market value
   d. gathering all necessary appraisal data

2. *The area that a structure's foundation rests upon is called a*
   a. footer.
   b. joist.
   c. pier.
   d. slab.

3. *Which is an example of general data on a subject property?*
   a. school district
   b. site topography
   c. utility source
   d. view

4. *Trade fixtures can best be described as*
   a. items attached to real estate for business purposes.
   b. items that were once personal property but are now real property.
   c. lights and plumbing items attached to the real estate.
   d. items that a landlord installs for the use of business tenants.

5. *Using the information in the following table, calculate the annual depreciation of a house using the straight-line method.*

Current Building Cost	$200,000
Effective Age	25 years
Actual Age	40 years
Expected Useful Life	50 years

   a. $2500
   b. $5,000
   c. $8,000
   d. $10,000

6. *In calculating square footage of a residential house, which is NOT considered part of the primary living space?*
   a. any room on the second floor
   b. living and dining rooms
   c. porches
   d. both a and b

7. *In counting rooms in the house, which would typically NOT be counted in the total number of rooms?*
   a. a basement recreation room
   b. bedrooms on the second floor
   c. living and dining room—only if above grade
   d. both a and b

8. *A functional problem (or obsolescence) in a home pertains to*
   a. items outside the boundary of the subject.
   b. location.
   c. proximity to shopping.
   d. the utility of the property, such as room layout.

9. *The value most often sought in an appraisal is*
   a. depreciated value.
   b. market value.
   c. replacement value.
   d. value in use.

10. *Using a GMRM, the income approach requires the appraiser to*
    a. convert net income into a value estimate.
    b. divide net income by the rate.
    c. multiply the gross rent by a multiplier.
    d. use gross rent divided by the property value.

11. *Market value is the most*
    a. probable annual income.
    b. probable selling price.
    c. recent annual rent.
    d. recent transfer price.

12. **In analyzing a comparable sale where the seller paid points, the appraiser must**

    a. adjust the comparable for any impact seller paid points may have had on the sale price.

    b. adjust the subject for any impact seller paid points may have had on the sale price.

    c. contact the lender to verify current interest rates and loan program information.

    d. contact the lender to verify the going rates for points.

13. **The rental amount according to lease terms is defined as _____ rent.**

    a. contract

    b. effective

    c. market

    d. term

14. **Using the information provided, calculate the value of an apartment building using direct capitalization.**

Annual Income	$150,000
Monthly Expenses	$2,000
Capitalization Rate	9%

    a. $1,134,000

    b. $1,400,000

    c. $1,644,444

    d. $1,666,667

15. **An external obsolescence pertains to**

    a. a family room located in the basement.

    b. the placement of bedrooms in relation to the bathroom.

    c. a railroad track running along side the lot.

    d. the size of the kitchen.

16. **Which approach to value deals primarily with the amount of money an owner can receive from a rental property?**

    a. cost approach

    b. income approach

    c. sales comparison method

    d. square foot method

17. **Which principle is the value of adjustments done for the sales comparison approach generally based on?**

    a. change

    b. conformity

    c. highest and best use

    d. substitution

18. **In residential appraisals, a commonly utilized method of depreciation is the _____ method.**

    a. age-life

    b. quantity of survey

    c. square foot

    d. unit in place

19. **The process of estimating the value of a property by adding the estimated cost to replace a building, minus depreciation, plus the estimated site value, is known as the**

    a. cost approach.

    b. functional obsolescence.

    c. physical curable valuation.

    d. quantitative survey method.

20. **The period of time during which a structure may reasonably be expected to perform the function for which it was designed is known as its**

    a. chronological age.

    b. effective age.

    c. physical life span.

    d. total economic life.

21. **An improvement to a property that is not likely to contribute its cost to the total market value of the subject property is known as**

    a. improvement depreciation.

    b. negative contribution.

    c. over improvement.

    d. physical loss amenity.

22. **The lack of sufficient information for sales of similar properties is a limitation of the _____ approach.**

    a. comparative unit

    b. cost

    c. rental valuation

    d. sales comparison

23. **In completing a market analysis, an item contributing value and representing a variance between the subject property and a comparable sale requires the**

    a. comparable to be adjusted accordingly.

    b. conclusions to be altered.

    c. principle of change to be used.

    d. subject property to be adjusted accordingly.

24. **The financial terms of a sale**
    a. are irrelevant if the buyer paid full asking price.
    b. have no influence on the price.
    c. may have an impact on the price paid.
    d. can be disregarded if it involved seller financing.

25. **Which approach to value for owner-occupied, single-family housing is based primarily on information obtained by analyzing comparable sales?**
    a. cost approach
    b. income approach
    c. sales comparison approach
    d. unit in place approach

26. **Which would likely result in functional obsolescence?**
    a. a company closing a factory in the area
    b. a house with five bedrooms and one bathroom
    c. a new freeway built near a neighborhood
    d. a zoning change

27. **While closed sales are required for the sales comparison approach, why would analyzing listed properties be useful?**
    a. A listing can be used as a third comparable property.
    b. Location adjustments can be extracted from listings.
    c. They are necessary for determining time adjustments.
    d. They provide evidence of substitution and the upper limit of value.

28. **After freeway construction, the volume of business on a street decreased by 50%. This can be considered a(n)**
    a. amenity.
    b. appurtenance.
    c. external obsolescence.
    d. functional obsolescence.

29. **Which would be considered an external obsolescence?**
    a. changes in zoning
    b. normal wear and tear
    c. poor architectural design
    d. termite and pest control

30. **A 25-year-old property sells for $125,000. If the site is worth $25,000 and the building would cost $200,000 to replace today, what is the annual rate of depreciation?**
    a. 0.5%
    b. 1.0%
    c. 2.0%
    d. 5.0%

31. **The capitalization approach using a GMRM means to**
    a. convert net income into a value estimate.
    b. divide the cost of a building by annual rent.
    c. divide the net income by the rate.
    d. multiply the gross rent by a multiplier.

32. **In applying the gross monthly rent multiplier to the subject property, the appraiser would use _____ rent.**
    a. current actual
    b. gross market
    c. historic
    d. net market

33. **The monthly rent being paid for a rental property is called _____ rent.**
    a. contract
    b. effective
    c. historic
    d. market

34. **In determining whether an item is a fixture, and therefore part of the real estate, which is least important?**
    a. annexation or attachment
    b. intent
    c. purpose
    d. value

35. **An unfurnished house rents for $6,000 per year. An appraiser estimates the value of the subject at $80,000. What's the monthly gross rent multiplier?**
    a. 7.50
    b. 13.33
    c. 133
    d. 160

36. **The most detailed method of estimating a reproduction cost for a structure is**
    a. comparative unit.
    b. index.
    c. quantity survey.
    d. square foot.

37. **The duration of time during which a structure may be financially efficient is its**
    a. chronological age.
    b. economic life.
    c. effective age.
    d. observable life.

38. **Real estate markets are said to be imperfect because**
    a. buyers and sellers are not always well informed.
    b. most properties are alike.
    c. property is easily and quickly developed.
    d. supply always exceeds demand.

39. **The land valuation method that uses a ratio of land to improved value is called**
    a. allocation.
    b. capitalization.
    c. extraction.
    d. land residual.

40. **A rectangular parcel of land containing five acres has 600 feet of road frontage. Depth is _____ feet.**
    a. 363
    b. 495
    c. 661
    d. 726

41. **A comparable sale that sold for $102,000 requires the adjustments below. What percent is the total of gross adjustments?**

Location	+ $5,000
Condition	- $7,500
Physical Characteristics	+ $2,500

    a. 0%
    b. 4.9%
    c. 9.8%
    d. 14.7%

42. **The sales comparison approach is based on the assumption that an informed buyer would pay _____ for a property than the cost of acquiring another property of the same utility.**
    a. less
    b. no more
    c. substantially less
    d. substantially more

43. **While actual sales are preferred for the sales comparison approach, properties that have recently been listed may have some influence on an appraisal because listings indicate a(n)**
    a. lower limit of value.
    b. market preference.
    c. market value.
    d. upper limit of value.

44. **The property described below is selling for $2,700 per acre. What is the total purchase price?**

    S ½ of SW ¼ of SW ¼ of Section 6 and the N ½ of NW ¼ of Section 7

    a. $216,000
    b. $243,000
    c. $270,000
    d. $324,000

45. **In the sales comparison approach, assume Sale #1 sold for $60,000 and, in the appraiser's opinion, it is 15% superior to the subject property. What is the value of the subject?**
    a. $9,000
    b. $51,000
    c. $55,000
    d. $69,000

46. **The second bedroom of a house must be accessed through the first bedroom. This is considered**
    a. an amenity.
    b. an aversion.
    c. eminent domain.
    d. functional obsolescence.

47. **Replacement cost new and reproduction cost new are**

    a. always the same.

    b. only different in custom-built homes.

    c. only the same in new construction.

    d. only the same for historical properties.

48. **If the gross monthly rent multiplier is 180 and monthly rent is $600, what's the value of the subject?**

    a. $108,000

    b. $110,000

    c. $160,000

    d. $180,000

49. **A house rents unfurnished for $500 per month. Using the gross monthly rent multiplier method, the appraiser estimates value of the subject at $80,000. What's the monthly gross rent multiplier?**

    a. 0.16

    b. 1.60

    c. 16.0

    d. 160.0

50. **The effective age of a house has been established at 30 years. The remaining economic life is 50 years. What is the percent of depreciation?**

    a. 16.7%

    b. 26.7%

    c. 37.5%

    d. 60.0%

Real Estate Appraisal Exams Answer Key

Exam 1		
1.	a	as of the effective date of the appraisal only.
2.	d	the contract price of the property.
3.	b	income approach
4.	c	$192,000
5.	b	the most probable selling price to a typical buyer.
6.	a	amount, in dollars, actually paid for the property.
7.	d	net operating income.
8.	d	future income is always more valuable than present income.
9.	c	$34,600
10.	c	location.
11.	c	scarcity and utility
12.	d	economic, governmental, social, and physical.
13.	b	change.
14.	a	its highest and best use.
15.	d	$39,945
16.	d	all of the above
17.	d	all of the above
18.	c	increases at a decreasing rate.
19.	d	$15,300.00
20.	a	building codes, restrictions, and zoning.
21.	b	+ 1,000
22.	d	physical
23.	d	the actual age of the house.
24.	b	exterior dimensions of the dwelling, not including the garage.
25.	d	site work, foundation, framing, and rough-ins
26.	c	Ranch
27.	d	substitution
28.	a	adjust the comparable sales to the subject property.
29.	d	Seller was not knowledgeable of value.
30.	d	transaction was arm's length.
31.	c	income
32.	d	names of the previous owners
33.	a	amount a typical buyer will pay for an item.
34.	d	recent sales
35.	c	adjustment
36.	b	plat map.
37.	a	school district
38.	b	higher
39.	d	vacant site sales are often scarce.
40.	d	subdivision analysis
41.	b	2,904 square feet
42.	b	plottage comparison
43.	d	a gross rent multiplier
44.	c	$10,800 - $13,500
45.	c	market's reaction in terms of dollars.
46.	b	cost approach
47.	c	physical deterioration.
48.	d	similar building using modern materials.
49.	b	depreciated cost new of improvements to estimated site value.
50.	d	no heating source

Exam 2		
1.	b	completing a survey of the site
2.	a	footer
3.	a	school district
4.	a	an item attached to real estate for business purposes.
5.	a	$2500
6.	c	porches
7.	a	a basement recreation room
8.	d	the utility of the property, such as room layout.
9.	b	market value.
10.	c	multiply the gross rent by a multiplier.
11.	b	probable selling price.
12.	a	adjust the comparable for any impact seller paid points may have had on the sale price.
13.	a	contract
14.	b	$1,400,000
15.	c	a railroad track running along side the lot.
16.	b	income approach
17.	d	substitution
18.	a	age-life
19.	a	cost approach.
20.	d	total economic life.
21.	c	over improvement.
22.	d	sales comparison
23.	a	comparable to be adjusted accordingly.
24.	c	may have an impact on the price paid.
25.	c	sales comparison approach
26.	b	a house with five bedrooms and one bathroom
27.	d	They provide evidence of substitution and the upper limit of value.
28.	c	external obsolescence.
29.	a	changes in zoning
30.	c	2.0%
31.	d	multiply the gross rent by a multiplier.
32.	b	gross market
33.	a	contract
34.	d	value
35.	d	160
36.	c	quantity survey.
37.	b	economic life.
38.	a	buyers and sellers are not always well informed.
39.	a	allocation
40.	a	363
41.	d	14.7%
42.	b	no more
43.	d	upper limit of value.
44.	c	$270,000
45.	b	$51,000
46.	d	functional obsolescence.
47.	c	only the same in new construction.
48.	a	$108,000
49.	d	160.0
50.	c	37.5%

Glossary

Addenda Additional parts of an appraisal report. Addenda usually consist of photos of the subject house and comparables, a sketch of the subject's floor plan, a table for calculating the area of the subject, a location map, or additional necessary comments that do not fit in the space on the appraisal form.

Amenity A tangible or intangible feature that enhances and adds value to real estate.

Annexer A person who owns an item of personal property and brings it onto real property, making it a part of the real property.

Anticipation An economic principle that says value is created by the expectation of future benefits, such as profit on resale, pleasure, tax shelter, production, income, etc. Anticipation is the foundation of the income approach.

Appraisal The act or process of developing an opinion of value; an opinion of value.

Appraisal Foundation A nonprofit organization, created by the leading appraisal organizations, which is recognized as the authority for professional appraisal standards.

Appraisal Institute (AI) A professional organization for appraisers; created in 1990 by the merger of the American Institute of Real Estate Appraisers and Society of Residential Appraisers.

Appraisal Review The act or process of developing and communicating an opinion about the quality of another appraiser's work that was performed as part of an appraisal, appraisal review, or appraisal consulting assignment.

Appraiser One who is expected to perform valuation services competently and in a manner that is independent, impartial, and objective.

Appurtenance A right that goes with ownership of real property. It is usually transferred with the property, but may be sold separately. This is a legal term referring both physical and non-physical appurtenances.

Arm's Length Transaction A transaction that occurred under typical conditions in the marketplace, with each of the parties acting in their own best interests.

Assemblage The combining of two or more parcels of land into one larger parcel.

Building Codes 1. A means of setting construction standards requiring builders to use particular methods and materials. 2. Regulations establishing minimum standards for construction and materials.

Bundle of Rights All real property rights conferred with ownership, including (but not limited to) the right of use, right of enjoyment, and right of disposal.

Buyer's Market A situation in the real estate market in which buyers have a large selection of properties from which to choose (advantage to the buyer).

Capitalization An income approach technique that converts the income of a property into a value opinion through the application of either a direct capitalization rate or a factor, such as a multiplier.

Change A principle affecting value in real estate that says all factors that influence real estate—physical, economic, governmental, and social—are constantly changing and thus, the property value itself is subject to constant change.

Comparable Properties Sold properties that ideally represent the most similar market conditions, physical design and features, and market appeal as the subject property.

Competitive Market Analysis (CMA) A method of determining a recommended listing price and anticipated sale price of a property by comparing the subject property to other properties that have sold, are presently for sale, or did not sell in a given area. *Also called* **Comparative Market Analysis**.

Concrete Footers A base that a foundation sits on; must be poured on solid ground, below frost depth, and wider at the bottom than the structure to be supported.

Contract Rent What tenants are actually paying for in rent, as stated in the terms of the lease.

Cost The dollars needed to develop, produce, or build something.

Cost Approach An appraisal method that develops an indication of the value of real property by figuring the cost of building the house or other improvement on the land, minus (-) depreciation, plus (+) the value of the vacant land.

Cost Manuals Books, electronic media, and online sources that give estimated construction costs for various types of buildings in different areas of the country.

Decline The third stage a neighborhood goes through in its life cycle, when property values begin to fall as demand falls.

Deed Restriction Limitations on real property use, imposed by a former owner through language included in the deed. Deed restrictions can be in the form of **Restrictive Covenants** or **Restrictive Conditions**.

Depreciation A loss in value to property for any reason.

Direct Capitalization An income capitalization method that takes a property's single-year net operating income (or NOI) divided by a direct capitalization rate: NOI ÷ Rate = Value.

Direct Capitalization Rate A rate of return, stated as a percent, used to derive a value opinion from the anticipated net operating income a property could generate. It is used for direct capitalization in the income approach. *Also called* **Cap Rate** or **Rate**.

Economic Base The main business or industry in an area that a community uses to support and sustain itself.

Economic Life The time during which a building can be used for its intended purpose, or generate more income than is paid out for operating expenses.

Effective Age The age of a structure based on physical deterioration, functional obsolescence, or external obsolescence.

Effective Gross Income Potential gross income less (-) vacancy and collection losses.

Environmental Hazard A situation in which there is potential for harm to persons or property from conditions that exist in a property or the surrounding area.

External Obsolescence When something outside of a property's boundaries makes a property less desirable.

Fee Simple The greatest estate (ownership) one can have in real property; it is freely transferable and inheritable, and of indefinite duration, with no conditions on title. *Also called* **Fee Simple Absolute** or **Fee Title**.

FIRREA (Financial Institutions Reform, Recovery, and Enforcement Act) An act passed in 1989 as a comprehensive savings and loan bailout and preventive measure against future savings and loan insolvency. This Act of Congress recognizes USPAP as the current industry standard for appraisal, and identifies the Appraisal Foundation as the authority for professional appraisal standards.

Fixed Expenses Ongoing operating expenses that do not vary based on occupancy levels of the property (e.g., taxes, insurance).

Fixture A man-made attachment; an item of personal property that has been attached or annexed to real property in such a way that it legally becomes part of the real property. Major fixtures are called **Improvements**.

Foundation The basic structure on which the rest of the building will sit. A foundation can be **concrete slab**, **pier and beams**, **crawl space**, or **basement**.

Framing The basic load bearing skeleton of the house to which interior walls, exterior walls, and roof are attached.

Functional Obsolescence When an improvement is less desirable because of something inherent in its design.

General Data Information that covers the forces that affect property values, but are not directly related to a particular piece of property. General data covers **p**hysical, **e**conomic, **g**overnmental, and **s**ocial factors (**P-E-G-S**) and can be local or national.

Gentrification The process of rapid revitalization of properties in a neighborhood which causes current residents to be displaced.

Government Survey System A legal description for land, referencing principal meridians and base lines designated throughout the country. *Also called* **Governmental Rectangular Survey**.

Gross Adjustments The overall total of all adjustments applied regardless of whether the adjustment is applied as positive or negative.

Gross Income The estimated income a property has the potential to generate, before vacancy and collection losses and expenses.

Gross Living Area (GLA) Residential space that is finished, livable, and above grade. Garages, finished basements, and storage areas usually do not count as GLA.

Gross Monthly Rent Multiplier (GMRM) A rate of return, stated as a factor or multiplier, used to derive a value opinion from the anticipated monthly rent a property could generate. The technique takes a single month's gross rent and multiplies it by the GMRM to indicate a value conclusion: Monthly gross rent x GMRM = Value.

Growth The first stage a neighborhood goes through in its life cycle when property values rise as development activity begins and continues.

Home Inspection A visual examination of the physical structure and systems of a home.

Income Approach An appraisal method that develops an indication of the value of real property by analyzing the amount of income the property could generate using market data.

Law of Diminishing Returns An economic principle that says beyond a certain point, the added value of an additional feature, addition, repair, etc., is less than the actual cost of the item. *Also called* the **Law of Decreasing Returns**.

Law of Increasing Returns An economic principle that says the added value of an additional feature, addition, repair, etc., is more than the actual cost of the item.

Lease A contract for which one party pays the other rent in exchange for possession of real estate.

Life Estate A freehold estate that lasts only as long as a specified person lives. That person is referred to as the **life tenant** or the **measuring life**.

Location Survey The process of verifying that an improvement properly sits within the boundaries of the property and there are no encroachments from neighboring land onto the subject property.

Lot and Block A legal description used for platted property. The description states only the property's lot and block number in a particular subdivision; to find the exact location of property boundaries, the plat map for that subdivision must be consulted at the county recorder's office.

Market Price The price property sold for in an actual transaction.

Market Rent What the property could rent for in the open market if unencumbered by any lease and available.

Market Value The most probable price that a property should bring in a competitive and open market.

Matched Pair Analysis The process of developing the contributory value of specific property characteristics or features by comparing pairs of similar properties. *Also called* **Paired Data Analysis**.

Metes and Bounds A legal description that starts at an easily identifiable point of beginning (POB), then describes the property's boundaries in terms of courses (compass directions) and distances, ultimately returning to the POB.

Multiple Listing Services (MLS) A listing service whereby local member brokers agree to share listings and commissions on properties sold jointly.

Neighborhood Any constant, contiguous area that may be identified by similar characteristics or physical boundaries. Also referred to as **Market Area**.

Net Adjustments The sum of the adjustments, taking into account whether the adjustment was positive or negative.

Net Operating Income (NOI) Net income after all operating expenses have been deducted.

Nuisance Anything outside property boundaries that interferes with the right of quiet enjoyment.

Partial Interest Any interest in real property one may have, other than the full bundle of rights.

Permits Official government documents that acknowledge work a person wants to do on a property and allow it to be done.

Personal Property 1. Tangible items not permanently attached to or part of real estate. 2. Any property that is not real property. 3. Movable property not affixed to land. *Also called* **Chattel** or **Personalty**.

Pitch A roof's vertical rise in inches, divided by its horizontal span in feet.

Plat A detailed survey map of a subdivision, or other grouped lots of land, recorded in the county where the land is located. Subdivided property is often called platted property. *Also called* a **Plat Map**.

Plottage Combining two or more parcels into one, with an increase in value over the value of the two parcels individually.

Police Power The constitutional power of state and local governments to enact and enforce laws that protect the public's health, safety, morals, and general welfare.

Potential Gross Income The income that could be produced by a property in an ideal situation, with no vacancy or collection losses.

Progression A principle that says the value of a home is positively affected by the other homes in an area. Usually said about the "worst" home in the "best" area.

Property 1. The rights of ownership in an object, such as the right to use, possess, transfer, or encumber real estate. 2. Something that is owned, real or personal.

Radon Gas A naturally occurring radioactive gas that emanates from the earth; it is odorless, colorless, and tasteless but has been identified as a cancer-causing agent.

Range Lines In the government survey system, north-south lines that run parallel to principal meridians at six-mile intervals.

Real Estate The actual physical land and everything, both natural and man-made, attached to it.

Real Property Not only the physical land and everything attached to it, but also the rights of ownership (**Bundle of Rights**) in the real estate.

Reconciliation Analyzing the values derived from the different appraisal approaches to arrive at a final opinion of value.

Regression A principle that says the value of a home is negatively affected by the other homes in an area. Usually said about the "best" home in the "worst" area.

Remaining Economic Life The period of usefulness (physically, functionally, and externally) that an improvement has remaining as of the day of the appraisal.

Replacement Building the functional equivalent (substitute) of the original building using modern materials, methods, and design.

Reproduction Building an exact duplicate (replica) of the original building.

Reserves for Replacement An amount of money, considered as an operating expense, set aside for future replacement of major items, such as the roof or heating system.

Revitalization The final stage a neighborhood goes through in its life cycle when property values rise again as demand increases, resulting in increased renovation and rehabilitation. (Rapid revitalization is called **Gentrification**.)

Rough-ins Any type of interior work to a house or building that is not part of the finish work (e.g., plumbing, HVAC, electrical).

Sales Comparison Approach An appraisal method that develops an indication of the value of real property by comparing the property being appraised with other recently sold properties. Data are collected and adjustments made for differences. *Also called* **Market Approach**.

Section Part of a township, one mile by one mile square, used for the government survey system; one section equals 640 acres; 36 sections equal one township.

Seller's Market A situation in the real estate market where property offerings are scarce and buyers have fewer properties being offered on the market to choose from (advantage to the seller).

Site A parcel of land with enhancements that make it ready for a building or structure.

Specific Data Information that is relevant to the subject property itself or specific comparable properties. There are two types of specific data: **Subject Property Data (**information on the subject property site and improvements) and **Comparative Purpose Data** (information about comparable sale properties, as well as income and cost information).

Stability The second stage a neighborhood goes through in its life cycle when the area is built up to the point where there is little, if any, vacant property. *Also called* Equilibrium.

Stigmatized Property A property made undesirable to most people by a past event, often a crime or environmental hazard.

Subject Property Property for which a value opinion is sought.

Supply and Demand A law of economics that says, for all products, goods, and services, when supply exceeds demand, prices will fall and when demand exceeds supply, prices will rise.

Survey The process of locating and measuring the boundaries of a property and identifying the improvements, encroachments, and easements associated with that land.

Transactional Brokerage An arrangement allowed in some states in which a licensee serves as a facilitator to assist in the timely and accurate conclusion of a sales transaction but does not act as an agent for either party. Also called Nonagency.

Townships Square divisions of land, six miles by six miles, in the government survey system. One township contains 36 sections.

Trade Fixture Personal property that a tenant or current owner installs for use in his trade or business that can be removed by the tenant before the lease expires or that the owner can remove prior to transfer.

Uniform Residential Appraisal Report (URAR) A standard appraisal report form used by lenders and appraisers; developed and approved by secondary mortgage market participants Fannie Mae and Freddie Mac.

Value The amount of goods or services offered in the marketplace in exchange for something else.

Variable Expenses Operating expenses necessary to the property, but typically dependent on the property's occupancy level.

Zoning laws Local ordinances dividing a city, county, etc., into zones, specifying different types of land use and requirements in different areas. This is a type of government restriction via police power.

Appendix

CMA SUPPLEMENT

What Is a Competitive Market Analysis?

A competitive market analysis (CMA) is a method of determining a recommended listing price and anticipated sale price of a property by comparing the subject property to other properties that have sold, are presently for sale, or did not sell in a given area. This is also called a comparative market analysis. A CMA is typically performed by a real estate professional. Properties are identified in the subject's marketplace based on similar characteristics that are shared with the subject property. These properties are chosen for comparison because they will attract similar buyers as the subject property. Remember, though, a CMA is not an appraisal. They may seem similar, but there are distinct differences. Let's compare the two.

How Are a CMA and an Appraisal Different?

The typical CMA may seem like an abbreviated version of the sales comparison approach found in an appraisal. A common format for reporting a CMA consists of a table of facts comparing features of the subject property to a series of comparable properties. The purpose is for the real estate agent to assist buyers or sellers by providing a range of probable selling prices for the subject property. This is done by comparing the subject property to other similar properties in the area.

 Remember: The CMA looks not only at houses that have sold in the area, but also at homes currently for sale and homes that didn't sell.

An important distinction between a CMA and an appraisal is that the CMA doesn't go into as much detail as a sales comparison approach in an appraisal would. A CMA compares only the primary features of the properties when identifying comparables. Size and style are two of the more important criteria in a typical CMA. Size compares lot size, square footage of the houses, and room counts. Style looks at number of stories, construction, and other visible attributes.

The CMA primarily focuses on the observable differences between properties that would draw a buyer to one property over another. If the subject property is lacking a significant feature that's present in the comparables, the agent may suggest a lower price to attract buyers to the property. But if a feature is present in the subject property that is not in any comparables, then a higher price may suggested, anticipating that potential buyers may be motivated by that feature. A CMA is much less detailed than an appraisal, but it can still provide useful information to sellers who need to know how to price and position their property in the market place, and buyers who need to decide how much to offer for a property.

Which Properties Should Be Considered?

As a general rule, a CMA should consider all properties that have been exposed to the market—typically during a more recent period of time. This could vary by market and/or property type. Properties to be examined should include:

- **Current offerings**—Properties currently listed for sale in the market, both from the multiple listing service (MLS) and any properties For Sale By Owner (FSBO)—the subject's potential competition

- **Sold offerings**—Properties that have sold (often within the past six months or one year) in the market and area where the subject is located
- **Expired offerings**—Properties where the listing agreements have expired because the property was not sold during the listing period
- **Withdrawn offerings**—Properties that were taken off the market

Why Consider Properties That Didn't Sell?

Properties that didn't sell can often provide more useful information to a real estate professional and prospective buyers or sellers than properties currently for sale. This is because the market's reaction to the property has already been determined. If a property didn't sell at a certain price after being tested on the market, that is most often a strong indication the property was overpriced, didn't have the features desired by the marketplace, or there was an oversupply of properties in the market. Regardless, the property has been tested on the market and potential buyers were not interested in the property at that price. Real estate experts agree that price can overcome any condition of a property. Thus, the indication here is the property should have been priced lower, and the subject (assuming the subject is comparable to the property that did not sell) should be priced lower as well, in order to attract buyers and market activity.

A seller may still insist on pricing his property higher—and perhaps this can be justified if the subject property has features or characteristics superior to the properties that did not sell—but the market has spoken. Marketing time is also a factor in pricing. The more a property is listed above what the market indicates it should be listed for, the longer it will take to sell the property. This will be discussed later in this supplement.

Can't I Just Look At Properties That Sold?

The next obvious question is: "Why can't I just look at properties that have sold?" The assumption is that if a property sold, then it must have been priced correctly. While this logic appears sound, it's not complete:

- It's possible there was a unique buyer who desired or needed a particular property or who was under duress to purchase something quickly, so an individual sale cannot be used to justify the price of the subject property.
- It is impossible to know all of the factors that went into an individual buying decision.
- The competition that existed in the marketplace at that time cannot be determined only by looking at properties that sold.
- The entire market must be considered to arrive at the best price for the subject property.

What Is a "Whole Market" Approach?

The "whole market" approach refers to a method of completing a CMA that considers sold, current, expired, and withdrawn offerings. Because of this, it is the most reliable method of performing a CMA. It provides the real estate agent and those who will rely on the indications produced by a CMA more complete information.

For Example

A real estate agent was making a recommendation to a seller regarding a property's listing price. The agent looked at four current listings and five listings sold in the prior six months. The price recommendation was made based on this analysis. The price was at the high end of the range, but deemed acceptable because it fell within the range.

After several weeks, and no showings, the seller was upset. It turns out the price was too high after all. The real estate agent had not considered the whole market. Examining the whole market revealed:

- 18 active listings
- 6 listings sold in past six months—average days on market: 125
- 12 listings expired in past six months—average days on market: 180
- 2 withdrawn or canceled listings in past six months

Upon examination of the whole market, the real estate agent realized the listing price was too high. But it was too late. The seller did not relist the property with the real estate agent (when the listing agreement expired) and listed with another real estate brokerage.

Days On Market (DOM)

In the previous example, you can also see another important reason for looking at the whole market. By looking at the days on market (DOM) for each of the properties examined in the CMA, you can observe how long the subject property might take to sell. You also need to consider the total number of competing properties currently for sale as an indication of the current supply and demand situation in the marketplace.

With only six comparable listings sold in the last 125-180 days (about one listing sold per month), it would take about 18 months for the market to absorb the 18 listings currently on the market. If the seller wants a property sold sooner, a more aggressive pricing strategy (e.g., lower price) should be considered to make the property more competitive and attractive in the marketplace.

How Much Weight Should Be Given To Properties Currently For Sale?

From the previous example, it looks as if current listings should receive the most attention. In fact, with a CMA, active listings are given significant emphasis from the standpoint of competition. Sold properties provide an indication of what property in the area might sell for, but the subject property's competition will be other properties currently for sale. The subject property has to be viewed from the perspective of a typical buyer.

Prospective buyers usually look at many properties before arriving at a decision. A competitive and favorably priced property will attract more buyers. If the property is at or exceeding the high end of the range indicated by the CMA without justification, the market will dismiss the property as being overpriced—buyers will move on to the competition, which may be more reasonably priced.

How to Present a CMA

There are several ways a real estate agent can present a CMA to prospective buyers or sellers. Often, a successful presentation will include ample facts and data. The presentation and style of a CMA can vary depending on a particular market and the particular tools available to the real estate professional to complete the CMA. There are numerous technology-based CMA applications available to real estate professionals.

Regardless, the facts and data used for the CMA would likely be presented in some sort of comparison grid.

The primary points of comparison in most CMAs are:

* Location
* Style
* Size (building and lot)
* Age
* Property details, features, and condition

A summary of how to interpret the information being examined is also included An interpretation of the market could be shown as follows :

SOLD PROPERTIES:
★ ★★★★   ★
$100K $110K $120K $130K

ACTIVE PROPERTIES:
★★★★   ★
$100K $110K $120K $130K

EXPIRED PROPERTIES:
★★★   ★★
$100K $110K $120K $130K

In this type of diagram, each star would represent a comparable property that was active, sold, or expired. The star's position would indicate the price point at which the indicated market activity took place. In this case, the visual helps the buyer or seller see that a price range of $100,000-110,000 is probably most realistic for the property. Additional supporting data, such as closing assistance or allowances that were, or are being offered, could help narrow the suggested price even further.

COMPETITIVE MARKET ANALYSIS

SUBJECT

ADDRESS	STYLE	BDRMS	BATHS	BSMT/FIN	FEATURES	AGE	CONDITION

COMPETING PROPERTIES

ADDRESS	STYLE	BDRMS	BATHS	BSMT/FIN	FEATURES	AGE	CONDITION	DOM	PRICE

SOLD PROPERTIES

ADDRESS	STYLE	BDRMS	BATHS	BSMT/FIN	FEATURES	AGE	CNDTN	DOM	SALE DATE	LISTED PRICE	SALE PRICE	FNNC

OFFERED, BUT DID NOT SELL

ADDRESS	STYLE	BDRMS	BATHS	BSMT/FIN	FEATURES	AGE	CNDTN	DOM	FINAL LIST PRICE

VALUE RANGE INDICATED _____ TO _____   ASKING PRICE RANGE _____ TO _____

CONSTRUCTION AND HOME INSPECTION SUPPLEMENT

Parts of Houses

All parts of a house are important. Other than the interior decor, each serves a useful function. We previously discussed some of the different types and styles of roofs commonly seen on homes. Let's build on that by identifying other parts of a house with the correct terminology.

The exterior is important to a home's strength, insulation, and weatherproofing. Windows provide a means of letting light in and keeping cold air out. Doors provide a means of security, entry, and insulation on the outside, and privacy on the inside. Let's look at the parts of a house, their types and terminology, starting with home exteriors, then looking at some common types of windows and doors.

Home Exteriors

Home exterior materials can contribute greatly to the look and value of a home. Materials are chosen for their ability to stand up to the elements, to protect the house, and keep it looking good with a minimum of maintenance.

Vinyl siding is a very common type of siding. It is popular because it is relatively inexpensive and easy to maintain. Vinyl siding typically needs some type of backing or insulation board before it can be installed over stud walls (see illustration on the next page). Vinyl can also be installed over existing house siding. Vinyl does not dent like aluminum siding can, and the finish and color are molded into the material so there is no need to worry about the finish wearing off, but it can fade in the sun. Vinyl can also crack from severe cold weather or a hard thrown baseball, but typically vinyl siding can last 25 years or so.

Aluminum siding is a common type of siding on older homes. Aluminum can also be installed over existing house siding. Aluminum siding typically needs some type of backing or insulation board before it can be installed (see illustration on the next page). In addition to being relatively inexpensive, aluminum is easy to maintain. The main drawback to aluminum is that it can dent easily and will need to be painted after the factory finish wears off in about 10-15 years.

Wood siding (also called **lapped siding**) is common on existing homes because it is tough, economical and enhances the appearance of a home. New homes that want an early American look may also turn to wood siding. It is more expensive than vinyl or aluminum, and will last longer, but needs regular maintenance and painting. Wood siding also adds insulating value that aluminum and vinyl do not.

Wood shakes and **wood shingles** are popular choices for homes, but are more expensive than wood siding. Wood shakes and shingles are often put over wood surfaces—hardboards or existing wood siding. Wood shakes are rough and have an irregular finish; wood shingles are milled and appear more regular and orderly on a house. Popular choices for wood are cedar or redwood. The wood can be left natural, stained, or painted. With some maintenance, wood can last 50 years or more.

Plywood (made of thin layers of wood glued together) and **hardboard panels** (made of pressed and glued wood fibers—e.g., particle board or wafer board) are cheaper than other types of wood siding. These boards add strength to a home and can be installed rather quickly on top of bare stud walls, but are not as durable as other types of siding.

EXTERIOR PARTS

1. Flashing
2. Fascia
3. Eaves
4. Soffit
5. Siding
6. Lintel
7. Foundation
8. Gutter
9. Downspout
10. Gable
11. Corner Board
12. Porch
13. Shed Roof
14. Post
15. Double Hung Window
16. Window Frame
17. Window Sash
18. Sill
19. Door

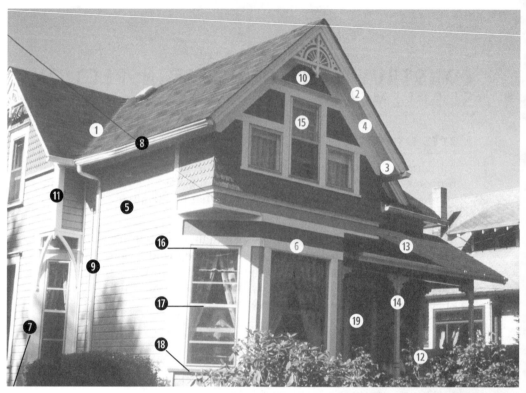

INTERIOR PARTS

1. Rafters
2. Studs
3. Beam or Girder
4. Joists
5. Header
6. Bearing Wall
7. Sheathing
8. Drywall, Plasterboard, or Wallboard
9. Basement/Crawlspace
10. Foundation Wall
11. Footer (below grade of foundation wall)
12. Subfloor
13. Sill Plate

They can be painted, but are often used as a backing for other types of exterior siding materials.

Stucco is a popular material used to cover houses. Stucco is durable because it has no seams to let water or moisture in, but can crack from repeated freeze-thaw cycles. Stucco can be applied over masonry block walls or over hardboard siding with wire mesh. It gives a good outward appearance at about half the cost of brick.

Brick and stone veneer sidings are the most expensive types of siding. They are arguably the most attractive and the most durable. Brick and stone are easy to maintain—even cleaning is not necessary. Older brick and stone exteriors may show signs of deterioration from the weather and water. If older brick has missing or crumbling mortar joints, they must be replaced with new mortar by a process called **tuckpointing**. Brick can be painted if desired, but then must be repainted when the paint starts to peel. New brick or stone walls need some type of backing and wire lath before being installed over stud walls or concrete block walls (see illustration below).

ALUMINUM OR VINYL SIDING

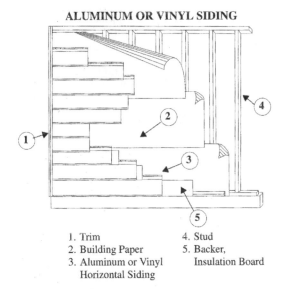

1. Trim
2. Building Paper
3. Aluminum or Vinyl Horizontal Siding
4. Stud
5. Backer, Insulation Board

BRICK OR STONE VENEER

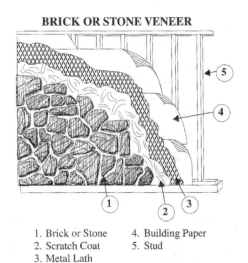

1. Brick or Stone
2. Scratch Coat
3. Metal Lath
4. Building Paper
5. Stud

Illustrations from Marshall & Swift's *Home Repair & Remodel Cost Guide 1997*, © 1997. Used with permission.

Typical exterior wall systems.

Windows

Windows provide beauty to a home, let light in, and keep cold out. Several types of windows appear below, along with common window parts. Single-hung windows have only one sash that moves vertically; double-hung windows have two sashes that move vertically; casement windows swing out right or left.

Common window materials are wood, vinyl, and aluminum. Wood is the best insulator, but needs upkeep so vinyl clad windows are an alternative. **Low-E glass (low-emissivity glass)** coated windows block summer heat wavelengths and trap winter sunlight. **Gas filled** windows have gas between panes to act as an insulator. The window type, material, features, and manufacturer may be noted in an appraisal.

Doors

Doors provide entry, security, and privacy. In addition to standard exterior doors, there are sliding glass doors, storm doors, and screen doors. Interior doors are passage doors between rooms, and passage, bi-fold, or bypass doors for closets.

WINDOW TYPES

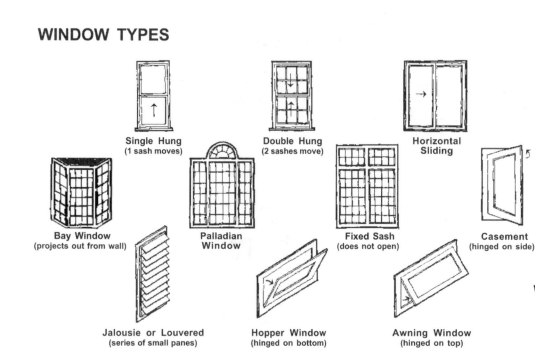

Single Hung
(1 sash moves)

Double Hung
(2 sashes move)

Horizontal
Sliding

Bay Window
(projects out from wall)

Palladian
Window

Fixed Sash
(does not open)

Casement
(hinged on side)

Jalousie or Louvered
(series of small panes)

Hopper Window
(hinged on bottom)

Awning Window
(hinged on top)

Illustrations from the *Old Building Owner's Manual*, Judith L. Kitchen, © 1983, published by the Ohio Historic Preservation Office of the Ohio Historical Society.

WINDOW PARTS

1. Lintel or Header
2. Top Rail
3. Jamb
4. Frame
5. Stile
6. Meeting Rail
7. Light (one pane of glass)
8. Mullions
9. Muntins
10. Bottom Rail
11. Sash
12. Sill

This double hung window is referred to as a 6/6 (six over six) window because there are 6 lights in the top sash and 6 lights in the bottom sash.

DOOR TYPES

Six Panel Door

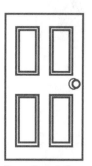

Four Panel Door

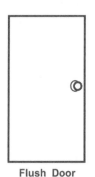

Flush Door

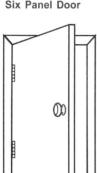

Right Hand Door

Door knob is on the right side when door opens toward you.

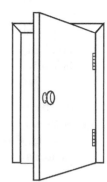

Left Hand Door

Door knob is on the left side when door opens toward you.

DOOR PARTS

1. Door
2. Lockset
3. Header/Top Casing
4. Casing or Trim
5. Jamb
6. Strike Plate
7. Door Stop
8. Door Frame
9. Stile
10. Rail
11. Panel
12. Threshold (exterior door)

Hinges are not shown in this diagram. Typically, hinges and strike plates are mortised. (A groove is cut so that they sit flush with the frame.)

Exterior doors can be solid wood, hollow wood (with insulating material inside), or metal (exterior metal sheets with supports and insulation inside). Interior doors can be solid wood, hollow core (wood), or formed particle board (hollow, imitating wood designs). **Lauan** (a wood originally from the Philippines) is popular for interior doors because it is lightweight and inexpensive. Many new doors can be bought **pre-hung**: The door comes already mounted on the hinges in the door frame.

Systems of Houses

There are three basic systems in a house:

*   Electrical
*   Plumbing
*   Heating

These are typically referred to as the "mechanicals" of a house.

Electrical System

The electrical system of a house is comprised of several elements, which include such things as the wiring, distribution box, circuit breaker box, circuit breakers, fuses, lights and lighting fixtures, light switches, and wall outlets. Standard electric service in the U.S. calls for a minimum of 100 amps and 110 volts for normal usage. Both of these can be higher, and for some types of appliances or equipment, they must be higher.

For Example

Many clothes dryers require a special line carrying 220 volts of electricity. Actually, most homes have 220 volts running to the home, but it is split in half at the distribution box to provide multiple 110 volt lines. By combining these lines, 220 volt service is achieved when needed.

As a real estate agent or appraiser, it's probably a good idea to at least open the distribution box or circuit breaker box to check for obvious signs of trouble. This is not intended to replace a home inspection, and agents and appraisers should never pass themselves off as experts, but they would be doing buyers a great service if they persuaded them to get a home inspection because they saw something that they knew didn't look right. Some of these warning signs are patched wiring in the box, sparks or light flashes, sounds coming from any part of the electrical system (including hums), and any part of the electrical system (including a cord) that is warm or hot to the touch. Additional warning signs are installed fuses that are rated higher than the amp capacity of a circuit, and lights that flicker when additional lights or devices are turned on.

Plumbing System

The plumbing system of a house is comprised of several elements, which include such things as the piping, drains, clean outs, vents, valves, faucets, sinks, toilets, tubs, showers, and hot water tank (gas or electric). The piping includes all supply lines (cold water), hot water lines, and waste water lines (sewer lines).

 Often, gas lines are also included as part of the plumbing system.

It's important to understand that supply lines carry water under pressure from the source. Hot water tanks are specially designed to retain this pressure when delivering hot water. Waste water lines, on the other hand, rely on gravity to move waste into the sewer. That's why vents are so important. Not only do they let sewer gases escape from the house, they also allow atmospheric pressure to come in and push waste water down the pipes (sewer pipes must be sloped according to code).

Although washing machines and dishwashers are connected to the plumbing, they are generally not included as part of the "plumbing system." Their valves, connections, and drains may be checked for leaks, but these machines are not routinely inspected except as "other mechanicals" or "other systems" (garbage disposals may or may not be included as well).

As a real estate agent or appraiser, it's probably a good idea to at least check the various plumbing fixtures to make sure that they work. Again, this is not intended to replace a home inspection and agents and appraisers should never pass themselves off as experts, but they would be doing buyers a great service if they persuaded them to get a home inspection because they saw something that wasn't right. Some of the things to look for are faucets that leak, drains that leak, toilets that don't flush properly, drains that are slow, drains that have odors emanating from them, drains that gurgle or make other noises as they empty, and excessive putty on fixtures or pipe joints. Additional warning signs are lack of water pressure when multiple faucets are turned on and/or a toilet is flushed, corroded fixtures or pipes, and lead pipes.

Heating System

The heating system of a house is comprised of several elements, including such things as a furnace or heat pump, flue, ducts and ductwork, registers, and thermostat. Depending on the type of fuel the system uses, there may also be electrical connections, gas lines, or oil/fuel storage. For houses with air conditioners, the air conditioning system is generally lumped together as part of the heating system because they usually share a common ductwork system. In fact, it's common to refer to all of these system components collectively as **heating and cooling systems** or **HVAC (**heating, ventilation, and air-conditioning**) systems**. "Ventilation" is added to the mix because the systems can also provide fresh air and cleaned air to the house as they circulate the heated or cooled air. In fact, indoor air quality (IAQ) is becoming a hot topic. In addition to standard filters, electronic filters and static filters are cleaning indoor air better than ever.

What Size Furnace or Air-Conditioner?

Determining the correct size of furnace or air conditioner that a house needs can be a difficult task—even for a professional. That's because some of the variables are unknowns. Not only must the size of the house be taken into consideration, but also the number of windows, type of foundation, amount of ventilation, and the biggest unknown—how well the house is insulated. What needs to be determined for a furnace is how fast heat moves out of the house. A furnace is chosen so that it can replace lost heat, and keep a house at the desired temperature.

For Example

Let's assume that we have a "normal" 2,000 square foot house, and it has been determined that it loses about 60,000 **BTUs** per hour. **BTU** (**British Thermal Unit**) is *the common measurement of heating capacity*. A **BTU** *is the amount of heat needed to raise the temperature of one pound of water by one degree Fahrenheit*. Since the example home is losing heat at a rate of 60K BTUs/hour, we could install a 60K BTU furnace—but then the furnace would have to run constantly. Instead, HVAC specialists will add 20-30% to their estimates. So, here, the house could comfortably have an 80K BTU furnace installed. Since 60K divided by 80K equals 75%, the furnace would run about 75% of the time.

Air-conditioning calculations are different than those for a furnace because additional factors are taken into account. And since heat rises and tries to escape, a less powerful air-conditioner is needed. As a general rule, every 500-1,000 square feet of living area needs one ton of air-conditioning capacity. Thus, a "normal" 2,000 square foot home could be cooled adequately by a two-ton air-conditioner.

 One ton equals 12,000 BTUs.

Types of Furnaces

There are two basic ways that central furnaces can distribute heat to the house. A **forced air furnace** has a fan or blower that moves the air through the ductwork. A **gravity furnace** relies on the natural phenomenon of heat rising to distribute it. Additional types of heat sources can include wall furnaces, electric baseboard heating units and wood burning stoves. An appraiser may need to make adjustments to the value of a home if the primary heat source is from something other than a central furnace.

Heat Pumps

Electric heat pumps are an alternative to traditional heating and cooling systems. With heat pumps, the same unit provides heat in the winter and cooled air in the summer. There are advantages and disadvantages to the system. The main advantages are that it uses energy more efficiently than a furnace that burns fuel, and that only one unit is needed instead of two. The main disadvantages are that it can be more expensive to obtain and operate than a furnace, and heat pumps aren't effective when temperatures drop below freezing for extended periods.

Other Non-System Items

Although window air-conditioners, space heaters, and fireplaces produce some of the same results as the HVAC system, these items are not included as part of the HVAC system. They are generally considered separate items for inspection purposes.

As a real estate agent or appraiser, it is probably a good idea to at least play with the thermostat to see if the furnace and/or air-conditioner are operable. This is not intended to replace a home inspection, and agents and appraisers should never pass themselves off as experts, but they would be doing buyers a great service if they persuaded them to get a home inspection because they found something that didn't seem to work right. Some of these warning signs are a furnace that runs constantly instead of cycling on and off with the temperature in the room, and loud noises coming from the ductwork—especially a bang after the furnace cycles off. This could indicate that the furnace does not have an adequate cold air return, and is trying to suck more air. Both of these problems may be symptoms that the furnace is undersized or overworked. Additional warning signs could be furnaces that look old, or that have old inspection dates written on them. Also, a furnace that is dirty or old and worn can give off carbon monoxide gas. The gas is a silent killer and should be checked for by an expert.

Other Systems

There are other systems that play a role in maintaining a properly functioning home. These include the roof, foundation, drainage, and may include other items such as appliances, a fireplace, a security system, or the telephone system. Some of these are of more concern to home buyers than others. Many of them are inspected during a home inspection (but may cost an extra fee).

Home Inspection

A **home inspection** is *a visual examination of the physical structure and systems of a home.* The home inspector is inspecting the house for quality and condition. Our discussion here of home inspections is the culmination of everything we discussed in Chapter 7. To be a good home inspector, one needs to have knowledge of the building process, building codes, parts of a home, and systems of a home. A home inspection will cover many areas of the home: Roof, mechanicals, and the foundation. It is different than a building inspection because the home inspector is not necessarily looking for code compliance. Code deficiencies will be pointed out, but this is not the primary focus of a home inspection since older homes do not necessarily have to be brought up to code.

The home inspection is geared towards finding items that are dangerous, items that are damaged, and items that don't work. The purpose of a home inspection is not to find every possible imperfection in the home—even new homes have imperfections. By concentrating on potential problems, the home inspection is trying to help a home buyer (or owner) make intelligent choices. Homes cannot "fail" a home inspection. The purpose of the home inspection is information and discovery. Upon completion of a home inspection, the buyer/ owner should know what:

- Repairs need to be done immediately
- Potential future repairs may be needed
- Are the repair priorities
- Major/minor repairs are recommended
- Preventive maintenance steps are recommended
- Significant deficiencies are in the home
- Are the risks of hidden damage
- Conditions are unsafe
- Areas may warrant further investigation

Professional Home Inspections

Professional home inspections can be performed by anyone who claims to be skilled in the area. This is where potential problems can arise, both in the quality of the inspection and in the area of liability. Let's look at each of these.

Quality Inspection

The best way to obtain a quality inspection is to use someone with a good reputation in the area. This can be done simply by asking around among other home owners, real estate agents, or brokers. A person can also seek out home inspectors that have some sort of certification or belong to a professional organization. This may indicate a level of training or expertise, and means that the inspector is adhering to the organization's guidelines and ethics.

The American Society of Home Inspectors® (ASHI) is the oldest and leading non-profit professional association for independent home inspectors. ASHI members must pass two written technical exams and perform at least 250 home inspections, plus obtain continuing education credits. Several other associations also exist.

A person might also choose to have an engineer inspect a home. The National Academy of Building Inspection Engineers (NABIE) is a non-profit, professional society which accepts as members only state-registered professional engineers specializing in the practice of building inspections. In addition to standard home inspection analysis, licensed engineers are also allowed to evaluate overall structural soundness and mechanical system adequacy as of the date of the inspection.

Potential Liability

A home inspection is generally not warranted, and does not provide any type of guarantee on the items or systems inspected. The home inspector provides a report to the buyer or home owner stating the condition as of the date of the inspection. Typically, though, a home owner can obtain a home warranty, purchased by buyer or seller, at closing. A home inspection company may offer this or make a referral, or the broker can refer the home owner to a home warranty company.

Where liability can become an issue, though, is if people pass themselves off as home inspectors, or others believe that they are home inspectors and rely on their opinion. Such misrepresentation or misunderstanding can get a person into serious trouble if a major defect in a home is missed. That's why it is very important for real estate agents to be careful so as not to be perceived as giving home inspection advice. The only advice that a real estate agent should give to potential buyers (or to sellers) is to urge them to have their own professional home inspection done.

Liability can also be a problem for home inspectors if they miss a serious problem with a home. Since home inspectors hold themselves out as having a higher level of competence, they are held to a higher standard of culpability. A home inspection must be thorough to avoid these types of problems.

Areas Covered By a Home Inspection

A thorough home inspection covers the areas discussed in this chapter, and more. From the roof to the foundation, and all parts and systems in between, home inspections are designed to let buyers know what they're getting into. A standard ASHI home inspection includes a visual inspection and written report on all home systems (heating, air-conditioning, plumbing, and electrical); the foundation, basement, and visible structure; the roof (including gutters and downspouts), attic, and visible insulation; windows and doors; interior and exterior walls; and floors and ceilings.

Other items that are usually inspected as part of a home inspection include garages, sidewalks and driveways, cabinets and countertops, appliances, fireplaces, security systems, and telephone systems.

 Some of these items may add to the standard fee.

Most inspectors also offer additional tests (often at additional cost) for wells, septic systems, drinking water, air quality, termites, lead, radon, and any number of other items.

APPENDIX 2: EXPLODED HOUSE DIAGRAM

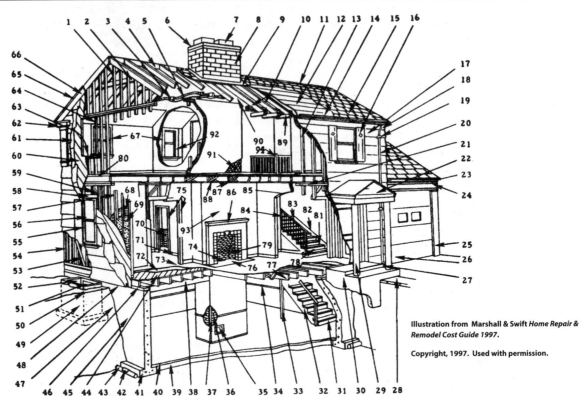

Illustration from Marshall & Swift *Home Repair & Remodel Cost Guide 1997.*

Copyright, 1997. Used with permission.

1. Gable Stud
2. Collar Beam
3. Ceiling Joist
4. Ridgeboard
5. Insulation
6. Chimney Cap
7. Chimney Pot
8. Chimney
9. Chimney Flashing
10. Rafters
11. Ridge
12. Roof Boards
13. Stud
14. Eave Trough/Gutter
15. Roofing
16. Blind/Shutter
17. Bevel Siding
18. Downspout Neck
19. Downspout Strap
20. Downspout
21. Double Plate
22. Entrance Canopy
23. Garage Cornice
24. Frieze

25. Door Jamb
26. Garage Door
27. Downspout Shoe
28. Sidewalk
29. Entrance Post
30. Entrance Platform
31. Stair Riser (Bsmt)
32. Stair Stringer
33. Girder Post
34. Chair Rail
35. Cleanout Door
36. Furring Strip
37. Corner Stud
38. Girder
39. Cinder, Gravel Fill
40. Concrete Floor
41. Footing
42. Tarpaper Strip
43. Drain Tile
44. Diag. Subflooring
45. Foundation Wall
46. Mudsill
47. Backfill
48. Termite Shield

49. Areaway Wall
50. Grade Line
51. Basement Sash
52. Areaway
53. Corner Brace
54. Corner Studs
55. Window Frame
56. Window Light
57. Wall Studs
58. Header
59. Window Cripple
60. Wall Sheathing
61. Building Paper
62. Frieze Board
63. Rough Header
64. Cripple Stud
65. Cornice Molding
66. Fascia Board
67. Window Casing
68. Lath
69. Insulation
70. Wainscoting
71. Baseboard
72. Building Paper

73. Finish Floor
74. Ash Dump
75. Door Trim
76. Fireplace Hearth
77. Floor Joists
78. Stair Riser
79. Fire Brick
80. Sole Plate
81. Stair Tread
82. Finish Stringer
83. Stair Rail
84. Balusters
85. Plaster Arch
86. Mantel
87. Floor Joist
88. Bridging
89. Lookout
90. Attic Space
91. Metal Lath
92. Window Sash
93. Chimney Breast
94. Newel Post

APPRAISAL MATH SUPPLEMENT

Lot and Land Measurements

There are four measurements necessary to understand in regard to appraisal work:

1. Front feet (frontage)
2. Square feet
3. Acreage
4. Mile

Front Feet

*Also known as **frontage**, the linear dimension across the access side of a parcel of land.* In a measurement, front feet is always the *first* number. This measures the portion of the lot that faces the street.

Example:

If a lot measures 250' x 200', what is the amount of frontage?

Since the first number is **250'**, that is the amount of frontage.

Square Feet

*The area of a parcel, calculated as **length x width**.*

This is a very simple calculation for squares or rectangles.

Example #1

If a lot measures 250' x 200', what is the area of the land?

250 x 200 = **50,000 square feet**

Example #2

What is total area of these two lots combined?

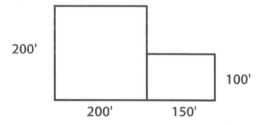

Calculate the area of each rectangle separately, then add them together.

200 x 200 = 40,000   150 x 100 = 15,000

40,000 + 15,000 = **55,000 square feet total for the combined parcels**.

Acreage

There are 43,560 square feet in an acre.

To calculate acreage, first calculate the square feet of the lot, then divide that number by 43,560.

Example

If a lot measures 220' x 396', what is the amount of acreage?

First, determine the area of the lot by multiplying 220 x 396 = 87,120.

Next, divide that result by 43,560: 87,120 ÷ 43,560 = 2 acres.

A lot that measures 220' x 100' is being sold for $88,000. Calculate the price per front foot, price per square foot, and price per acre.

Step #1: Calculate price per front foot by dividing price by frontage.

$88,000 ÷ 220 = $400 per front foot

Step #2: Calculate the price per square foot by first calculating the area of the lot (length x width), then divide price by lot size.

220 x 100 = 22,000 square feet of lot area

$88,000 ÷ 22,000 = $4 per square foot

Step #3: Calculate price per acre by dividing the area of the lot by 43,560, then dividing price by lot acreage.

Cost per acre: 220 x 100 = 22,000 square feet of lot area

22,000 ÷ 43,560 = 0.505050 acres

$88,000 ÷ 0.505050 = **$174,240.17 per acre**

In this last calculation, note the price per acre is *greater* than the price of the lot because the lot is smaller than one acre.

Mile

There are 5,280 feet in a mile.

Very often, the road frontage of a parcel might be stated as a percent or fraction of a mile.

Example

If a parcel of land is 1/8 of a mile by 250', how many acres are in the parcel?

Step #1: Find the frontage of the parcel in feet.

5,280' ÷ 8 = 660'

Step #2: Calculate the total square feet of the parcel.

660' x 250' = 165,000 square feet

Step #3: Determine the acres in the parcel.

165,000 ÷ 43,560 = **3.7879 acres**

Extra Problems

1. A commercial lot is priced at $1,800 per front foot. If the lot measures 170' x 550', what is the price of the lot?

2. If the same lot is priced at $2.75 per square foot, calculate the price of the lot.

3. What is the price of a parcel of land selling for $ 9,000 per acre and that is a quarter mile squared?

Gross Living Area (GLA) Calculations

To review, **gross living area (GLA)** is *residential space that is finished, heated, and above grade.* Garages and spaces below grade are specifically excluded.

This means garages, finished basements, and storage areas should typically not be counted as part of the total GLA. Finished attics may count as GLA if they have heat and electricity, finished walls, and normal ceiling height. Square footage is always calculated by using the *outside* dimensions of the structure—the building costs need to include the outside walls as well. For residential property, non-living areas (e.g., garage space, screened-in porch, etc.,) are always subtracted from the outer building dimension totals when calculating square footage.

When calculating square footage, there are two formulas you need to know: One for the area of a square or rectangle, and one for the area of a triangle.

SQUARE or RECTANGLE—length x width

area = length x width

area = l x w

TRIANGLE—one half x base x height

area = 1/2 x base x height

area = 1/2 x b x h

Apply these formulas to each part of the structure until you have calculated its entire square footage. Remember that all measurements *must* be in the same units—feet, inches, etc.,—before starting any calculations.

Example 1

A house being appraised has the following layout. The measurements of the exterior walls are indicated in the diagram below.

What is the gross living area?

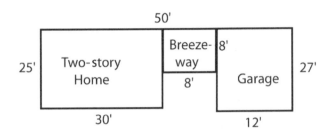

Step #1: Calculate the area of the house using length x width.

Do *not* count the area of the breezeway or garage.

First floor area: 30' x 25' = 750 square feet

Step #2: Multiply the first floor area by 2 to account for the area of the second story.

Total floor area: 750' x 2' = **1,500 square feet**.

Example 2

Calculate the cost to build the following structure if cost manuals set the cost at $9.81 per square foot.

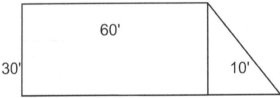

Step #1: Calculate the area of the building using length x width for the rectangular portion, and 1/2 x base x height for the triangular portion. Since there is no indication of building usage, assume that all parts use the same cost.

Rectangular area: 30' x 60' = 1,800 square feet

Triangular area: 1/2 x 10' x 30' = 150 square feet

Step #2: Add both parts for the total area, and then multiply the total by the cost of the building given in the problem.

Total area: 1,800' + 150' = 1,950 square feet

Total cost: 1,950' x $9.81 = **$19,129.50**

Extra Problems

1. Calculate the cost of building a structure that is 120' x 75', if the cost is $11.25 per square foot.

2. A warehouse that is 700' x 300' can be built for a cost of $8.00 per square foot, but part of that space is a 100' x 100' office area that will cost $12.75 per square foot. What is the total building cost?

Cubic Foot Calculations

Sometimes, certain types of building area, such as a warehouse, might be stated by cubic feet. Calculation of cubic feet is also often required for state examinations. This method of determining the gross building area will be used when the height of an area is relative to utility.

Calculations for a cube are similar to the calculation for gross living area and gross building area, except the height of the structure is also used in the calculation.

area = length x width x height

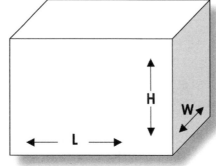

Example

A storage warehouse is 100' long, 75' wide, and 22' tall. What is area of the building in cubic feet?

100' x 75' x 22' = **165,000 cubic feet**

Extra Problems

1. What is the length of a building that has 15,000 cubic feet if the height is 15' and the width is 20'?

2. A building is being constructed for $4.80 per cubic foot. The building is 18' tall and contains 1,250 square feet. What is the cost of the building?

Calculating Sections

The **government survey system** is a type of legal description for land that references principal meridians and base lines designated throughout much of the country. This is also called the **rectangular survey system** or **military survey** system. This system divides land into six-mile-square townships, which are further divided into sections. A particular parcel of land is identified by directions and coordinates within these sections.

It is important to remember that there are 640 acres in a section.

Example 1

Find the amount of acreage in the S 1/2 of the NW 1/4 of a section.

Since an entire section of land always contains 640 acres, start with 640 and divide by the denominators (bottom number) of each fractional part in the description, starting with the last number.

640 ÷ 4 ÷ 2 = **80 acres in the S 1/2 of the NW 1/4 of the section**.

Example 2

Locate the S 1/2 of the NW 1/4 of a section.

Since the indicated area is located in the NW 1/4, look at the upper left corner of the section, then read the next part of the description to determine which part of the NW 1/4 is indicated. Finally, find the S 1/2 of that part. This is the shaded area in the diagram.

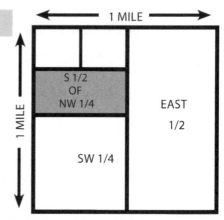

SECTION: 1 SQUARE MILE, 640 ACRES

Example 3

Calculate the number of acres in the parcel of ground described as the N 1/2, NE 1/4, NE 1/4 of the section.

Since we know the total number of acres in a section is 640, we simply calculate the following: 640 ÷ 4 ÷ 4 ÷ 2 = 20 acres; therefore, there are **20 acres in the N 1/2, NE 1/4, NE 1/4 of the section**.

Example 4

Write a description for the diagram at right:

A description for the dark area would read **W 1/2, NW 1/4 of the section**.

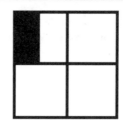

Extra Problems

1. Write a description for the diagram at right:

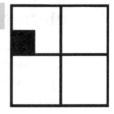

2. Calculate the number of acres in the parcels described as the SW 1/4, SW 1/4 of Section 17 and the NW 1/4, NW 1/4, NW 1/4 of Section 20.

Math Needed for the Valuation Approaches

Each of the three approaches to value requires different mathematical skills. Some of these were used earlier when the **sales comparison approach**, **cost approach**, and **income approach** were introduced. This section serves as a review of those math concepts, beginning with the cost approach, since it has the simplest math. In fact, one important calculation for the cost approach is the area of a building, which was reviewed earlier in this supplement. The other important cost approach calculation is **depreciation**, which is discussed first. From the sales comparison approach, this section reviews **matched pair analysis** and making **adjustments**. Finally, from the income approach, overall **capitalization rates** and **gross rent multipliers** are discussed.

Cost Approach: Depreciation

Recall that the **cost approach** is *an appraisal method that estimates the value of real estate by calculating the cost of building the house or other improvement on the land plus the value of the vacant land*. **Depreciation** is *a loss in value for any reason*. Since the land itself is never said to depreciate, depreciation only affects the building or structure on the land.

There are several methods of determining depreciation. One used for accounting purposes takes a set amount of depreciation as a loss each year during the useful life of a building. This is usually not equal to the actual number of years the building would be expected to last and often does not consider actual wear. Rather, it is a form of tax benefit. This method of depreciation is not discussed here. Instead, the focus is on the **age-life method** and **the breakdown method**.

Age-Life Method

Find the percent of depreciation by dividing the effective age by the total economic life of the building. Then, multiply the total cost of the building by the percent of depreciation. This produces a depreciation amount for the building.

Example

Determine depreciation of a building costing $500,000, with an effective age of 10 years. The building has a total economic life of 50 years.

Step #1: Calculate the percent of depreciation as follows:

effective age ÷ total economic life = percent of depreciation

10 ÷ 50 = 0.20 or 20%

Step #2: Multiply the cost of the building by the percent of depreciation

building cost x percent of depreciation = depreciation amount

$500,000 x 20% = **$100,000**

Breakdown Method

The **breakdown method** is *a method of calculating the observed depreciation by breaking down the total depreciation into categories*. Let's look at an example of the breakdown method due to physical deterioration.

Physical deterioration is actual wear and tear on a property due to age, the elements, or other forces. A depreciation figure is calculated by taking the new price of the item and subtracting a percentage for wear and tear actually used. If an item must be replaced, the new cost is used.

Example #1

A furnace costs $5,000 new and wear and tear makes it appear to have used 20% of its life. The amount of depreciation (20% of $5,000) for that item is $1,000.

Example #2

The roof would cost $8,000 and it has been determined that 80% of its life has been used up. The amount of depreciation (80% of $8,000) would be $6,400.

Extra Problems

1. Using the breakdown method, what is the amount of depreciation of carpeting costing $6,000, with 75% of its life remaining?

2. A house has an effective age of 15 years, if the remaining economic life is 45 years, what is the percent of depreciation?

Sales Comparison Approach: Matched Pair Analysis

Recall that the **sales comparison approach** is an appraisal method that develops an indication of the value of real property by comparing the property being appraised with properties that are comparable. The value of the subject property is determined by comparing it to the other comparable properties, then adjusting the comparables for differences that are present or absent in the subject.

Matched pair analysis (also called **paired data analysis**) is the *process of determining the value of specific property characteristics or features by comparing pairs of similar properties.* By isolating a different characteristic between the pairs of properties being analyzed, the difference in sale price between the two properties can be attributed directly to that feature's **contributory value**.

Example

An appraiser is trying to find the value of a larger-than-market-garage. In researching recent sales in the area, the appraiser finds two properties that have nearly identical features and were on the market for about the same amount of time. The one with a one-car garage sold for $145,000; the one with a two-car garage sold for $150,000. From this, the appraiser concludes that the larger garage has a contributory value of $5,000 in this market area.

It is important to note that paired data analysis can be performed between any two similar properties. The subject property does not have to be included in the matched pair analysis

When performing a paired data analysis, the following steps should be followed to determine adjustment values:

Step #1: *Locate as many sales as possible with similar characteristics, where only one factor can be isolated as being different.*

Step #2: *Find the difference in price between the two properties to arrive at a value figure for the different feature*

Step #3: *If the item difference is a physical feature, then a dollar value is used. Other items may require a percentage adjustment*

Use the following matched pair data grid to find the adjustment amounts. Assume having a wooded lot and not having an easement are superior features.

	Subject	Sale #1	Sale #2	Sale #3	Sale #4
Sale Price	----	$14,750	$13,750	$13,000	$13,500
Depth	150'	175'	150'	150'	150'
Easement	Yes	Yes	Yes	Yes	No
Amenities	Wooded	Yes	Yes	No	No

The dollar adjustments, based on matched pairs, are:

Easement: $500 for easement influence, comparing Sales #3 and #4

Amenity: $750 for woods, comparing Sales #2 and #3

Depth: $1,000 for additional depth, comparing Sales #1 and #2

Extra Problem

1. Based on the previous matched pair data grid, complete the following sales comparison grid and derive the subject's value.

	Subject	Sale #1	Sale #2	Sale #3	Sale #4
Sale Price	----	$14,750	$13,750	$13,000	$13,500
Depth	-0-	_____	-0-	-0-	-0-
Easement	-0-	-0-	-0-	-0-	_____
Amenities	-0-	-0-	-0-	_____	_____
Net Adjustment	-0-	_____	-0-	_____	_____
Adjusted Sale Price		$_____	$_____	$_____	$_____
Final Value Opinion for Subject	$_____				

Income Approach: Direct Capitalization

Appraisers need to be able to calculate property's value based on its ability to generate income. Direct capitalization uses **net income**. Depreciation and annual debt service are not considered building expenses and should not be used if they are included in the problem; they are considered owner expenses.

The formula for direct capitalization is remembered as **IRV**. This is the basic formula for developing a value opinion using the income approach:

INCOME ÷ RATE = VALUE

From a mathematical standpoint, this formula can be used to solve for any variable needed to answer the question or find the requested variable. By knowing any two variables, you can find the third using this equation.

Appraisers need to be familiar with the following terms:

Potential gross income: The income a property would generate if every unit were occupied 100% of the time.

Effective gross income: Potential gross income minus vacancy and collection losses.

Net income: Effective gross income minus building expenses.

Example #1

Given the following data, find the value of the property:

Gross income	= $250,000
Expenses	= $130,000
Depreciation	= $ 50,000
Debt service	= $ 25,000
Cap rate	= 15%

Remember two important things:

1. Always use *net income* (net income = gross income - expenses).

2. Depreciation and debt service do *not* count as expenses.

As is common on the test, this question is confusing, because it provides extra information you do not need. Sometimes the expenses are a list of items you must add together or they may be one figure, as in this example. Either way, ignore depreciation and debt service numbers. Calculate the answer as follows:

INCOME ÷ RATE = VALUE

($250,000 - $130,000) ÷ 15% = ?

$120,000 ÷ 15% = $800,000 is the **value** of the property

Example #2

Given the following data, find the capitalization rate.

Gross income = $250,000

Expenses = $130,000

Depreciation = $ 50,000

Debt service = $ 25,000

Value = $800,000

The same *net income* rules apply, but we need a different formula:

INCOME ÷ **VALUE** = **RATE**

($250,000 - $130,000) ÷ $800,000 = ?

$120,000 ÷ $800,000 = 0.15 = 15% is the **direct capitalization rate**

Example #3

Given a property value and investor's desired capitalization rate, find the net income needed to achieve the desired return.

Value = $800,000   Capitalization rate = 15%

VALUE x RATE = INCOME

$800,000 x 15% = $120,000 **net income** needed

A property generates $100,000 in annual income. If monthly expenses are $3,000 and the capitalization rate is 9%, what is the value of the property?

Step #1: Find the net (annual) income. Take the gross annual income minus annual expenses (monthly expenses x 12);

$100,000 - $36,000 = $64,000 in annual net income

Step #2: The value of the property can be found by IRV:

net **I**ncome ÷ **R**ate = **V**alue:

$64,000 ÷ 9% = $711,111.11 is value of the property

Extra Problems

1. A property has annual income of $75,000 and monthly building expenses of $3,200. Annual debt service is $19,200 and depreciation is 5% of value. Using a capitalization rate of 9%, determine the value of the building.

2. An apartment building has four units, each of which rents for $550 per month. The building has an occupancy rate of 88% and monthly building expenses of $460. If the capitalization rate is 12%, determine the building's value.

Income Approach: Gross Monthly Rent Multiplier (GMRM)

A property's relative value can be derived by comparing the potential gross rent among similar properties. The value or selling price for each property is divided by the gross rent that the property commanded (or could command) in the marketplace, arriving at a gross monthly rent multiplier (GMRM) figure:

VALUE ÷ GROSS MONTHLY RENT = GROSS MONTHLY RENT MULTIPLIER

or

Rental property sale price ÷ gross rent = GMRM

The gross monthly market rent of the subject property is then multiplied by the GMRM derived in the first step to give an estimate of value for the subject property:

Gross Monthly Market Rent x GMRM = Indicated Value

A rental property generates income of $800. Calculate the gross monthly rent multiplier if the value of the property is $100,000.

Value ÷ Gross Income = GMRM

$100,000 ÷ $800 = 125

Extra Problems

1. A property valued at $150,000 generates annual income of $30,000. Building expenses run $1,500 per month, leading to a net income of $12,000. Calculate the gross monthly rent multiplier.

2. Calculate the value of a property that has a gross monthly income of $5,000 if the GMRM in the area is 160.

Other Useful Real Estate Math

You may encounter many other math problems in your appraisal career. These include various measurements, points on loans, property tax assessments, and return on investment calculations. Let's briefly review these.

Measurements—Carpets, Sidewalks, and Driveways

It is useful to know how to calculate the area, amounts, and costs for various types of common construction materials—especially when completing a cost approach appraisal.

Carpet area formula: Length x Width

Carpet is often sold by the square *yard*, yet appraisers usually measure a room in *feet*. They must convert from feet to yards:

Length x Width = Square Feet

square feet ÷ 9 = square yards

Example

If a room measures 20′ x 20′, how much carpet is needed?

20′ x 20′ = 400

400′ ÷ 9 = 44.4 square yards of carpet

Sidewalk and Driveway area formula: Length x Width x Depth

Remember these important considerations when working with sidewalks and driveways.

1. There is a *depth component* to the measurement, so you will have three numbers to multiply.
2. All numbers must be in the same units. Often, you will have length and width in feet, but the depth in inches—convert inches to feet (divide by 12).
3. Concrete is usually sold by the cubic yard, so you must convert.

Length x Width x Depth = Cubic Feet

cubic feet ÷ 27 = cubic yards

Example

A driveway measures 50′ x 8′ x 3″. How much concrete is needed?

50′ x 8′ x 0.25′ = 100′ (Don't forget to convert inches to feet: 3″ = 0.25′)

100′ ÷ 27 = 3.70 cubic yards of concrete

Find the cost of a sidewalk that is 40′ x 8′ x 6″ if concrete costs $75 per cubic yard?

Step #1: Calculate sidewalk size:

40′ x 8′ x 0.5′ = 160′ (don't forget to convert inches to feet: 6″ = 0.5′)

160′ ÷ 27 = 5.93 cubic yards of concrete

Step #2: Calculate total cost as size x the price per cubic yard:

5.93 x 75 = $444.75 for the concrete

Extra Problems

1. How much would it cost to carpet two rooms if one room is 10' x 16', the other room is 8' x 12', and carpet costs $12 per square yard?

2. How much will a driveway cost if it is 40' x 8' x 4", and concrete costs $6 per cubic yard?

Points

Points are defined as a percent of the mortgage loan amount. One point equals one percent of the mortgage. Points may also be referred to as "discount points" or "loan origination fees." They are all calculated the same way.

If you are given information on sale price and down payment amount, you may need to calculate the mortgage amount from this information (sale price - down payment = loan). Your only goal is determining the mortgage loan amount.

Remember: 1 point = 1% of the mortgage loan amount, *not the sale price.*

The loan on a property is $100,000, and the borrower will pay three points. How much will the borrower pay in points?

$100,000 x 3 (%) = $3,000

Extra Problems

1. A buyer is buying a property for $100,000 and will make a $10,000 down payment. If charged two points, how much will the buyer owe in points?

2. John is buying a property for $125,000 with a 20% down payment. He will be charged two points. How much will John owe in points?

Property Taxes

At some point you may need to determine property taxes. Consider them on an annual basis, although they are often paid every six months. Of course, it is convenient to look them up, but it is useful to understand the calculations behind the tax.

To determine property taxes, you need three pieces of information:

1. The market value or appraised value of the property

2. The assessment ratio

3. The "mills" (representing the tax rate)

Note: consider one mill as one dollar per thousand dollars of assessed value.

1 mill = 1/1000 = .001

Calculate annual taxes based on the following information:

Market value = $100,000

Assessment ratio = 35%

Mills = 45

The following steps answer the question:

Step #1: *$100,000 x 35% = $35,000 assessed value*

Step #2: *$35,000 ÷ 1000 = 35 (treat mills as dollars per thousand)*

Step #3: *$35 x 45 mills = $1,575*

Extra Problems

1. A property is appraised at $150,000 and assessed for tax purposes at 35% of value. Calculate the annual taxes if the mills total is 80.

2. A home is valued at $100,000 and assessed for tax purposes at 35% of value. If mills are 47.5, calculate the annual taxes.

Return on Investment (ROI)

If you need to calculate the **return on investment (ROI)** for a property, you are trying to determine the percentage of profit made on the investment. If you know the original purchase price of the property and the eventual selling price, you can determine how much ROI someone made on the property.

A simple formula comes in handy:

WHAT YOU MADE divided by WHAT YOU PAID

or

WHAT YOU MADE ÷ WHAT YOU PAID = RETURN ON INVESTMENT

= PERCENT OF RETURN

A parcel of land is purchased for $100,000 and later sold for $115,000. What is the percent of profit?

Step #1: *Determine what you made:*

$115,000 - $100,000 = $15,000 profit

Step #2: *What you made ÷ what you paid:*

15,000 ÷ 100,000 = 0.15 = 15% is the percent of profit

Extra Problems

1. A buyer purchases land for $50,000 and divides it into three lots that are sold for $20,000 each. What is the return on investment?

2. You purchase an investment property for $125,000. You later sell it at a loss of $20,000. What is your percent of loss?

Chapter Quiz Answer Key

Chapter 1—Introduction to Appraisal

1. c opinion of value.
2. d USPAP
3. a bailout the savings and loan industry and try to prevent future insolvency.
4. c based on the gathering and analysis of objective facts and data.
5. d Scope of Work Rule
6. b Ethics Rule
7. c Jurisdictional Exception Rule
8. a Competency Rule
9. d It allows an appraiser to take on any type of assignment.

Chapter 2—Real Estate and Appraisal

1. a barbecue grill
2. d window seat
3. d What was the cost of the annexed property?
4. d right of litigation
5. a air
6. d zoning
7. d above-ground pool

Chapter 3—Value and the Real Estate Market

1. c houses for sale than buyers.
2. c more than other big ticket items because mortgages are long term.
3. c They provide insurance or make loan guarantees to lenders.
4. d there is a limited supply that cannot be moved, destroyed, or created.
5. b no two properties are exactly the same.
6. c a seller's market
7. b economic base.
8. c both conformity and highest and best use.
9. a benefits from the principle of progression.
10. c increasing returns.

11. a demand, utility, scarcity, transferability, and purchase ability are present.
12. d theoretical price that real estate is most likely to bring in a typical transaction.
13. d buyer and seller have agreed upon payment terms for a land contract

Chapter 4—The Appraisal Process

1. a comparative market analysis
2. d racial makeup of a neighborhood
3. c any interest in real estate that is less than the entire bundle of rights.
4. a all factors that influence real estate are constantly changing and, thus, the property value itself is subject to constant change.
5. c The appraisal is valid only as of the effective date on the appraisal.
6. d specific data on the transfer history of the property going back to the original deed
7. d What is the ideal improvement for the land if it were vacant?
8. c Land devoted to highest and best use will always result in a loss of income.
9. b never
10. d clearly and accurately set forth the appraisal in a manner that will not be misleading.

Chapter 5—Appraisal Data

1. d general data on current mortgage interest rates.
2. c look at general trends that may affect value in the real estate market.
3. b personal inspection.
4. b both analysis of data and verification of data
5. d cost manual data

Chapter 6—External and Environmental Influences

1. a ethnic origin of residents
2. b growth, stability/equilibrium, decline, and revitalization.
3. d rapid revitalization of the neighborhood.
4. d imposing deed restrictions
5. a affects some of the owner's bundle of rights.
6. b is one that may be undesirable to some people because of a past event.
7. d Sellers must hire a contractor to remove any lead-based paint.
8. a can present a problem indoors if allowed to build up to dangerous levels.

Chapter 7—Residential Construction and Home Inspection

1. b sloped joists
2. c rise of the roof in inches, divided by the span of the roof in feet.
3. c rough-in
4. c interior finish
5. a completion
6. a one-story.
7. b one-and-a-half-stories.
8. a is built one story at a time.
9. a footer.
10. c rough-ins.
11. d truss.
12. d sheathing.

Chapter 8—Site Valuation

1. b improvements
2. b assemblage.
3. a government survey system
4. c 640
5. b plat map.
6. d township markers
7. c location survey.
8. c size.

9. d zoning.
10. c location of the lot with regard to market demand.
11. c sales comparison method
12. a allocation method
13. d subdivision analysis method

Chapter 9—Sales Comparison Approach

1. d cost manuals
2. a is a means of determining the contributory value of specific property features by comparing similar properties.
3. b financing concessions, terms of sale, date of sale, location, and physical features
4. d any tangible or intangible feature that enhances and adds value to real estate.
5. c never
6. d evidencing competition and the upper limit of value.
7. c the need for an adjustment is not supported.
8. b 10%
9. b 5%
10. c effective date.

Chapter 10—Cost Approach

1. d matched pair data
2. d a loss in value for any reason.
3. c a residential condo in a complex with 50% occupancy and many recent sales.
4. a Replacement / most of the time, a similar building is an acceptable, less expensive alternative.
5. b a building's effective age
6. c effective age / economic life
7. d incurable physical deterioration.
8. a related to things outside the property boundaries.
9. d incurable functional obsolescence.
10. b The appraiser considers what the purpose of the appraisal is before deciding how much weight to give the cost approach.

Chapter 11—Income Approach

1. d   debt service

2. d   value is created by the expectation of future benefits.

3. a   debt service

4. d   determined by analysis of market data.

5. d   sale price

6. c   the lack of very similar comparable data.

7. b   effective gross income (EGI).

8. c $86,500

9. b $115,000

10. a   6.15%

11. d   217.78

12. c   market rent

Chapter 12—Reconciling Estimates of Value and Reporting Conclusions

1. b   the appraiser decides which approach or approaches to give the most weight.

2. d   reference the listing or sales contract price of the subject property as a factor in developing the value opinion.

3. d   gross rent multiplier

4. c   may be given the most weight if the data is reliable and the approach is applicable.

5. d   other approaches may be used to support that opinion.

Appraisal Math Extra Problems Answer key

Extra Problems (Page 207)

1. A commercial lot is priced at $1,800 per front foot. If the lot measures 170' x 550', what is the price of the lot?

$306,000

(170' x $1,800 = $306,000)

2. If the same lot is priced at $2.75 per square foot, calculate the price of the lot.

$257,125

(170' x 550' = 93,500 square feet
93,500 x 2.75 = $257,125)

3. What is the price of a parcel of land selling for $9,000 per acre and that is a quarter mile squared?

$360,000

(5,280' ÷ 4 = 1,320
1,320' x 1,320' = 1,742,400 sq. ft.
1,742,400 ÷ 43,560 = 40 acres
40 x $9,000 - $360,000)

Extra Problems (Page 208)

1. Calculate the cost of building a structure that is 120' x 75', if the cost is $11.25 per square foot.

$101,250

(120' x 75' = 9,000 square feet
9,000 x $11.25 = $101,250)

2. A warehouse that is 700' x 300' can be built for a cost of $8.00 per square foot, but part of that space is a 100' x 100' office area that will cost $12.75 per square foot. What is the total building cost?

$1,727,500

(700' x 300' = 210,000 sq. ft.
100' x 100' = 10,000 sq. ft.
210,000 – 10,000 = 200,000 sq. ft.
200,000 x $8.00 = $1,600,000
10,000 x $12.75 = $127,500
$1,600,000 + $127,500 =
  $1,727,500)

Extra Problems (Page 209)

1. What is the length of a building that has 15,000 cubic feet, if the height is 15' and the width is 20'?

50 feet
(15' x 20' = 300
15,000 ÷ 300 = 50')

2. A building is being constructed for $4.80 per cubic foot. The building is 18' tall and contains 1,250 square feet. What is the cost of the building?

$108,000
(1,250 sq. ft. x 18' (height) = 22,500 cubic feet
22,500 x $4.80 = $108,000)

Extra Problems (Page 210)

1. Write a description for this diagram:

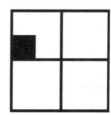 **SW 1/4 of the NW 1/4** The upper left quarter is the northwest quarter of the section. The shaded area is the southwest quarter of the northwest quarter of the section.

2. Calculate the number of acres in the parcels described as the SW ¼, SW ¼ of Section 17 and the NW ¼, NW ¼, NW ¼ of Section 20.

50 Acres

Section 17 = 640 Acres
SW ¼ = 160 Acres
SW ¼ of SW ¼ = 40 Acres

Section 20 = 640 Acres
NW ¼ = 160 Acres
NW ¼ of NW ¼ = 40 Acres
NW ¼ of NW ¼ of NW ¼ = 10 Acres

40 + 10 = 50 Acres Total

Extra Problems (Page 212)

1. Using the breakdown method, what is the amount of depreciation of carpeting costing $6,000, with 75% of its life remaining?

$1,500
(100% - 75% = 25%
$6,000 x 25% = $1,500)

2. A house has an effective age of 15 years, if the remaining economic life is 45 years, what is the percent of depreciation?

25%
(15 + 45 = 60
15 ÷ 60 = 25%)

Extra Problems (Page 215)

1. A property has annual income of $75,000 and monthly building expenses of $3,200. Annual debt service is $19,200 and depreciation is 5% of value. Using a capitalization rate of 9%, determine the value of the building.

$406,667
$75,000 - $38,400 (12 x $3,200) =
$36,600
$36,600 ÷ 0.09 (9%) = $406,667
(rounded)

2. An apartment building has four units, each rents for $550 per month. The building has an occupancy rate of 88% and monthly building expenses of $460. If the capitalization rate is 12%, determine the building's value.

$147,600
$26,400 ($550 x 4 x 12) x 0.12
(100% - 88%) = $3,168
$26,400 - $3,168 = $23,232
$23,232 - $5,520 ($460 x 12) = $17,712
$17,712 ÷ 0.12 (12%) = $147,600

Extra Problem (Page 213)

1. Based on the previous paired data grid, complete the following sales comparison grid and derive the subject's value.

	Subject	Sale #1	Sale #2	Sale #3	Sale #4
Sale Price	????????	$14,750	$13,750	$13,000	$13,500
Depth	-0-	- $1,000	-0-	-0-	-0-
Easement	-0-	-0-	-0-	-0-	- $500
Amenities	-0-	-0-	-0-	+ $750	+ $750
Net Adjustment	-0-	**- $1,000**	-0-	**+ $750**	**+ $250**
Adjusted Sale Price		**$13,750**	**$13,750**	**$13,750**	**$13,750**
Final Value Opinion for Subject	**$13,750**				

Final value opinion for the subject: **$13,750**

Extra Problems (Page 216)

1. A property valued at $150,000 generates annual income of $30,000. Building expenses run $1,500 per month, leading to a net income of $12,000. Calculate the gross rent multiplier.

60
$150,000 ÷ $2,500 ($30,000 ÷ 12) = 60

2. Calculate the value of a property that has a gross monthly income of $5,000 if the GRM in the area is 160.

$800,000
$5,000 x 160 = $800,000

Extra Problems (Page 218 top)

1. How much would it cost to carpet two rooms if one room is 10' x 16', the other room is 8' x 12', and carpet costs $12 per square yard?

$341.33
10' x 16' = 160 sq. ft.
8' x 12' = 96 sq. ft.
160 + 96 = 256 sq. ft.
256 ÷ 9 = 28.4444
28.4444 x $12 = $341.33

2. How much will a driveway cost if it is 40' x 8' x 4", and concrete costs $6 per cubic yard?

$23.70
40' x 8' x 0.3333 = 106.656 cubic feet
106.656 ÷ 3.9502
3.9502 x $6 = $23.70 (rounded)

Extra Problems (Page 218 bottom)

1. A buyer is buying a property for $100,000 and will make a $10,000 down payment. If charged two points, how much will the buyer owe in points?

$1,800
$100,000 - $10,000 = $90,000
$90,000 x 0.02 (2%) = $1,800

2. John is buying a property for $125,000 with a 20% down payment. He will be charged two points. How much will John owe in points?

$2,000
$125,000 x 0.20 (20%) = $25,000
$125,000 - $25,000 = $100,000
$100,000 x 0.02 (2%) = $2,000

Extra Problems (Page 219)

1. A property is appraised at $150,000 and assessed for tax purposes at 35% of value. Calculate the annual taxes if the mills total is 80.

$4,200
$150,000 x 0.35 (35%) = 52,500
$52,500 ÷ 1,000 = 52.5
52.5 x 80 = $4,200

2. A home is valued at $100,000 and assessed for tax purposes at 35% of value. If mills are 47.5, calculate the annual taxes.

$1,662.50
$100,000 x 0.35 (35%) = $35,000
$35,000 ÷ 1,000 = 35
35 x 47.5 = $1,662.50

Extra Problems (Page 220)

1. A buyer purchases land for $50,000 and divides it into three lots that are sold for $20,000 each. What is the return on investment?

20%
3 x $20,000 = $60,000
$60,000 - $50,000 = $10,000 profit
$10,000 ÷ $50,000 = 0.20 (20%)

2. You purchase an investment property for $125,000. You later sell it at a loss of $20,000. What is your percent of loss?

16%
-$20,000 ÷ $125,000 = 0.16 (16%)

Index